Conservatism

Short Histories

Agenda Short Histories are incisive and provocative introductions to topics, ideas and events for students wanting to know more about how we got where we are today.

Published

Conservatism
Mark Garnett

Thatcherism
Peter Dorey

Conservatism

Mark Garnett

agenda
publishing

First published in 2023 by Agenda Publishing

Agenda Publishing Limited
The Core
Bath Lane
Newcastle Helix
Newcastle upon Tyne
NE4 5TF
www.agendapub.com

ISBN 978-1-78821-503-9 (hardcover)
ISBN 978-1-78821-504-6 (paperback)

British Library Cataloguing-in-Publication Data
A catalogue record for this book is available from the British Library

Typeset by JS Typesetting Ltd, Porthcawl, Mid Glamorgan
Printed and bound in the UK by TJ Books

Contents

Preface

In December 2019, it looked as if the British Conservative Party had performed a feat of electoral escapology to match anything in its long history. The party had been in office since 2010, but never with a secure parliamentary majority. Its implementation of dramatic cuts in public spending – "austerity" – had incurred considerable public hostility during its coalition with the Liberal Democrats (2010–15), and although the party won a narrow overall majority in May 2015 the ensuing months were dominated by a bitter internal debate over an impending referendum on Britain's membership of the European Union (EU). When this took place in June 2016 a small majority of those who voted rejected the advice of the prime minister, David Cameron, and opted for withdrawal. Theresa May, chosen as Cameron's successor in preference to more colourful candidates, was unable to recreate a semblance of unity among her own party, let alone the public; a "snap" election called in 2017 in order to bolster her parliamentary position had the opposite effect. From the ensuing constitutional melee over the implementation of "Brexit", none of the branches of British government emerged with enhanced public esteem; baulked by parliament and the courts, May had exhausted her personal authority long before standing down in July 2019.

To its critics – and, indeed, to many senior figures in its own ranks – this was a mess almost entirely of the Conservative Party's own making. The erstwhile "party of Europe", and its allies in the mainstream media, had developed an obsession with the EU, ensuring that this potent source of division was a constant presence in the newspaper headlines which confronted a largely uncomprehending electorate. Spooked after 2012 by a surge in media and public support for the United Kingdom Independence Party (UKIP), which made their own brand of "Euroscepticism" seem tepid, the Conservatives had responded by giving the voters a chance to channel their varied resentments into a one-off, single-issue decision. Cameron had been so confident of a victory for "Remain" that no serious preparations had been made in case the verdict went the other way. Whatever the merits of the rival arguments over the EU, the episode thus exposed the Conservatives as masters of mismanagement. Yet in the election of December 2019 the party was rewarded rather than punished, with an overall majority of 80. Under a new leader, Boris Johnson, it had presented itself as a party which had been wholly committed to Brexit all along, while its opponents, who lamented the referendum result to varying degrees, could be portrayed as bad losers or opponents of "the will of the people".

For tribal Conservatives this seemed almost too good to be true, and the jubilation was reflected faithfully in the pages of the *Daily Telegraph* – a newspaper which could claim with justice to represent the conscience of the party. Johnson the vote-winning premier was a long-standing *Telegraph* columnist, whose baiting of the Brussels bureaucracy had forged his reputation in Eurosceptic circles. The paper had covered the 2019 contest to succeed Theresa May like a coronation for its favourite son, adorning almost every front page with headlines which included the magical name "Boris".

Yet the *Telegraph*'s support was not unconditional; if anything, its connection with Johnson made its columnists more watchful after he had become party leader and secured his "mandate" from the voters in December 2019. In the same month a new virus, Covid-19, had been detected in China. The first confirmed deaths in the UK were recorded in March, and Johnson announced stringent limitations on freedom of movement and association – a national "lockdown". The *Telegraph* viewed these developments with a dismay which deepened as restrictions were eased, then reimposed in response to a "second wave" of the virus in autumn 2020. By the summer of 2021 the newspaper's columnists had concluded that the pandemic had exposed the superficiality of Johnson's principles. Indeed, according to Allister Heath, under Johnson the country had lurched to the left, so that "Decadent Britain" was now "sleepwalking into a vortex of permanent decline" (Heath 2021a). A few weeks later another *Telegraph* columnist contributed pieces which successively announced that "The Tories have lost touch with Conservatism" and that the announcement of a new levy to fund health and social care "sounded the death knell for Conservatism" (Tominey 2021a, 2021b). Shortly before Johnson's enforced departure from the party leadership in July 2022, a *Telegraph* editorial asked plaintively, "What happened to Conservatism?" (*Daily Telegraph* 2022). Its preferred successor to Johnson, who regarded himself as a reborn Winston Churchill, was Liz Truss, whose impersonation of Margaret Thatcher was even more blatant and (at least) equally unpersuasive. During Truss's swiftly-terminated premiership, several *Telegraph* columnists expressed enthusiasm for a "philosophical" approach to politics which inspired her to promise lower taxation and a smaller state.

The proper principles of the Conservative Party have been a persistent preoccupation for the *Telegraph* newspaper group. In July 2017, after Theresa May's election gamble had backfired, another of the paper's contributors had suggested that "Conservatism" should be taught in schools, and Allister Heath later supplied a list ("Burke, Locke, Hayek, Friedman and Oakeshott") of supposedly relevant thinkers whose legacy the party was busily betraying (Heath 2021b). While it would be a mistake to assume that the *Telegraph*'s ideological preoccupations are universally shared among members of the Conservative Party, the newspaper knows its audience and, judging from its correspondence columns, plenty of its readers really are engrossed by such debates.

On this evidence, although the nature of "Conservatism" might not be contested as urgently as it was during the Thatcher years, it is still a topic worthy of very serious consideration. A second conclusion arising from the *Telegraph*'s commentary during the pandemic is that Conservatism, as a set of principles, cannot simply be equated with the stated views and policy proposals of Conservative Party politicians at any given time. If the *Telegraph* columnists are to be believed, it is even possible for senior members of the party to be committing "treason" against its true principles. This, of course, is a recurrent refrain whenever supporters of a party feel that their views are not being respected by their leaders. However, the claim coincides with a view held by some (although by no means all) academic commentators, who have attempted to characterize an ideology which may, or may not, be reflected in the Conservative Party's approach to political questions.

The main objective of the present study is to explore these issues in greater depth, by presenting parallel intellectual histories – of the British Conservative Party, and of the ideology with which it is commonly

associated. Such a twin-track approach confronts an awkward termi-
nological difficulty. Academics almost invariably use an upper-case "C"
when referring to intellectual developments within the Conservative
Party, and a lower-case "c" in relation to ideas which, though obviously
associated with the party in some way, are analytically distinct from its
stated principles at any given time. However, journalists and politicians
feel no obligation to discriminate in this way. The promiscuous use of
the upper- and lower-case terms is chiefly characteristic of observers
and participants who assert that there can be no difference between
"Conservatism" and "conservatism" – in short, that "C/conservatism"
is whatever the party of that name chooses it to be. However, some
authors – like the *Telegraph* columnists quoted above – designate ideas
with the upper-case "C", even when arguing that the Conservative Party
has deserted Conservatism..

There is no hazard-free path through this methodological mine-
field: it would, for example, be wrong to impose uniformity on original sources, amending "Conservatism" to "conservatism" in quotations
which are clearly referring to ideas. Hopefully this will not give rise to
undue confusion in the following pages. My own approach is to use
the (upper-case) word "Conservatism" as sparingly as possible. It is relatively straight-forward to examine the development of ideas within
the Conservative *Party* from its origins in the early 1830s, focusing on
politicians and intellectuals who chose to be associated with the organization and have sought to influence its policy direction. However, from
the outset these individuals disagreed on fundamental matters of principle – particularly concerning religious toleration, voting rights and
free trade (see Chapter 2). Academic observers are well aware that the
Conservative Party does not "think" collectively; they have little choice
but to take the views of its leading figures (as expressed in speeches,
election literature, etc) as authoritative statements of (upper-case "C")
"Conservatism", while taking note of significant dissenting voices. This
is the approach I have tried to follow in this book.

Since the late nineteenth century similar observations could apply to
"conservatism" as a body of ideas. "Representatives" of this lower-case
species of conservatism could be office-holders within the party looking
to address philosophical questions rather than specific issues, or indeed
might be writers with no party affiliation who simply see themselves
as "conservative" in outlook. In comparison to liberals and socialists,

British conservatives were relatively late in claiming membership of an intellectual tradition. As we shall see, this was due not least to the tendency even of self-consciously "conservative" writers to focus on ideas which they *opposed* rather than engaging in a dialogue with the works of those who broadly shared their outlook. Nevertheless, by the early twentieth century writers commonly referred to a "conservative tradition" which could be cited in relation to contemporary policy discussion but was taken to exist independently of the party's current stance. The obvious question guiding an inquiry of this kind is: has the Conservative Party always followed distinctive conservative principles, since its foundation in the early 1830s? As we shall see, the evidence prompts a reworded question: has the Conservative Party *ever* followed principles which are distinctively conservative?. The answer suggested by this book is "not for long", which raises the further task of explaining the nature and causes of any divergence between principles and practice. Some readers might wish to speculate about the possibility of a reconciliation between the Conservative Party and distinctively conservative views. The present study, however, is concerned with the past rather than the future, and only proffers some tentative hints.

The book has plenty of ground to cover, within a relatively limited space. There is, therefore, no attempt at comparative analysis, although of course Britain does not enjoy a monopoly of "conservative" ideas, or of parties which claim to be "Conservative" with varying degrees of plausibility. Although it focuses on a single country – and, perforce, on England at the expense of the UK as a whole – hopefully it will also have some value for scholars and general readers in other nations who take an interest in the relationship between principles and practical politics.

Also for reasons of space, I have been unable to devote anything like adequate attention to academic analysis of British conservatism. This is certainly not intended as a discourtesy to the scholars who have laboured in this field. I have included a separate section in the bibliography for the convenience of readers who might want to enquire further.

These omissions, I hope, can be excused because the intention was always to concentrate on *participants* rather than *onlookers*, however erudite, and so far as possible to allow the former to testify for themselves. The usual interplay between personalities, principles, events and institutions is particularly complex in the case(s) of British C/conservatism. As a result, many people feature in this study as both "thinkers" and "doers". In his posthumous heyday, for example, Benjamin Disraeli was hailed in Conservative Party propaganda as a masterly thinker as well as a tactical genius; the 3rd Marquess of Salisbury, Stanley Baldwin and (more recently) Sir Keith Joseph can also be said, in their very different ways, to straddle a divide between ideas and action which, for academic observers, is more difficult to discern because supporters of the party leadership have tended to insist that it could not exist. In this respect – although perhaps not in others – the present author is content to rest on the authority of writers in the *Daily Telegraph*, but readers are of course at liberty to make up their own minds.

I am most grateful for the patient guidance of Alison Howson and Steven Gerrard at Agenda, and for the helpful suggestions of the anonymous reviewers of my proposal and a draft of the manuscript. My friends David Denver, Dave Smith, Brian Garvey and Kieron O'Hara also saved me from some glaring errors: any that remain are entirely my responsibility.

1

The contestable conservative tradition: Burke to Southey

Most commentators on modern conservatism agree in identifying the Irish-born author and politician Edmund Burke (1726–97) as its first major figure. In 1930 a former MP, Arthur Baumann, published *Burke: The Founder of Conservatism*. For the American historian Peter Viereck, conservative thought "begins with Burke", and the publication of Burke's *Reflections on the Revolution in France* in 1790 was an ideological landmark to match the appearance of *The Communist Manifesto* in 1848 (Viereck 1956: 10). Lord Hugh Cecil even gave conservatism a birthday – 6 May 1791, when Burke's opposition to the French Revolution produced a public breach with the leadership of the Whig Party (Cecil 1912: 43; where the nativity is misdated to 1790). More recently, the MP Jesse Norman argued that "in many ways [Burke] was the first conservative, the founder: the first person who can properly lay claim to having forged conservatism as a distinctive body of thought" (Norman 2013: 282).

There are alternative and earlier candidates for the parentage of modern conservatism – Benjamin Disraeli, for example, was a passionate admirer of Henry St John, Viscount Bolingbroke (1678–1751), author of *The Idea of a Patriot King*, and the sceptical Scottish philosopher David Hume (1711–76) anticipated Burke in important respects. However, although Burke's *Reflections* was written in response to a single, momentous historical development, it incorporated numerous passages whose implications reached beyond revolutionary France, and could be said to constitute an appeal to "first principles". Burke had two immediate aims – to attack the ideas which, he felt, had inspired the revolutionary movement in France, and to quash symptoms of a similar insurgency in Britain itself. The danger of such ideas, Burke argued, lay chiefly in their propensity to encourage *radical* change. No system of government could be perfect, and it was the duty of responsible politicians to propose reforms once defects became too glaring to ignore. But even such imperative changes should be introduced gradually. Root-and-branch reform could lead to a breakdown of political and social order. This was particularly the case if the radical proposals were inspired by abstract ideas which showed insufficient respect for established practices.

Scholars of political ideologies are generally agreed that such belief systems are "action-oriented" – that is, ideologies provide the motivation for political decisions of various kinds (Bell 1960). This would fit even the most simplistic definition of "conservatism" – i.e., one which depicts a conservative as being a stubborn, unreflective defender of any status quo. In times of general contentment such an outlook would promote *inaction* ("if it's not broke, why fix it?"); in other circumstances, it could imply a readiness to respond to demands for reform with repression rather than arguments.

In contrast to this approach – a combination of complacency and bone-headed "reaction" – Burke offered a more flexible and sophisticated doctrine. In his view, the constitutional settlement established after Britain's Glorious Revolution of 1688–89 was basically sound – a judicious blend of liberty and authority. However, even within this laudable framework reforms might become necessary in response to changing circumstances or inherent imperfections in the machinery of government. Far from being a recipe for inaction in quiet times, Burke's political approach suggested that public-spirited politicians should make constructive use of such interludes, always scanning the horizon for clouds which might swell into storms and taking timely precautions. In homespun terms, Burke's approach is not "if it's not broke, why fix it?", or "what we have, we hold"; but, rather, "a stitch in time saves nine". Incremental reform was the best preventative of revolution: as he put it, "A state without the means of some change is without the means of its conservation" (Mitchell 1989: 72).

Yet while Burke provided a clear rationale in favour of piecemeal change, the celebrity of his *Reflections* was due chiefly to his condemnation of the alternative, radical approach. Burke had become alarmed at the tendency of British radicals (notably the unitarian minister Richard Price (1723–91)) to greet the collapse of the *Ancien Régime* in France as an opportune moment to re-examine Britain's own "revolution settlement", whose hundredth anniversary Price had marked by delivering a *Discourse on the Love of our Country* (1789). Burke's response – one of fury mixed with ice-cold contempt – came as a considerable surprise to those (such as Price himself) who remembered his sympathy with an earlier "revolution" – the American War of Independence. But in that instance the "rebels" could be seen as "conservatives", organizing to *resist* innovations in the relationship between the colonies and the metropolitan power. The French revolutionaries, by contrast, were trying to overthrow the existing order of government – one which Burke (improbably) claimed was amenable to his preferred model of reform by gentle instalments. By rejecting reformism and fomenting revolution, the French radicals had unleashed forces which, Burke (rightly) predicted, they could not hope to contain.

Rather than simply arguing for political stability from the standpoint of those who benefited from the established order in Britain, Burke insisted that radical change hurt *everyone*. In Burke's view, the British admirers of French revolutionaries were not to be patronised as naïve intellectuals who overlooked the possibility that their good intentions might be paving the road to hell. In *Reflections* he wrote as if the hellish results of revolution should be self-evident, and he judged the intentions of British radicals like Price accordingly. *Reflections* gave ample warning that the French Revolution would, eventually, devour its own children; it would result in mindless bloodshed rather than any noticeable long-term improvement in the governance of that country because the ideological advocates of revolution were simply wrong about human nature. Contrary to the view of "enlightened" philosophers from the Voltaire stable, the influence of "reason" over human actions is tenuous at best. When established authority is overthrown, lawlessness ensues rather than the idyllic scenario envisaged by irresponsible intellectual scribblers.

"The myth of ideological purity"

The present study is based on the view that, whether or not Burke was the founder of modern conservatism, his understanding of human nature, society and politics is highly distinctive and can serve as a kind of ideological "template" against which other thinkers may be evaluated. However, this approach to the study of conservatism has not escaped criticism, and although the debate deserves much closer scrutiny it is important at least to note some of the key points of contention. Robert

Eccleshall, for example, has argued that since Burke had belonged to a different political party – the Whigs – his place in "the Tory pantheon" is the result of "an audacious twentieth-century trick", intended "to portray modern conservatives as heirs to a robust intellectual tradition" (Eccleshall 1990: 2–3). In a thorough and insightful survey of the historical evidence, Emily Jones dates the construction of a "conservative" Burke more precisely, to the debate over Irish Home Rule in the 1890s (see Chapter 2). On this account, Burke's latter-day admirers rationalized his work to serve their current purposes, leading "to his abstraction from his original historical context" (Jones 2015: 1138).

It is true that ideological liberals continued to venerate Burke, and not just because of his pre-Revolutionary speeches and writings. However, the notion that conservatives commandeered Burke chiefly for reasons of intellectual prestige is difficult to square with the evidence. Lord Hugh Cecil could be regarded as an early ideological body-snatcher, since he regarded Burke as "Conservatism's first and perhaps its greatest teacher". Notwithstanding his party affiliation, according to Cecil "Burke was a conservative all his life" (Cecil 1912: 40). Yet, far from supposing that Burke's dazzling contemporary reputation would provide some undeserved kudos for a "conservative tradition", Cecil was not an unqualified admirer of *Reflections*. Apart from imperfections in Burke's knowledge of conditions in France, Cecil argued that "the arrangement of the book is by no means clear or attractive", much of the detail is uninteresting and the style is unfashionable. As a result, *Reflections* is "not so much read now as it deserves to be". Whatever his attractions to the intellectual elite, Burke was not a household name whose association with conservatism could help to win widespread popular support for the Conservative Party. Why, then, should conservatives of the early twentieth century bother with Burke? According to Cecil, for all his failings Burke "is constantly digressing into general disquisitions of deep and permanent interest" (Cecil 1912: 45, 47). In other words, Burke gave eloquent expression to ideas which, in the view of people who considered themselves to be conservative, transcended their context, conferring on him the right to be preferred to other plausible candidates as the founder of their tradition.

An assault with more deadly potential was launched by W. H. Greenleaf, in his exhaustive study of *The British Political Tradition*. Greenleaf insisted that "The myth of ideological purity dies hard. But …

there is no single correct version of any political creed". In his view, the lack of any perfect exemplar of a political doctrine means that it must be fruitless to search for the "essence" of ideologies. By implication, anyone who tries to assemble a coherent conservative tradition on the basis of "objective" criteria such as core principles, common themes or "family resemblances" is engaged in an exercise which is futile at best: indeed, Greenleaf accuses those who make the attempt of "a bad and fundamental error of analysis" (Greenleaf 1983: 14).

On Greenleaf's account, ideologies are subject to change and their associated principles often overlap. His own preference is to explain British politics since the early nineteenth century in terms of "collectivism" and "individualism". This follows an approach used by the late Victorian jurist A. V. Dicey (see Chapter 3; Dicey 1905). Greenleaf's extensive research into (often obscure) primary sources indicated that, since its foundation, the Conservative Party has been supported by people who can be assigned to either of his "individualist" or "collectivist" camps. Therefore, he concludes, "Conservatism" must include both individualist and collectivist "strands". The balance of these elements has never been fixed: individualism might prevail at one time, and collectivism at another. A party which encompasses such conflicting viewpoints can scarcely be identified with a single, distinctive ideological position.

Thus, for Greenleaf, the term "Conservatism" is almost endlessly elastic; the only apparent limit is that there should be a relationship of some kind between the ideas under discussion and one faction or another within the Conservative Party. Accordingly, Greenleaf eschews lower-case "conservatism" throughout his monumental study; for example, the entry for "Conservatism" in the index of his volume on *The Ideological Heritage* is followed by "*see also* Conservative Party". This promises to simplify the life of academic commentators, who would no longer have to keep ringing the changes between upper- and lower-case versions of the same word. However, as a means of explaining the relationship between political ideas and practice the approach leaves something to be desired. How, for example, can we decide if a political party's ideological position has changed? By implication, this has occurred when it adopts a new position on an issue of fundamental importance. Presumably, for Greenleaf, the key criterion is the party's attitude towards state intervention. However, this seems to elevate "individualism" or "collectivism" into the "core principles" or "essences" which Greenleaf finds so objectionable in respect of ideological traditions.

On inspection, there are no "pure" exemplars either of individualism or of collectivism in the British political tradition. Many advocates of state intervention, indeed, have argued that collective provision in fields such as education and health actively *promote* individualism. This argument was advanced by Winston Churchill as a reforming minister in the Liberal Asquith governments; for example, in 1909 he insisted that unemployment insurance and old-age pensions would help people to become more self-reliant (Churchill 1970: 146). It is surely significant that Churchill receives scant attention from Greenleaf, because his political peregrinations make him a fascinating case-study. On Greenleaf's view, presumably, it would be entirely proper to refer to Churchill's Conservatism in his early political career, his "Liberalism" between 1904 and 1923, and his renewed "Conservatism" after he formally rejoined the Conservative Party in 1924. Between leaving the Liberals and working his passage back to the Conservative fold, Churchill stood for parliament as an independent "anti-socialist" and as a "Constitutionalist". His zig-zagging path across the floor of the Commons was partly prompted by personal ambition, but also by changes in his policy *priorities*: issues which had once seemed crucial to him (e.g., free trade) faded in significance or were superseded by others. After the 1917 Russian Revolution opposition to "Bolshevism" became much more important to Churchill, but he had expressed a strong dislike for socialism long before then. Throughout his career Churchill's position is best understood as that of a moderate liberal in ideological terms, a judgement based not on any "core principles" as such but on a more general appraisal of his stated views and decisions (see Chapter 2).

Greenleaf's study has particular relevance to conservatism, since his first two volumes appeared at a time (1983) when the nature of the Conservative Party's ideas was being warmly contested. Both the supporters and opponents of the party leader, Margaret Thatcher, claimed to be upholding "true" conservatism (see Chapters 3 and 4). Greenleaf's analytical framework suggested that the contestants were equally wrong-headed, since there was no such thing as "true conservatism". However, he was unable to conceal his personal hostility towards collectivism, and barely stopped short of wishing Thatcher good luck in her attempt to "roll back the frontiers of the state". Reviewers like Michael Freeden took a charitable view of this dramatic demonstration of partisanship; others might describe Greenleaf's ideological bias as "a bad and fundamental error of analysis" (Freeden 1985: 854–6).

Despite its serious flaws, Greenleaf's work on the subject does have some cautionary value for students of ideology in Britain. He is right to insist that "there is no single correct version of any political creed". Ideologies are intellectual constructs which necessarily over-simplify the stated or implied beliefs of real political actors. They are best characterized as relatively coherent worldviews whose broad, basic assumptions do not change; rather, these assumptions inform varying political responses to changing circumstances. Understood in this way, the concept of ideology can be an invaluable tool for those who appreciate the importance of political ideas and approach the subject in the spirit of objectivity rather than partisanship.

Burke on human nature, society and the state

Burke, then, is rightly regarded as the first exemplar of modern British conservatism because he gave eloquent expression to a range of propositions which inform a distinctive political approach – an aversion to radical change. Among these ideas, perhaps the most important is the view that political upheaval gives rise to incalculable consequences since human beings are imperfectly rational. As Burke put it, "We are afraid to put men to live and trade each on his private stock of reason; because we suspect that this stock in each man is small" (Mitchell 1989: 138).

Although *Reflections* is not a systematic treatise, Burke develops his view of human nature into what can be presented as a coherent understanding of society, the state and political judgement. Rather than acting in accordance with abstract reason, humans tend to rely on what Burke called "prejudice". This was a kind of instinctive guide to conduct, not too distant from the idea of "common sense". Among other things, prejudice encourages people to take a positive view of long-established institutions and practices, which must be deemed to be beneficial precisely because of their longevity. Despite his repudiation of individual rationality, Burke saw veneration for a country's past as evidence of a *collective* wisdom, expressed in his view that "the individual is foolish, the species is wise" (Burke 1816: 47). The individual who supposes that her or his unassisted reason can dream up a blueprint for a more successful political and social order was the most foolish (and dangerous) of all; the existing dispensation, after all, embodied not only the wisdom of existing people but also the accumulated acumen of previous ages. Thus, reform within the existing system should build on the inheritance of the past as well as being carefully calibrated to avoid the risk of more radical repercussions.

Burke seems to have ranked general acceptance of a social hierarchy in Britain, marked by extreme inequalities of status and wealth, as one of the well-founded "prejudices" of his day. Society was much more than an assemblage of self-sufficient individuals; it was interdependent, so that even the most humbly-born Britons could recognize their value to the continued health of society as a whole. In *Reflections*, Burke rhapsodised the British state as the embodiment of the wisdom of ages and the ultimate expression of an "organic" population. As such, the state could be characterized in mystical terms: "it is not a partnership in things subservient only to the gross animal existence of a temporary and perishable nature. It is a partnership in all science; a partnership in all art; a partnership in every virtue, and in all perfection" (Mitchell 1989: 147). Emily Jones is right to point out that Burke's "organic" view of society was given undue prominence by later writers, under the influence of idealist philosophy. Nevertheless, this anti-individualist aspect of his thought has been over-emphasized rather than invented (Jones 2015: 1138).

Some of Burke's admirers (notably Hugh Cecil and the American academic Russell Kirk) have emphasized the spiritual element of his thinking, reflecting his view that "man is by his constitution a religious animal" and his belief that approval of the established Church of England was "the first of our prejudices". To a more secular-minded age, it might appear that Burke valued religion as a useful support to the established social and political order, generating "a wholesome awe" amongst ordinary citizens who might otherwise be tempted to transgress. Burke's emphasis on the importance of religion as the source of ultimate sanctions against wrong-doers – even those in the most exalted stations of earthly life – explains why his most splenetic outbursts against France's revolutionary ideologues were reserved for impious worshippers at the altar of human reason ("Atheists are not our preachers; madmen are not our lawgivers"). In the absence of religion, he believed, it was inevitable that human beings would fall prey to "all the lust of selfish will" (Mitchell 1989: 137, 145)

Burke and the aristocratic ideal

Although Burke's defence of religious faith and of the existing British ecclesiastical order was undoubtedly sincere, it is possible to assent to his general views on politics, society and human nature without bringing in the prospect of eternal damnation as a disciplinary back-stop. So far as the "lower orders" were concerned, the legal system of late eighteenth-century Britain included earthly penalties, even for trivial offences, which would deter most would-be offenders. Careful contemporary readers of *Reflections* would have been more struck by the relevance of Burke's religious views to the conduct of the privileged classes. Burke saw religious faith as a form of moral leverage to ensure that privileged members of society remembered their duties; its precepts reminded "persons possessing any portion of power" that one day they would have to make a reckoning for "their conduct in that trust to the one great master, author, and founder of society" (quoted in Mitchell 1989: 142). Such passages would have made awkward reading for Burke's political allies within the Whig Party, few of whom could be considered as paragons of fleshly self-denial. An average day in the life of the Whig leader Charles James Fox featured lapses from moral rectitude which would have cost a humble farm-worker his livelihood (if not his life). Fox's epicurean lifestyle could hardly have appealed to the austere Burke, long before the disagreement over the French Revolution which put an end to their political and personal relationship.

The successful operation of Burke's preferred social order depended crucially on responsible, public-spirited behaviour by the aristocratic class which also enjoyed a virtual monopoly of political offices; relatively low-born interlopers like Burke himself might be recruited from time to time, but only if they showed truly outstanding abilities (and an appropriate level of deference towards their social superiors). Burke assumed that such individuals could exercise a degree of moral influence over their "betters". In this respect, he was unlikely to have been impressed by the prominence in Whig circles of another Dublin-born literary figure, Richard Brinsley Sheridan (1751–1816), whose extravagant spending and capacity for alcohol matched that of Fox himself. Although Sheridan became a boon companion of the Prince of Wales (later George IV), neither he nor Burke could ever be part of the charmed circle of high-born politicians who were regarded as candidates for the highest positions.

After the publication of *Reflections*, Burke's differences with his former Whig friends became impossible to conceal and he was ostracized from the party. In compensation, Burke's anti-revolutionary writings had earned him the gratitude of Fox's sworn enemy King George III, who wanted to bestow a peerage on Burke but instead granted him a substantial annual pension. When Fox's friends, including the Whig grandee the Duke of Bedford, attacked this attempt to relieve Burke from some of his debts the latter responded with a coruscating polemic (*A Letter to a Noble Lord*, 1796). Burke, as had become his custom, went out of his way to lambast the philosophers whom he blamed for the French Revolution: "Nothing can be conceived more hard than the heart of a thoroughbred metaphysician. It comes nearer to the cold malignity of a wicked spirit than to the frailty and passion of a man. It is like that of the principle of Evil himself, incorporeal, pure, unmixed, dephlegmated, defecated evil" (McDowell 1991: 176).

Aristocrats like Bedford could present an even greater threat to Britain's political stability than low-born compatriots if they identified themselves with such monsters. While venting his anger against Bedford, Burke alluded to the origins of his enemy's title – bestowed by a bloody and bloated tyrant, Henry VIII – and dwelt in some detail on the extent of his inherited estates. Burke had allowed his rhetoric to outrun his own small stock of reason. He went beyond the debating-point which would have been compatible with his more considered thinking – i.e., that although individual representatives of their class might be foolish, the aristocracy as a whole was wise and this justified an hierarchical society – and trespassed on the terrain of his revolutionary opponents, who (along with aristocratic fellow-travellers like "Philippe Égalité") argued that human beings should be judged on their inherent qualities rather than unearned privileges. Some British radicals of the 1790s might have been equally rude about the aristocracy in general, but very few could rival Burke's *Letter* in terms of direct personal effrontery.

In *Reflections*, Burke's defence of the role of aristocracy within the existing political and social order is excessively abstract – an early and unconvincing exercise in "spin". He argued that a "prejudice", on closer inspection, will almost invariably be found to contain "latent wisdom" (Mitchell 1989: 138). His uncritical portrait of the aristocracy could be regarded as the product of prejudice; the *Letter to a Noble Lord* provides the detailed scrutiny which shows this prejudice to be unfounded. The same reliance on rhetoric, rather than empirical evidence, characterizes Burke's depiction of the lower end of Britain's social scale. In a notable passage in *Reflections*, he likened the common people to "great cattle, reposed under the shadow of the British oak", who were unlikely to be disturbed by "the importunate chink" of "half a dozen grasshoppers" (i.e., the home-grown radicals, who make all the noise in the field but are ignored by the other inhabitants who merely "chew the cud and are silent": Mitchell 1989: 136). As applied to British society in 1790, this unflattering metaphor was significant; it portrayed a predominantly *rural* population. A society in which the balance of political power reflected the ownership of land rather than wealth gained from trade or financial speculation could be supposed to exhibit the stability which Burke craved: for the inhabitants of a rural society, change was climatic and seasonal, rather than arising from human choice. But urban-dwellers were a different matter, as Burke knew very well having witnessed the unacceptable face of prejudice, displayed by bigoted London Protestants during the 1780 Gordon Riots. In an urban context, the tendency towards cud-chewing passivity could easily be transformed in the face of real or imaginary public grievances. Again, the *Letter to a Noble Lord* is more instructive on this point; at the time of the riots, Burke recalled, "Wild and savage insurrection quitted the woods, and prowled about our streets in the name of reform" (McDowell 1991: 152).

Burke and the problem of poverty

Although the established order had survived the Gordon Riots, Burke was worried that the subversive "grasshoppers" might be more successful in the 1790s, emboldened by events in France and the failure of Britain's propertied classes to present a united front in defence of the established order. Yet his account suggested that radical ideas alone could not precipitate a revolution; social conditions were also relevant. At around the time that he was writing his *Letter to a Noble Lord* – and apparently in response to a request from the prime minister, William Pitt the Younger – Burke set down his thoughts on the appropriate response by the state to economic distress. Such occasions – usually brought on by the failure of a harvest – were often accompanied by localized social disorder. Such outbreaks could become more general, encompassing cities as well as isolated rural areas (Gilmour 1992: 224–46). As such, famine in the incendiary context of the 1790s was a pressing matter of national security, as well as internal social stability.

Burke began his advice to Pitt with the argument that "To provide for us in our necessities is not in the power of Government". Rather, relief of the poor was a duty which should be acknowledged by "the Rich – [who] are the pensioners of the poor", since those who labour "in reality feed both the pensioners and themselves". This could be read as a surreal satire on the author himself, since almost exactly at the time of writing the king (and Pitt's government) had provided his own family with a pension which covered rather more than "necessities". Burke proceeded with an argument which was to become very familiar among apologists for economic inequality: if the "extremely small" number of rich people were expropriated, the ensuing redistribution of wealth "would not give a bit of bread and cheese for one night's supper to those who labour" (McDowell 1991: 120–1).

Robbing the rich would in fact be self-defeating according to Burke, since they "are trustees for those who labour". Essentially he meant that the rich could be trusted to help those in genuine need – as opposed to "able-bodied" workers, whom he sought to exclude from the ranks of the poor even in times of economic hardship – through the judicious exercise of charity. However, his confidence in his own claim seemed less than complete: "Whether they mean it or not, [the rich] do, in effect, exercise their trust – some with more, some with less fidelity and judgement". It would be wrong to disguise the realities of economic life from the poor, through "flattery"; "The poor in that case would be rendered as improvident as the rich, which would not be at all good for them". Advocates of private charity frequently appealed to a distinction between the "deserving" and "undeserving" poor. Burke's own testi mony, like his Letter to a Noble Lord, inadvertently drew attention to the failings of the "undeserving", "improvident" rich.

The historian of poverty in the early nineteenth century, Gertrude Himmelfarb, noted the stark discrepancy between the Burke of

Edmund Burke: the flawed founding father

Reflections and the author of *Thoughts and Details on Scarcity*. For example, she pointed out that Burke had departed from his earlier praise of time-honoured institutions and practices: organized relief of the poor had been an acknowledged feature of English local government since the Elizabethan Age, but Burke was now proposing to scrap it. In *Reflections*, Burke had eulogized a society whose individual members were bound together by ties which were far more profound than any short-term "contract" agreed for short-term mutual convenience. Yet *Thoughts and Details* presents a conflictual relationship between rich and poor, resembling the socio-economic apartheid lamented decades later in Disraeli's novels (Himmelfarb 1984: 66–73).

Himmelfarb's penetrating analysis can be taken even further. In *Reflections*, Burke had recommended an approach to political questions which could be described as "pragmatic": when judging whether reform of existing institutions was required or not, the responsible politician must take contemporary circumstances into account even while maintaining a preference for institutions which had stood the test of time. Yet in *Thoughts and Details* Burke recommended that long-established approaches to the problem of poverty were *least* appropriate in the context where they were *most* necessary if the overall goal of policy is social stability rather than ideological purity. He wrote that

> The cry of the people in cities and towns, though unfortunately (from a fear of their multitude and combination) the most regarded, ought in *fact*, to be the *least* attended to upon this subject; for citizens are in a state of utter ignorance of the means by which they are to be fed, and they contribute little or nothing, except in an infinitely circuitous manner, to their own maintenance (McDowell 1991: 129, emphasis in original).

In short, the very urban dwellers who present the greatest potential threat to social order "ought in *fact*" to be treated with less empathy than anyone else because of their supposed ignorance of economic realities.

In the first paragraph of his memorandum, Burke even managed to undermine his previous praise of "prejudice" as opposed to "reason". Relief of the poor in times of hardship, he argues, is unusually problematic for decision-makers because "there is nothing on which the passions of men are so violent, and their judgement so weak, and on which there exists such a multitude of ill-founded popular prejudices" (McDowell 1991: 120). While Burke had not claimed that "prejudice" was *always* a reliable guide to conduct, in *Reflections* he had strongly implied that it had a particular application to morality: "Prejudice renders a man's virtue his habit: and not a series of unconnected acts. Through just prejudice, his duty becomes part of his nature" (Mitchell 1989: 136). However, in the instance of poor relief the moral "prejudice" in favour of remedial action should be overridden by the "rational" dictates of political economy. Burke, in fact, had convinced himself that the laws of the free market were divinely inspired, which seemed to entail that those who failed to suppress undiscriminating charitable urges were guilty of blasphemy (Macpherson 1980: 59).

In *Reflections*, Burke had lamented that "the age of chivalry" had been replaced by the rule of "sophisters, economists and calculators" (Mitchell 1989: 127). *Thoughts and Details* implies that he had decided to join the winning side, following the emerging school of "economists and calculators" in attempting to prescribe strict limits to government activity in general. He argued that the state

> ought to confine itself to what regards the State … namely, the exterior establishment of its religion; its magistracy; its revenue; its military force by sea and land; the corporations that owe their existence to its fiat; in a word, to every thing that is *truly and properly* public, to the public peace, to the public safety, to the public order, to the public prosperity (McDowell 1991: 143).

In its tone, this depiction of the role of the state was more like the radical liberal ideologue Thomas Paine than the "conservative" Edmund Burke. However, far from being a blueprint for limited government, Burke's list of approved state activities was susceptible to endless expansion; for example, if the effects of poverty were proving to be a menace to "the public peace, to the public safety, to the public order", then on Burke's own argument the state should undertake the kind of organized relief of the poor which the remainder of his tract had ruled out. Indeed, if what is "*properly* public" includes "public prosperity", Burke could have been enlisted by John Maynard Keynes and his twentieth-century "collectivist" followers as an early advocate for continuous government intervention in the economy.

The contrasts between *Reflections* and *Thought and Details on Scarcity* are so numerous and significant that the possibility of mental disturbance cannot be excluded. In printed caricatures during his lifetime Burke was often portrayed as slightly dotty; compared to Fox and Pitt, who could deliver lucid speeches when they were semi-stupified by alcohol, the relatively abstemious Burke was prone to flights of oratorical fancy which baffled (and often bored) his listeners. During the parliamentary debates on the Regency Bill in 1789 he had expressed views on the apparent madness of George III which suggested that he was suffering sympathetic symptoms, declaring that the king had been "smitten by the hand of Omnipotence, and that the Almighty had hurled him from his throne" (Stanhope 1879: 337). The historian Edward Gibbon wrote in May 1791 that "Poor Burke is the most eloquent and rational madman that I ever knew" (Prothero 1896: 252). In December 1792, in preparation for a debate on an Aliens Bill, Burke smuggled a dagger into the House of Commons; when he brandished it during his speech, Sheridan, from the Whig benches which Burke had abandoned, cried out "Where's the fork?". These eccentric exhibitions happened before the death of Burke's son Richard – an event which by all accounts left him prostrate with grief and guilt, not least because it extinguished his chance of establishing an aristocratic political dynasty of his own. If Richard had lived, Burke would almost certainly have crowned his career by accepting the peerage offered by King George. In the absence of any male heirs, he turned down that honour. Almost a century later, the title he would have chosen was bestowed on the childless Benjamin Disraeli, who thus became the one and only Earl of Beaconsfield. It is unlikely that Burke would have appreciated the coincidence.

Burke's literary productions – even pamphlets which were drafted rapidly in response to contemporary developments – were revised carefully prior to publication. On a charitable view of *Thoughts and Details*, it was left as a very raw first draft and Burke would have subjected it to judicious editing if it had ever looked like being published in his lifetime. The fact remains, however, that he drafted the memorandum in earnest and based his crucial arguments on the kind of abstract theorizing which he had denounced in *Reflections*. In that tract he had denounced revolutionary ideologues as "metaphysically mad". Even if Burke was not clinically insane when he wrote *Thoughts and Details*, he was certainly a bitterly disappointed man. In addition to its insistence on a (relatively) humane response to scarcity, Pitt's government had signalled its readiness to negotiate with the "regicide" regime in France. Its attitude suggested what Burke already had good reason to sense: i.e., that it did not regard the conflict in which Britain had (belatedly) engaged as part of a "war of ideas" which could only end with a conclusive victory for the forces of order, but rather as a disruption of the European balance of power which, however serious, was still amenable to a pragmatic settlement. Ironically, the unsuspecting economist Adam Smith had flattered Pitt and Burke in similar terms, implying that they both understood his ideas better than he did himself. Whether or not Pitt was really interested in Burke's thoughts on the relief of poverty, shortly after receiving the memorandum the prime minister proved himself the more faithful of Smith's disciples by declaring that the translation of abstract free-market principles into inflexible dictums would constitute "the most absurd bigotry" (Himmelfarb 1984: 74).

Romanticism and conservatism

Burke was not alone in exaggerating the importance of ideas in precipitating the French Revolution. Thanks to the revolution, prominent political writers found that governments, whatever their professed nature, had a limited tolerance for free speech: Thomas Paine's life was in equal danger in England (for being too radical) and France (where he was far too moderate for Robespierre's taste). On both sides of the debate among intellectuals, the appearance of *Reflections* was accorded a vital role in rallying counter-revolutionary forces. Burke himself seemed to detect no contradiction between his praise for traditional British liberties in *Reflections* – not to mention his support for a limited state in *Thoughts and Details on Scarcity* – and a vigorous campaign to turn the full force of the law against political dissidents. While admitting that Burke was a "great man", the essayist William Hazlitt claimed that "the consequences of his writings as instruments of political power have been tremendous, fatal, such as no exertion of wit or knowledge or genius can ever counteract or atone for" (Howe 1932: 308–9). Hazlitt continued to differ from Burke while paying tribute to his eloquence, but some initial sympathizers with the French Revolution experienced something akin to an ideological conversion once it became apparent to them that Burke had been right all along in his predictions of murderous mayhem. For example, in 1796 James Mackintosh – the author of *Vindiciae Gallicae: A Defence of the French Revolution and its English Admirers* (1791), which was widely considered to be the most effective reply to *Reflections* – told Burke that he considered his "general Principles … as the only solid foundation both of political Science and of political prudence" (McDowell & Woods 1970: 193).

Another supporter of the French Revolution who became an ardent admirer of Burke was the poet William Wordsworth (1770–1850), who included a grovelling posthumous tribute in his autobiographical poem *The Prelude*. Other radicals reconsidered their initial view of the Revolution without Burke's assistance. For example, in 1794 – after the most notorious revolutionary atrocities, and when Britain was already at war with France – Samuel Taylor Coleridge (1772–1834) addressed a sonnet to Burke which recognized his genius but bemoaned his apparent abandonment of the cause of liberty. Coleridge's subsequent renunciation of radicalism was triggered by anxiety that the Revolution had become a serious threat to his own country's security, as expressed in his poem "Fears in Solitude: Written in April 1798, During the Alarm of an Invasion". This scare, along with French aggression towards republican Switzerland, turned Coleridge's thoughts towards understanding and trying to improve the existing British system of government rather than hoping for radical reform whose consequences could not be predicted.

With a voracious capacity for eclectic reading, and a remarkable ability to synthesize contrasting ideas, after his conversion Coleridge was never likely to become an unthinking disciple of any writer. Despite the "marked similarities between Coleridge's political philosophy and that of Burke", Coleridge owed more to earlier British "Republican" thinkers (notably James Harrington (1611–77)), along with Immanuel Kant and other German idealist philosophers (Morrow 1990: 161), Even Coleridge's journalistic productions were infused with this intoxicating intellectual brew; he could not help himself from alluding to unfamiliar concepts in phrases which seemed to have been written in a different language, then translated by someone with a grudge against Anglophone readers.

Coleridge had no conscious intention of refining or supplementing Burke's conservatism, but his work did have this effect. Following Harrington, he was acutely aware of the relationship between property and power and recognized that the constitutional settlement of the 1688–89 Glorious Revolution could only be provisional. While he exhibited a Burkean bias in favour of the long-established landed interest, he appreciated the claims to political influence of more "mobile" forms of property derived from commerce and industry. In Coleridge's terminology, power based on landownership tended towards "permanence", while the newer forms of wealth constituted forces of "progression".

Thus, for Coleridge, society in early nineteenth-century Britain contained contrasting tendencies which (in the style of his beloved German idealists), he believed could, and should, be brought to a workable accommodation.

This was a novel rationale for the kind of gradual political change which Burke had extolled in *Reflections* (where he had coined another alliterative phrase with similar implications, "conservation and correction"). Unlike Burke, who suggested that subversive writings were best answered by legal sanctions, Coleridge offered a constructive long-term remedy. His book *On the Constitution of the Church and State* (1830), was published shortly after the parliamentary decision to remove the most egregious forms of discrimination against Roman Catholics (see Chapter 2). Coleridge was willing to accept this reform, subject to measures which guaranteed the privileged position of the established Anglican church. However, that institution itself needed to change; it should become a truly "national church", a source of organic unity rather than division. Its mission would be moral and educational: it would provide the resources for a "clerisy", an intellectual elite which was charged with the task of spreading knowledge and enlightenment in the widest sense, inculcating virtue throughout the population and inoculating it against seditious arguments.

Whatever the practical problems associated with Coleridge's scheme, it did at least promise to address some of the flaws in Burke's defence of the status quo. As we have seen, Burke was not disposed to diagnose defects in the existing social order – even when some of its most favoured members turned against him. Coleridge perceived much more clearly that the interests of stability could not be served merely by preaching passive obedience to the poor – the type of thing epitomized by the condescending homilies of William Paley (1743–1805) and Hannah More (1745–1833). Poverty was an inescapable facet of human existence, and Coleridge's clerisy would provide direct material relief for the elderly and infirm. Private charity could help in other cases, but only if the propertied classes remembered their duties towards human beings who, whatever the differences in station, were still part of an interdependent society (or, as Coleridge characteristically put it in a 1817 letter to the prime minister, Lord Liverpool, "sprigs and boughs in a forest, tossed against each other, or moved all in the same direction, by an agency in which their own will has the least share"). Without a recognition of the responsibilities which came with wealth, no amount of preaching could prevent people who "are brutalized by ignorance and rendered desperate by want" from regarding the rich with "malignant envy" (Harris 1969: 225).

The main source of "brutalization" was manufacturing industry. This might not be evil in itself, but Coleridge foresaw that its impact on society would be devastating while it continued to be guided by "a false philosophy" – an atomistic view of life which, as Coleridge told the uncomprehending Lord Liverpool, had even infected "our gentry and clergy". As a result, "a few brilliant inventions have been dearly purchased". The most dangerous manifestation of the "false philosophy" was the so-called "science" of political economy embraced by the laissez-faire misinterpreters of Adam Smith. Thomas Robert Malthus (1766–1834) attracted Coleridge's harshest criticisms, and for good reasons: his coupling of endemic poverty with overpopulation seemed to verify the cold-hearted attitude towards the poor exemplified by Burke; he was an ordained clergyman; and like Coleridge he was an alumnus of Jesus College, Cambridge. Coleridge scoffed at the argument of political economists that the victims of industrialization were "free" to strike a bargain with employers; rather, "if labour were indeed free the employer would purchase and the labourer sell, what the former had no right to buy, and the latter no right to dispose of, namely, the labourer's health, life, and well-being. These belong not to himself alone, but to his friends, his parents, to his King, to his country, and to God" (Brinton 1926: 80). In 1818 Coleridge duly offered public support to Sir Robert Peel's Factory Bill, an early legislative attempt to address the most deleterious effects of free market practices. The measure passed in 1819 despite considerable parliamentary opposition, and only after the original proposals had been watered down.

In 1798 Coleridge had brought his conflict of loyalties to an end by accepting that he had been too optimistic about human nature and learning to look more favourably on his imperfect country. However, his profound patriotism never blinded him to the failings of British policy-makers: unlike Burke, who could write that "to make us love our country, our country ought to be lovely" without acquainting himself with real conditions in Britain, Coleridge retained a sincere mission to elevate the condition of the people in material as well as spiritual terms. John Stuart Mill was a great admirer of Coleridge's poetry and was attracted by some of his political ideas, particularly the clerisy. Importantly, in an 1840 essay Mill recognized that Coleridge was a "Conservative" – a word he was clearly using in an ideological, rather than a party-political sense – and was thus an opponent of his own liberalism. This was annoying, since Coleridge's philosophy had "so much in it, both of moral goodness and true insight". Thankfully for Mill, Coleridge was not always right: "In political economy especially he writes like an arrant driveller, and it would have been well for his reputation had he never meddled with the subject" (Mill 1840: 302, 293). Before his death, Mill had learned to adopt a less haughty attitude towards the opponents of liberal political economy.

Coleridge's ideological odyssey is often compared with that of his fellow-poet, Robert Southey (1774–1843), not least because during his own radical years the latter had joined with Coleridge and others in a plan to establish a "utopian" community by the Susquehanna River in New England – a scheme whose only practical result was that Southey and Coleridge became brothers-in-law (having married the Fricker sisters, Edith and Sara). Southey was a prolific prose writer, whose posthumous reputation as a political thinker would almost certainly have been higher if it could have been freed from the inevitable comparison with the more sophisticated Coleridge. It would also have helped if Southey had never written a line of poetry; in that sphere, even Coleridge's unfinished efforts betrayed considerable talent, whereas Southey's verse was sufficiently mediocre to win him (in 1813) the post of Poet Laureate after Sir Walter Scott turned it down. It is somehow fitting that, although Southey deserves immortality as the author of the first published version of "Goldilocks and the Three Bears", he rarely receives credit even for that low-brow literary achievement. Yet for the purposes of the present book Southey is more significant than Coleridge, since his polemical articles were far less demanding for practically-minded readers, especially politicians.

During his lifetime and later, Southey's critics attributed his change of political heart to material motives. His own testimony indicates an ideological overreaction, from speculations about communal bliss on the banks of the Susquehanna to the realization that "Man is a beast, and an ugly beast" (Brinton 1926: 89). As in Coleridge's case, Southey might have lost his faith in "the natural goodness of man", but he was always a *humanitarian* – i.e., he recoiled from the idea of human suffering, and continued to rage against it even though he accepted that it was inevitable. Once he had changed his own mind, Southey turned his wrath against people who continued to believe that radical reform could make the world better, and (on paper, at least) he recommended the forcible suppression of political dissent. For some (including Lord Byron, whose epic poem *Don Juan* featured a mocking dedication to Southey), this was intolerable hypocrisy. Byron was right in this instance, but in relation to the manufacturing system he and the renegade Southey were on the same page. After reading a report into factory conditions, Southey ranted to a friend that "I wonder (as far as I can wonder at anything in these times) that none of these cotton and worsted and flax kings have yet hanged themselves; that none of them have been pulled to pieces; that none of their factories have been destroyed; that the very pavement of the streets has not risen and stoned them" (Brinton 1926: 92).

Southey, Macaulay and Mill

In 1829 Southey published *Sir Thomas More: or, Colloquies on the Progress and Prospects of Society*, an imaginary discussion between More's ghost and the author himself (under the name of "Montesinos"). Montesinos and More enjoy a meeting of minds; in the nineteenth-century context the saintly author of *Utopia* turns out to be a sound conservative. In particular, they agree that religion is the foundation of all government; that no state can be secure unless it trains its people to respect its institutions; and that the manufacturing system produces degradation in human beings and "unqualified deformity" in the landscape.

For Southey and Sir Thomas, the proper scope of government intervention extends far beyond education. In direct contrast to Burke, they insist that in times of scarcity the state should provide employment through public works; indeed, they envisage that governments should intervene in good times as well as bad, since "A liberal expenditure in national works is one of the surest means for promoting national prosperity" (Macaulay 1898: 473). Taxation and the national debt – those bugbears of the liberal political economists – are perfectly acceptable to the poet and his spectral interlocutor.

Thanks to the *Colloquies*, Southey was also the inspiration (or rather the victim) of one of the most celebrated of all critical notices. In the

Edinburgh Review, the historian and Whig politician Thomas Babington (later Lord) Macaulay (1800–59), launched a blistering attack on the *Colloquies* and its author, accusing Southey of being "utterly destitute of the power of discerning truth from falsehood" (Macaulay 1898: 451). Southey should really have known that he was asking for trouble in exhuming Sir Thomas More to comment on England's current misfortunes, rather than using the orthodox didactic device of a visitor from a distant land. A prolific contributor to the Tory *Quarterly Review*, in modern parlance Southey was confined within an ideological "echo-chamber", which prevented him from realizing that he had presented eloquent opponents like Macaulay with an open invitation to play the man rather than the ball. Macaulay has great fun in lampooning Southey as a dabbler in matters far too deep for his understanding, but his attack could only be regarded as a successful *refutation* of Southey's

Robert Southey: Byron's "Epic Renegade"

arguments by occupants of Macaulay's own "echo-chamber" – i.e., readers of the rival, liberal-leaning *Edinburgh Review*. The exchange is thus best understood as a statement of one worldview in response to another, making it an invaluable guide to ideological debates in Britain just before the 1832 Reform Act.

In a significant passage, Macaulay compared Southey to "a much greater man, Mr Burke". The latter's views were dictated by his "fierce and ungovernable sensibility"; reason played a part in his writings and his oratory, but "It did whatever work his passions and his imagination might impose". For a disciple of David Hume and/or Burke, this was not a criticism but rather a plausible account of all human motivation, which would apply with particular force to the composition of a polemical political tract. However, according to Macaulay, Southey's "reason" was not simply "the slave of the passions"; rather, in his work "reason has no place at all, as either leader or follower, as either sovereign or slave" (Macaulay 1898: 451–2).

Thus the disagreement between Macaulay and Southey could be reduced to a single sentence: Macaulay had faith in human reason, whereas Southey (in his post-Revolutionary guise) did not. This fundamental difference was also reflected in sharply contrasting views on the nature of the human condition. Southey used the imaginary Thomas More to debunk the liberal claim that industrialization was a "progressive" development. For his part, Macaulay conceded that there was "great distress" in the country at the time of writing. However, no-one could dispute that Britain was richer than it had been in 1790, despite the effects of "a war, compared to which all other wars sink into insignificance" (indeed, Macaulay tacitly admitted that general prosperity had risen despite unprecedented levels of debt and taxation, thus coming perilously close to accepting one of Southey's arguments). But Southey had argued that rising *overall* prosperity could conceal increasing disparities between the condition of the rich and the poor, and Macaulay deliberately overlooked this point. In the same passage Southey had also argued that "Great capitalists become like pikes in a fish pond, who devour the weaker fish" (Macaulay 1898: 500, 502). For a writer of 1829 to anticipate Keynes and Marx within a couple of sentences is surely an achievement to rival the composition of "Goldilocks".

Macaulay's response echoes the Burke of *Thoughts and Details on Scarcity*, and scarcely differs from the anti-collectivist rhetoric of subsequent generations. "The intermeddling of Mr Southey's idol, the omniscient and omnipotent state", Macaulay insisted, is not only wrong in principle but counter-productive in practice. If government confines itself to its proper sphere ("maintaining peace, … defending property … diminishing the price of law … observing strict economy in every department of the state"), Macaulay thought it possible that by 1930 "a population of fifty million, better fed, clad, and lodged than the English of our time, will cover these islands" (Macaulay 1898: 500, 502). In some respects Macaulay's guesswork was inspired, but the shades of Southey and Sir Thomas, now properly united, would have been forgiven for thinking that history had enjoyed the last laugh over the great Whig historian. Thanks to the repercussions of the Wall Street Crash, by the end of Macaulay's chosen year of 1930 UK unemployment had soared to 2.5 million and governments even in democratic states like Britain and the United States felt it necessary to extend the scope of intervention to address the apparent failure of economic liberalism.

Belief in a minimal state, combined with faith in the findings of political economists and an equation of "progress" with material conditions rather than moral or spiritual concerns are hallmarks of laissez-faire liberalism. Macaulay was also a prominent parliamentary supporter of electoral reform, the key liberal demand of the time. As a young radical, Southey had written a poem about the depopulated borough of Old Sarum, near Salisbury, characterizing the right of its proprietor to nominate two MPs as an indefensible blot on the British political system. By 1832, Southey had come to regard Old Sarum and its ilk as highly eccentric, but nevertheless functional, anomalies which deserved preservation. Macaulay agreed with the young rather than the mature Southey.

Nevertheless, the American historian Russell Kirk credited Macaulay with a "service to the conservative cause" in the year before his diatribe against Southey (Kirk 1954: 194). Macaulay had engaged in a prolonged intellectual skirmish with the utilitarian Mills, James (the father) and John Stuart (the son). However, Kirk's praise only makes sense in the spirit of "my enemy's enemy is my friend", or if one takes seriously John Stuart Mill's 1840 claim that "every Englishman of the present day is by implication either a Benthamite or a Coleridgian" (Mill 1840: 260). Indeed, Macaulay did close his side of the debate – which extended over three articles in the *Edinburgh Review*, while John Stuart Mill replied in the radical *Westminster Review* – by confessing that he almost preferred "the venerable nonsense which holds prescriptive sway over the ultra-Tory" to the "prejudices and sophisms" of the utilitarians (Macaulay 1898: 411). Given that John Stuart Mill suspected ultra-Tories of crass stupidity, this was a verbal punch which landed below the belt.

According to Kirk, in his assault on the utilitarians Macaulay showed "more than a touch of Burke's genius, and ... a spirit which Burke would have commended" (Kirk 1954: 192). However, Macaulay's purpose in this controversy was to save his own (liberal) causes from utlilitarian contamination. He argued that the unpopularity of the utilitarians had "already made the science of political economy – a science of vast importance to the welfare of nations – an object of disgust to the majority of the community. The question of parliamentary reform will share the same fate if once an association be formed in the public mind between Reform and Utilitarianism" (Macaulay 1898: 409).

Macaulay was particularly exercised by the Mills' claim that all theories of government ultimately arose from interpretations of human nature. All that he would allow on this score was that "men always act from self interest", but this could have few political implications because, when examined closely, it merely meant that "a man had rather do what he would rather do" (Macaulay 1898: 365–6). This was a world away from the views expressed by Coleridge, or by Burke in his *Reflections*. Instead of advancing a systematic theory of his own, Macaulay recommended that policy-makers should adopt the method "which, in every experimental science to which it has been applied, has signally increased the power and knowledge of our species" – i.e., "by the method of Induction". This "noble Science of Politics", as Macaulay called it, did bear a superficial resemblance to an important element of the Burkean approach; it would give rise to proposals for reform which were based upon and tested against "facts", including "the history of past ages" (Macaulay 1898: 369–70). However, the outcome of such an inductive process depended on the nature of the "inputs" – in particular, despite Macaulay's disclaimer, assumptions about human nature. In Macaulay's case, induction inspired a "fervent wish" for an extension of the franchise which would make the House of Commons into "the express image of the opinion of the middle orders of Britain". He advocated a property qualification which would ensure that "every decent farmer and shopkeeper" would have the right to vote: "And this would content us" (Macaulay 1898: 449). "Decency", in Macaulay's mind, translated as "politically responsible": and induction had persuaded him that such qualities could be discerned in individual people on the basis of the property they owned.

In a parliamentary debate of March 1832 Macaulay claimed that Britain was faced with the alternatives of "Reform, or anarchy", and that he had reached this conclusion by means of his favourite "inductive" method. The next speaker, the Conservative John Wilson Croker, attested that his personal process of induction had confirmed his long-held opinion that extension of the franchise would inevitably plunge Britain into revolutionary mayhem (Hansard HC Deb., 19 March 1832). Their contrasting conclusions had been dictated by incompatible ideological perspectives; and they turned out to be equally ill-founded. So much for induction, and "the noble science of politics"!

These debates, leading to the passage of the Great Reform Act of 1832, took place when Burke's warnings against radical constitutional change seemed less relevant, not just because of Britain's avoidance of revolution but also because in 1830 France had undergone another upheaval, this time (relatively) bloodless and resulting in the installation of a "constitutional monarchy" under the Anglophile King Louis Philippe. Although Coleridge took the view that in political matters people should be "*weighed, not counted*", his chief objection to electoral reform was that it had passed after extreme pressure from public opinion (Harris 1969: 233). Macaulay, by sharp contrast, argued that the popular clamour was a key argument *in favour* of reform. His proposed (and, as it proved, unsustainable) compromise was that all *property*-owners should be treated equally; he hoped for a reform of the franchise which would "see an end put to all the advantages which particular forms of property possess over other forms". That is, being a substantial land-owner with a real and lasting "stake in the country" should provide no more political influence than wealth derived from commerce or industry. Macaulay was thus, in Coleridge's terms, a strong proponent of "progression" over "permanence", rather than a defender of consti-tutional arrangements which embodied a judicious balance between those antagonistic forces (Macaulay 1898: 449).

Associating political actors like Macaulay and Southey with different ideological traditions, on the basis of a range of relevant evidence, helps us not merely to understand the individuals concerned, but also the nature of the debates in which they took part. Macaulay versus Southey was not an exact reenactment of Paine versus Burke; the issues which had provoked polarization in the 1790s were still keenly contested but the context was far less toxic. The nature of ideologies does not change, but new political developments call forth different expressions of consistently-held beliefs, often exposing nuances which are less apparent in the whitest heat of controversy. If the voices of conservatism and liberalism could be heard distinctly in 1832, over the next few decades the "battle of ideas" would become more complicated.

Summary

While the case for tracing a distinctive tradition of modern conservatism to the Whig politician Edmund Burke is very strong, it is a mistake to regard him as an infallible exponent of his own general position. Some of his views were inconsistent with his key principles concerning human nature, society and political activity. The inconsistency was most marked in relation to economics. The former radicals Samuel Taylor Coleridge and Robert Southey reached very different conclusions on the key issues of poverty and the emergence of an atomistic, anonymous industrial society. Their stated principles offered a coherent basis for a critique of liberal-inspired reforms in church and state between 1828 and 1832 – the time when commentators had begun to refer to conservatism as a distinctive position, and the old Tory party adopted the "Conservative" label.

2

The Conservative Party from Peel to Salisbury

As Benjamin Disraeli wrote in 1835, "In times of great political change and rapid political transition, it will generally be observed that political parties find it convenient to re-baptise themselves" (Hutcheon 1913: 217). For the British Tory Party, the early 1830s was such a time. In 1832 the Whig Party – its rival since the late seventeenth century – pushed through a reform of the electoral franchise which marked the first significant step towards democracy in the United Kingdom. If Tories were to compete for office in this new context, they would have to discard their historic label; and "Conservative" seemed the most suitable substitute.

Some important details are missing from the Conservative birth certificate. For many years the parentage was attributed to John Wilson Croker (1780–1857: see Chapter 1), an Irish-born MP and journalist who was closely connected with many influential figures within the Tory Party. It turned out that a more obscure author had pre-empted Croker, using the term "conservative" in an article for the pro-Tory *Quarterly Review*, in January 1830 (Stewart 1978: 69). Robert Southey referred to "conservative" principles and a conservative party in the same journal the following year (Southey 1831: 315, 317). By the time of the Reform Act the label had been accepted in some unexpected places: even the maniacally partisan Duke of Newcastle-under-Lyne (1785–1851) switched from "Tory" to "Conservative" in his diary without missing a beat (Gaunt 2006: 201–202). However, no precise date of birth can be given. Indeed, the word "Tory" continues to be used, either by supporters who are proud of its traditionalist resonances, opponents who find that it fits better than "Conservative" in insulting slogans, or commentators for the sake of variety.

Between the Hanoverian succession in 1714 and the last, unsuccessful Jacobite rebellion of 1745 the name "Tory" had a clear political meaning. It denoted a stickler for the hereditary principle, who hoped for the reinstatement of the Stuart dynasty deposed in 1688–89. However, between the mid-eighteenth century and the late 1820s allusions to a cohesive "Tory Party" must be taken with a pinch of salt, despite the notable scholarship which has been devoted to its history (e.g., Wood 1924; Feiling 1924, 1938). It tended to be a label which could be attached to any politician who accepted government office on the understanding that the monarch – whether the product of "Divine" choice or not – was and should remain the central actor in the British political system. Since the monarchy enjoyed considerable electoral influence in that pre-democratic age, and government could not function without the cooperation of a bureaucratic elite which was loyal to the state rather than to any political party, it made sense for any incoming administration of the eighteenth century to reach an accommodation with the monarchy, even if this entailed a subservient relationship. Ministries which challenged this arrangement – most notably the Fox–North coalition of 1783 – tended to be short-lived.

Not even supposed Tory totems, like William Pitt the Younger (prime minister 1783–1801 and 1804–06), can easily be associated with the party. Pitt regarded himself as an "independent Whig" throughout his parliamentary career and resigned in 1801 because of a sharp disagreement with the king, George III, on the issue of Catholic emancipation. However, Pitt had initially become prime minister as the beneficiary of George's vendetta against the Fox–North coalition; and when he resumed the office in 1804 he promised George that he would never propose emancipation again. Pitt's place in the Tory pantheon was only assured once death (in 1806) silenced his protestations of Whig affiliation; when his rival Charles James Fox rapidly followed him to a grave in Westminster Abbey, "Whig" and "Tory" partisanship could readily be assigned on the basis of posthumous allegiance to either of those statesmen, either because of principle, personal friendship, or a mixture of both (Sack 1993: 83–90).

Even after Pitt's death it was more helpful to estimate the balance of forces in the House of Commons on the basis of support for various individual political actors (including the monarch) rather than party loyalties. Thus, although George Canning (1770–1827) is usually designated as a Tory, he pursued an ostentatiously liberal approach in his two spells as foreign secretary (1807–09 and 1822–27), and included several Whigs in the government he formed just a few months before his death in 1827. He is best understood as an admirer (and protégé) of Pitt (although this did not prevent him from fighting a celebrated duel in 1809 with Lord Castlereagh, another Tory (and a fellow-Pittite to boot)). Like Pitt before him, Canning's personal influence was felt long after his death; the "Canningite" Tories included Sir John Gladstone (1764–1851), the slave-owning father of the future Liberal prime minister.

However, while accidents of biography often explained the attribution of "Tory" allegiance to office-seekers, the parliamentary foot-soldiers of the party saw themselves as public-spirited, patriotic and independent-minded custodians of the interests of the localities they felt honoured to represent. The Tory archetype was the squire, not over-burdened with brains but heavily-freighted with integrity and common sense. Even in Jacobite years, one of them had proudly told a friend that "I go out a-hunting to show I am a Tory, and drink bumpers to show I am a churchman" (Feiling 1938: 11). Opponents, however, saw the average Tory in a very different light, especially after the sharpening of ideological battles in the aftermath of the French Revolution. In 1819 the radical essayist William Hazlitt presented a lengthy and unflattering portrait:

> A Tory is one who is governed by sense and habit alone. He considers not what is possible, but what is real; he gives might the preference over right. He cries Long Life to the conqueror, and is ever strong upon the stronger side – the side of corruption and prerogative …. He does not, like a fool, contest for modes of faith; but like a wise man, swears by that which is by law established. He has no principles himself, nor does he profess to have any, but will cut your throat for differing with any of his bigotted dogmas, or for objecting to any act of power that he supposes necessary to his interest …. He is not for empty speculations, but for full pockets. He is for having plenty of beef and pudding, a good coat to his back, a good house over his head, and for cutting a respectable figure in the world …. Truth and falsehood are, to him, something to buy and sell; principle and conscience, something to eat and drink. He tramples on the pleas of Humanity and lives, like a caterpillar, on the decay of public good. (Howe 1932: 17–18)

The rapid acceptance of the Conservative label by parliamentarians who had previously been known as Tories suggests a combination of push and pull factors – a recognition that the word "Tory" was toxic in some quarters and a feeling that "Conservative" was a more apposite short-hand term to encapsulate a political approach which the more thoughtful Tories had previously approved. As J. J. Sack has shown, over the years between Pitt's death and the passage of the Reform Act alternative names to "Tory" were canvassed – often by Pitt's devotees (Sack 1993: 89). It was the prospect of parliamentary reform, however, which provided the decisive impetus.

In June 1831 a group of prominent Tories met in London's Charles Street and agreed to subscribe to a fund which could finance a rudimentary party organization (Stewart 1978: 72). At the same time, opponents of the Whig Reform Bill were planning to expand the social attractions available to fellow-believers – an initiative which led to the opening of the Carlton Club in March 1832. A house on Carlton House Terrace soon proved too small for the club, which migrated to Pall Mall – conveniently situated between Westminster and Buckingham Palace.

London's clubland already provided opponents of electoral reform with ample opportunities for refreshment and reactionary banter. The only rationale for new social venues at this time was an increased sense of partisanship, so that Tories could vent their spleens over contemporary developments without any risk of being overheard by political opponents, as they could easily have been at White's, an existing club which was mainly (but not exclusively) Tory. By the same token, a "safe haven" of this kind could serve as a kind of organizational headquarters for opponents of electoral reform.

The new club had only been in business for a few weeks when political and social developments reinforced the arguments in favour of a new party name and an invigorated organization. The general election of May 1831, which provided the Whigs under Lord Grey with a majority estimated at more than 130 seats, had been called after the government was thwarted in its first attempt to modify the franchise. Despite this significant indication of public support for electoral reform, in October 1831 the government's proposals were rejected by the Tory-dominated House of Lords. A revised Reform Bill was presented, only to fall foul of the Lords a second time. When Grey resigned as prime minister the Tory leader, the Duke of Wellington – whose London residence had been attacked more than once by pro-reform mobs – accepted the King's commission to form a government. As recently as November 1830 Wellington had declared that the existing electoral arrangements in Britain could not be improved, making him an implausible architect of the compromise solution which now seemed unavoidable. New manifestations of civil disobedience (including mass withdrawals of funds from the Bank of England) forced the "Iron Duke" to retreat. Lord Grey returned to office, armed with an assurance from the king (William IV) that any further resistance in the House of Lords would be overridden by the creation of a sufficient number of pro-reform peers.

Thus the Tory peers who had obstructed reform found themselves undermined by their own vaunted principles. As staunch defenders of the royal prerogative, they could hardly deny the monarch's theoretical ability to affect the composition of the legislature by stuffing the upper house with newly-ennobled recruits: indeed, their ancestors had rejoiced when Charles II had deployed his constitutional weapons against Whigs. Their adherence to the hereditary principle made it difficult for them to grumble about the monarch himself, although William IV was not a great advertisement for the principle of divine right. His adult life had mostly been spent without a serious expectation of inheriting the throne, allowing him to become the carefree sire of ten children with an actress. Prior to 1832, Tory support for the monarchy included an assumption that the institution would always rally in defence of the established order. Afterwards, those who wanted to avert what they considered to be ruinously radical change could no longer make that assumption: they would have to marshal their own resources.

The constitutional settlement of 1688–89, which underpinned the monarchical-aristocratic state and was praised so rhapsodically by Edmund Burke, had undergone significant changes even before the passage of the Reform Act. In 1828 the Test and Corporation Acts, which debarred people who had not taken Anglican communion from holding either political or military offices, were repealed. In practice, the Acts had rarely been used against non-Anglican Protestants, but they retained more than a symbolic importance; while they persisted on the statute book, they reminded religious dissenters of all kinds that their enjoyment of civil rights was strictly provisional. Since Protestant dissent was widely equated with the political doctrines which had helped to inspire the seventeenth-century's Civil War, the legal classification of dissenters as second-class citizens (at best) had been a key objective for the original "Tories" under the restored monarchy.

Apart from a tiny, enlightened minority, both sides in the Civil War had been happy to agree that Roman Catholics should be persecuted. However, after the removal of legal penalties from Protestant dissenters in 1828 it was difficult to sustain the logic of anti-Catholic legislation, especially since (as Pitt had recognized in 1801) a continued regime of religious persecution in Ireland would jeopardize any benefits arising from the recent union of that country with Great Britain. According to the historian J. C. D. Clark, however, when Catholic emancipation duly arrived in 1829 it constituted "a shattering of the old order" (Clark 2000: 548). To make matters even worse, the prime minister who presided over the dismantling of the Restoration religious settlement was a Tory – none other than the Duke of Wellington, aided and abetted by his home secretary and effective deputy, Robert Peel (1788–1850). Having previously adopted a staunchly anti-Catholic position, Peel felt he could not remain as MP for Oxford University without a fresh endorsement from his constituents: in the ensuing by-election he was defeated by a fanatical anti-Catholic, Sir Robert Inglis.

While Clark's views remain controversial among historians, his insistence that the religious reforms of 1828–29 dealt a staggering blow to a governing system which had prevailed for more than a century – rendering subsequent reform of the electoral franchise little more than a footnote – is an important corrective to the tendency of scholars to focus on the more secular events of 1832. Even if Clark's verdict on the earlier, religious reforms – namely, that "a whole social and political order had been destroyed" – is exaggerated, it cannot be denied that the Conservative Party began its life on the back foot in terms of its overall purpose, and that its most senior figures seemed to be imbued with a culture of concession, in which the friends of the established order might "talk the talk" but were not prepared to act in accordance with their own rhetoric (Clark 2000: 548).

The ascendancy of Peel

Far from unleashing the forces of anarchy, as J. W. Croker and other alarmists had predicted, the Reform Act as eventually passed embodied a compromise of sorts; voting rights were still restricted to substantial property-owners, and the redistribution of seats created additional county constituencies where potential Conservative support was strong. However, the first general election held under the new provisions (December 1832) resulted in a crushing victory for the Whigs, who won more than two-thirds of the 658 seats in the House of Commons. A Conservative comeback from this dismal showing would depend crucially on good organization and inspired leadership. A more professional approach to organization, with the Carlton Club at its heart, had already been identified as a priority. As for leadership, it seemed that the party was well placed since it could call on the services of Peel (now Sir Robert), probably the best debater in the Commons at the time and also a proven administrator.

Peel's career is an excellent illustration of the interplay between individual personality, ideas, institutions and events at this time. A Harrow school contemporary of Lord Byron before graduating from Oxford with a double first in the unlikely combination of classics and mathematics, Peel was embarrassingly over-qualified as an ornament of the British landed classes. However, his father (another Robert) had become one of the richest men in Britain through his own efforts; his money (and his baronetcy) arose from his career as an enlightened employer in the cotton industry. Peel *père* had entered parliament in 1790 as a supporter of the Younger Pitt, rather than attaching himself to the reformist Whigs led by Charles James Fox; his parliamentary seat of Tamworth, Staffordshire, was secured by his purchase of the neighbouring estate of Drayton Bassett. The highlight of his parliamentary career was the introduction of the first legislative measure to regulate factories – the Health and Morals of Apprentices Act (1802); he also championed the Cotton Mills Act of 1819, which had won Coleridge's support (see Chapter 1).

As such, the first Sir Robert Peel and his namesake son personified Coleridge's elements of "progression" and "permanence". In terms of the national interest in the aftermath of reform, Sir Robert the younger thus seemed an ideal candidate for the highest office; but his prospects depended crucially on the ability of his party to attract support from moderate "progressives" – those who had backed the Whigs through the reform process but were unsettled by the prospect of further changes in church and state.

Disunity in the Whig ranks gave William IV an opportunity to dismiss the reforming government (now led by Viscount Melbourne) in late 1834. In Peel's absence (on holiday in Italy) the Duke of Wellington agreed to form a minority administration, with the proviso that the premier should sit in the Commons rather than the Lords. Thus Peel left the country as an opposition MP and returned as prime minister. Parliament was dissolved in December 1834, in advance of a general election to be held in the new year. With cabinet agreement, Peel issued a declaration of principle to voters within his Tamworth constituency, which he had inherited from his father in 1830.

The first "official" party proclamation of its kind, Peel's "Tamworth Manifesto" is often identified as the founding document for the Conservative Party. As we have seen, however, the party had adopted its new name before 1834. Also, while one Conservative Party historian was wrong to assert that the manifesto suffered from "a conspicuous absence" of "any specifically conservative principle", Peel himself felt it necessary to address the issue at greater length in a speech of 1838, admitting that his party had been "so often taunted with the use of vague generalities" (Hearnshaw 1933: 200; Gash 1965: 132–3). In the manifesto itself Peel focused on controversies of the present and the recent past, in a manner which was calculated to reassure moderate Whigs rather than to inspire his own side. Although he had opposed the 1832 Reform Act, in 1834 Peel tacitly accepted that he might have exaggerated its likely short-term consequences (a conclusion assisted by his knowledge that, as usual, he was about to be returned unopposed for Tamworth). The changes to the franchise could now be considered "a final and irrevocable settlement of a great constitutional question – a settlement which no friend to the peace and welfare of this country would attempt to disturb, either by direct or by insidious means" (White 1950: 157).

Under Peel's leadership, the Conservative Party would not embark on a Quixotic attempt to turn back the clock. Moderate Whigs should be more worried about the radical members of their own party:

> … if, by adopting the spirit of the Reform Bill, it be meant that we are to live in a perpetual vortex of agitation; that public men can only support themselves in public estimation by adopting every popular impression of the day, – by promising the instant

redress of anything which anybody may call an abuse – by aban-
doning altogether that great aid of government – more powerful than either law or reason – the respect for ancient rights,
and the deference to prescriptive authority; if this be the spirit
of the Reform Bill, I will not undertake to adopt it. But if the
spirit of the Reform Bill implies merely a careful review of institutions, civil and ecclesiastical, undertaken in a friendly temper
combining, with the firm maintenance of established rights,
the correction of proved abuses and the redress of real grievances, – in that case, I can for myself and colleagues undertake
to act in such a spirit and with such intentions (White 1950:
157–8).

This was not too far from the approach of the moderate Whig Macaulay
(see Chapter 1), but there were subtle differences. While, like Macaulay,
Peel insisted that his attitude to reform would derive from "facts", in his
case public clamour on behalf of change would, if anything, strengthen
the argument against it. Also, while Macaulay supported reform which
would give a preponderance of electoral power to the middle classes,
Peel promised that a Conservative government would give "just and
impartial consideration of what is due to all interests – agricultural,
manufacturing, and commercial". For Conservatives, as for Coleridge,
"just and impartial consideration" would result in a preference for the
forces of "permanence" (i.e., agriculture) over "progression". Peel's form
of words in 1834 suggested a similar outlook; years later it transpired
that he had very different ideas.

As a tactical device, the manifesto promised to bring dividends even
if the Conservatives did not win the election outright. When parliament reassembled, Peel's prescription would be available as a basis for
Conservative cooperation (or even conjunction) with any wavering
Whig MPs. Among the moderates who might be tempted into a Peel-led
party, the lowest-hanging fruit was Lord Edward Stanley (1799–1869),
later 14th Earl of Derby. In May 1834 Stanley had been one of four
Whigs who resigned from Earl Grey's government. The immediate issue
concerned the revenues of the established church in Ireland, but Stanley
had been considering his options for some time.

As it was, although the Conservatives made considerable gains in the
1835 general election they were still outnumbered by the Whigs and

their Irish allies, and could not coax Stanley into a government which included too many "Tory ultras" for his taste. However, after Peel's stop-gap government had resigned Stanley and his closest confidant, Sir James Graham, gradually disengaged themselves from the Whigs. The historian Robert Stewart has estimated that between the Reform Act and 1841, when Stanley finally joined the Carlton Club, a total of 58 Whigs gravitated towards the Conservatives (Stewart 1978: 117).

Although Peel was well aware that his party included MPs and peers who had not forgotten – or forgiven – his U-turn over Catholic emancipation, he was supremely confident of his own judgement and regarded "ultras" in his own ranks with ill-disguised contempt. Another development of 1834 suggested that he was right to discount his internal opponents. Inspired by the utilitarian Edwin Chadwick and the political economist Nassau Senior, the Whig government had introduced legislation to amend the Poor Laws, proposing to abolish outdoor relief for the able-bodied poor and establishing a system of workhouses overseen by elected boards. The measure stood in clear contravention of the social views expounded by Coleridge, Southey and (in *Reflections*, at least) Edmund Burke. Above all, it was a tacit acknowledgment that pleas for a moral renaissance among the propertied classes had not been heeded; they were not performing their duties to the poor, so the task had to be taken on by administrators who turned out to be more penny-pinching than paternalistic. Benjamin Disraeli (1804–81) argued that the legislation "announce[d] to the world that in England poverty is a crime" (Himmelfarb 1984: 182). Yet in 1834 Disraeli was not an MP. Parliamentary Conservative opposition was loud but limited; the most prominent dissidents either considered themselves to be "Tories" rather than Conservatives (like Richard Oastler (1789–1861)), or had been elected under the "Radical" label (like the veteran William Cobbett (1763–1835)). When Oastler lobbied senior Conservatives on the subject the response was lukewarm; the former chancellor Lord Eldon, usually considered as a violent ultra-Tory, was sympathetic but reportedly took the view that resistance was pointless since "nowadays they will pass anything" (Driver 1946: 285). Underneath the defeatism was a more venal calculation: Conservative politicians, like other landowners, were concerned at the rising cost of poor relief, and were glad to serve on the Poor Law boards so long as less well-heeled citizens were being required to share their financial burdens (Roberts 1979: 129–48).

"Young England", Catholicism and the Corn Laws

Conservative revulsion against the New Poor Law was more clearly (though still unsuccessfully) registered in the early 1840s. By that time, parliamentary opposition had been augmented by a group of idealists given the collective name of "Young England". The group looked to Coleridge for intellectual and spiritual inspiration, but Disraeli, its most dynamic representative, was something of an outrider, lacking the advantages of birth and education of his collaborators. Disraeli, indeed, had first stood for parliament (in an 1832 by-election) as an independent Radical. By 1837 he had charmed his way into the Conservative fold and was duly elected for Maidstone. His most effective arguments for the cause of "Young England" came in the form of novels (notably *Coningsby* (1844) and *Sybil* (1845)), which appeared as the group itself was losing its cohesion.

By that time the Conservative Party was in office, defying the doomsayers by securing an overall majority in the 1841 general election under the reformed franchise. However, the party rank and file was soon growing restless at the perceived continuity between Peel's new administration and the defeated Melbourne ministry. Peel's 1842 budget reinstated income tax (which had been abolished in 1816 and now became a permanent fiscal fixture) while reducing the duties on imported corn which had protected domestic agriculture since 1815. Although the parliamentary party acquiesced in these measures, backbench rebellions became more frequent; in March 1844, 95 Conservatives supported an attempt by Lord Ashley (later Lord Shaftesbury, 1801–85) to limit the hours of factory labour to ten. In the previous year, Ashley himself had told a cabinet minister that Peel's government had "introduced no mischievous legislation, & made no wicked appointments" – scarcely a ringing endorsement of his party's performance (Stewart 1978: 184).

In *Coningsby*, Disraeli provided a more pithy expression of a similar viewpoint in a remark by the fictional careerist politician Mr Taper, who characterized "A sound Conservative government" as a combination of "Tory men and Whig measures". This Peelite recipe began to seem less appetising within months of the novel's publication. In 1845 Peel decided to increase a government grant, first awarded by Pitt the Younger in 1795, to the Catholic seminary at Maynooth in County Kildare. This decision provoked the resignation of the president of the

Board of Trade, William Gladstone (1809–98), who had opposed the Maynooth grant in his 1838 book, *The State in its Relations with the Church*. In his review of Gladstone's book – which was heavily influenced by Coleridge – Macaulay had described the author as "the rising hope of those stern and unbending Tories". In the debate over Maynooth Gladstone proved excessively bendy, supporting from the backbenches (in a speech laced with references to Pitt and quotations from Burke) the very measure which had provoked his resignation. In reply, Disraeli poked fun at Gladstone's expense but heaped invective on his own party leader, Peel the alleged "Conservative dictator" (Hansard HC Deb., 11 April 1845). Although the legislation passed, the voting figures showed that the party was almost equally split, while anti-Catholic petitions attracted more than a million signatures (Stewart 1978: 193).

Stanley had supported Peel over Maynooth, but resigned from his cabinet position in December 1845 over an even more ominous issue – the Corn Laws. Although the decision to repeal the protectionist duties was taken in response to famine in Ireland, Peel had accepted the theoretical argument for such a step shortly after forming his government in 1841. He was accused of contradicting the Tamworth Manifesto by caving in to extra-parliamentary opinion (as expressed by the Anti-Corn Law League) and betraying the agricultural interest. Although Peel prevailed in the Commons, a majority of Conservative MPs voted against their own government on 15 May 1846. On 25 June the long-suffering Duke of Wellington cajoled the Lords into passing the necessary legislation; but later that day Peel was heavily defeated on an Irish Coercion Bill, which was opposed by many Whigs and Radicals as well as dissident Conservatives, and promptly resigned.

This is not the place for a detailed discussion of the ensuing party split and the gradual recovery under Stanley (who had been elevated to the House of Lords in 1844 and succeeded his father as Earl of Derby in 1851). The anti-Peelites – initially known as "Protectionists" – were led at first in the House of Commons by Lord George Bentinck, an extraordinary amalgam of enlightenment and pig-headedness, who shared Stanley's obsession with horse-racing but little of his political acumen. In December 1847 Bentinck delivered an impassioned speech in support of Jewish emancipation. On this subject his views were opposed with equal vehemence by many Protectionists (notably the bigoted Anglican Sir Robert Inglis, Peel's conqueror at Oxford University back in 1829), and Bentinck resigned as Protectionist leader. Ironically, the ultimate beneficiary of this antisemitic effusion was the Jewish-born Disraeli, who (after an unseemly attempt to find a more "orthodox" candidate) was recognized as the Commons' leader of what (at Stanley's insistence) was once again known as the Conservative Party.

The mover of the motion to remove Jewish "disabilities" was Lord John Russell, the son of the Duke of Bedford who had been attacked by Burke in his *Letter to a Noble Lord*. In that magnificent polemic Burke had compared Bedford's inherited power with his own laborious path into politics: "At every step of my progress in life (for in every step I was traversed and opposed), and at every turnpike I met, I was obliged to show my passport, and again and again to prove my sole title to the honour of being useful to my country" (McDowell 1991: 160). Disraeli encountered even stiffer opposition, but stormed through every turnpike without offering even a flash of his passport. The final obstacle to becoming leader of a reunited Conservative Party in the Commons was the fact that he had made himself persona non grata to Peel's followers (including Gladstone and Graham) through his calculated insults. His early career furnished even more cogent objections to his prominence within a party dedicated to the interests of the landed classes. In a personal manifesto issued in support of his third unsuccessful attempt as a Radical candidate (1833), Disraeli had proclaimed (with his own emphasis) that "THE ARISTOCRATIC PRINCIPLE HAS BEEN DESTROYED IN THIS COUNTRY, NOT BY THE REFORM ACT BUT BY THE MEANS BY WHICH THE REFORM ACT WAS PASSED". It was now "utterly impossible to revert to the aristocratic principle". However, Disraeli had also written that "He is a mean-spirited wretch who is restrained from doing his duty by the fear of being held up as insincere and inconsistent … A great mind that thinks and feels is never inconsistent, and never insincere" (Hutcheon 1913: 18-20). By casting in his lot with the Conservatives and deciding that "the aristocratic principle" had some mileage left in it after all, Disraeli gave the first of many demonstrations of his immunity from mundane considerations like consistency and sincerity.

As Robert Stewart has noted, Disraeli and Derby were colleagues, rather than friends: even if they had overcome their very different social origins, "temperamentally they were poles apart" (Stewart 1978: 262). However, consultations with his lieutenant, as well as the responsibilities

Benjamin Disraeli: the failed Radical and legendary
Conservative populist

of leadership, pushed Derby's thought-process in a Disraelian direction.
Thus, in March 1851 he told the ageing Croker that he was tempted to
fight the next election on the "war cry" of "Protestantism, Protection,
and down with the Income Tax". In effect, Derby was proposing to campaign on an explicit repudiation of the legacy of Sir Robert Peel (who
had died in a riding accident the previous year). This was not calculated
to improve the chances of reunion with the "Peelites". One must presume
that Derby's expression of distaste for the income tax, at least, came
from the heart; but the other proposed campaign slogans were cynical,
if not hypocritical. Derby's sincere Anglicanism had not prevented him
from supporting the Maynooth grant, and while stoking the Protestant
fire he was well aware of "its evils and all its dangers". At least his idea of

a new party platform was a means to what he considered to be a worthy end; it would help the Conservatives to ensure the continued supremacy of the landed interest and the preservation of the monarchy, which in his "deliberate judgement" would be destroyed if effective power passed into the hands of manufacturers (Stewart 1978: 252). Nevertheless, by 1851 Derby was coming to share Disraeli's view that the party should wean itself away from its Protectionist preoccupations and accept that the Corn Laws would never be restored.

The tawdry tactics paid off; there were significant Conservative gains in the 1852 general election, and Derby accepted the queen's request to form a government. However, the party lacked an overall majority and in December it was brought down after the defeat of Disraeli's budget, which had proposed a small but significant shift in the burden of taxation from agriculture to middle-class householders and shopkeepers. On 16 December 1852 Gladstone replied to Disraeli's speech (which, including a short intermission, stretched over five hours) with a lengthy oration of his own, replete with crushing rebukes. An ex-Tory was conducting a furious assault on a Conservative Party budget introduced by a former Radical. The government's fall was followed by the installation of a coalition government under Lord Aberdeen (1784–1860), who had excellent claims to be regarded as the last surviving protégé of Pitt the Younger yet now headed a coalition whose common theme was dislike for the Conservative Party.

Before the formation of Derby's government in 1852, Gladstone had argued that "a Liberal policy would be worked out with the greatest security to the country through the medium of the Conservative party" (Stewart 1978: 257). Gladstone was not the only senior figure at this time to echo the views of Disraeli's Mr Taper; in March 1852 Aberdeen wrote that "a Government of progress in these times is indispensable. None can be too liberal for me, provided it does not abandon its conservative character" (Gash 1965: 155–6). In 1856, the journalist Walter Bagehot claimed that "To a great extent, every Liberal is now a Conservative" (St John-Stevas 1974: 98). In 1862 James Fitzjames Stephen observed that the terms "Liberal-Conservative and Conservative-Liberal" were now "constantly in use" (Stephen 1862: 70; see Chapter 3). To paraphrase W. S. Gilbert, after the defeat of the radical Chartist movement it seemed that in mid-Victorian Britain "every boy and every gal" was either a little conservative-liberal or a little liberal-conservative. It was certainly not an age of "ideological purity": the conditions were thus ideal for Disraeli.

"The Conservative Surrender"

In November 1868 the novelist Anthony Trollope spent "the most wretched fortnight of my manhood" fighting the constituency of Beverley. In a campaign which was corrupt even by the standards of the time, the £400 he spent had proved too paltry for the voters and he came last of the four candidates (Trollope 1980: 290–300). Trollope, whose unsentimental observations of human nature made him a particular favourite of a cynical future Conservative premier, Harold Macmillan, was no advocate of radical change. This did not prevent him from feeling a tribal identity with the Liberal Party (formerly the Whigs), and from showering his better-funded political opponents with condescension. Trollope's 1871 novel *The Eustace Diamonds* included a sympathetic portrait of Frank Greystock, an amiable individual who "gets the girl" despite having been elected as a Conservative MP. The status of a Member of Parliament, which Trollope himself craved so desperately, was bestowed on the fictional Frank almost against his will; the Conservatives who invited him to put his name forward "knew probably but little of his own political beliefs or feelings, – did not probably know whether he had any". Trollope used Greystock's unsolicited situation as an excuse to exhibit his own animosity towards the Conservative Party, whose candidates had bested him at Beverley: "They feel among themselves that everything that is being done is bad, – even though that everything is done by their own party". The Reform Act was bad, the repeal of the Corn Laws was bad, the erosion of the privileged status of the Church of England was bad, and "Emancipation of Roman Catholics was the worst of all". Despite all of these fearful setbacks, Conservatives continued to think that "old England is of all countries the best in the world to live in, and is not at all the less comfortable because of the changes that have been made" (Trollope 1982: 33).

Trollope's Conservative stereotype bore some resemblance to the real-life Robert Gascoyne-Cecil, a Conservative MP from 1853 to 1866, Viscount Cranborne from 1865–68 and afterwards the 3rd Marquess of Salisbury. In October 1867 the *Quarterly Review* published an article by Cranborne (as he then was), entitled "The Conservative Surrender". It lamented the passage of a new piece of offensive legislation – a second Reform Act, which extended the vote in borough constituencies to virtually all householders. As a result, Britain and its empire had been placed "under the absolute control of the poorest classes in the towns"; and, to make matters even worse, the measure had been passed by a Conservative government – of which Cranborne himself had been a member until resigning over the issue.

Reflecting on the passage of the Second Reform Act, Cranborne oscillated between accusing his party of suddenly "surrendering" to public opinion, and claiming that its leaders had been planning such a betrayal for the best part of a decade. Neither explanation was particularly flattering to Derby or Disraeli (the real culprit, according to Cranborne). Cranborne insisted more than once that it would be premature to predict the consequences of reform, while giving his readers every reason to expect that the whole thing would prove to be a total disaster. At one point he wrote that "It is an opinion generally entertained that the nation is on the whole 'Conservative'; not in the party sense of that word, for that meaning has disappeared, but in the sense of a general preference of our institutions to those of any other nation" (Cranborne 1867: 558). This boy who cried wolf proved more fortunate than the original in Aesop's fable; the cabinet post he had left in disgust in 1866 was Secretary of State for India, but by 1874 he was back in the same role, at the invitation of the new prime minister – Benjamin Disraeli.

Cecil/Cranborne/Salisbury made important contributions to the conservative ideological tradition, as well as being one of the greatest figures in the history of the party. In the latter context, "The Conservative Surrender" has two significant features which could easily be missed by contemporary readers. First, the article played down the significance of the numerous constitutional and political changes since the late 1820s, implying that previous "Conservatives" had cried wolf when the beast in question had really been a poodle. Even if "the nation is on the whole 'Conservative'" in a non-party sense, it had succumbed to complacency. The Conservative classes "have pursued their business and made their money, and enjoyed their success without much solicitude as to the future of the system under which they have prospered. They know that no serious change has happened in their time, or their father's time, or for many generations before that" (Cranborne 1867: 552–3). The latter comment would have come as a surprise to Cranborne's own father, who during debates on the 1832 Reform Bill had exclaimed that supporters of reform would be stigmatized by history "as destroyers of their country" (Hansard HL Deb., 17 May 1832).

The second notable feature of Cranborne's article was his admission that the Conservative Party had become renowned for "Elaborate and successful electioneering" which was capable of yielding "brilliant results" (Cranborne 1867: 559). In Cranborne's view, such techniques would, at best, yield short-term benefits; unless the party's leaders stayed true to their principles, Conservative supporters would soon grow disillusioned. This section of Cranborne's article reads like an attempt to grasp straws by a man whose party was not really drowning. In fact, by "dishing the Whigs" and introducing their own Reform Bill in 1867, the Conservative leadership had taken the kind of calculated gamble which would appeal to a racing buff like Derby. The most radical effect of the Second Reform Act was its expansion of the electorate in borough constituencies where the Conservative Party had fared worst, especially since the 1832 reform. The new instalment of electoral reform thus produced a host of voters who could easily prove susceptible to distinctively Conservative messages. Rather than alienating Conservative campaigners in borough constituencies, this promised to increase their motivation. For them, rather than a "leap in the dark", as Derby described it, the 1867 Act was a shot in the arm; it certainly could not make matters worse for the party.

Contrary to Cranborne's view, although Disraeli was a political adventurer he was a strategic thinker as well as a gifted tactician. The circumstances of 1867 had given him the chance to realize, if imperfectly, the political visions which had informed his early ventures into politics. Standing as a Radical in 1833, he had advocated reforms associated with the Chartist movement – more regular parliaments, election by ballot, etc. But Disraeli approved of this radical agenda because it would allow the unrevolutionary voice of the people to be heard, drowning out the corrupt Whig oligarchy. In his *Vindication of the English Constitution* (1835) Disraeli had claimed that:

> The Tory party in this country is the national party; it is the really democratic party of England. It supports the institutions

of the country because they have been established for the common good, and because they secure the equality of civil rights,
without which, whatever might be its name, no government
can be free, and based upon which principle every government,
however it might be styled, is in fact a Democracy (Hutcheon
1913: 216).

Thus, more than three decades before he rushed through the final turnpike and became prime minister, Disraeli had sketched in very bold
outline his idea of "Tory Democracy". By 1867 there were additional
pages in his playbook. Foreign policy had been a neglected field for
the Conservatives, not least because it had been dominated since the
1830s by the bombastic, gunboat-toting Lord Palmerston, who had
entered parliament as long ago as 1809 as a Tory but had been lost to
the Conservatives thanks to his liberal stances on Catholic emancipation and parliamentary reform. Attempts to entice him back into the
party fold proved unavailing, and (following three lengthy stints as
foreign secretary) Palmerston served almost continuously as a Whig
prime minister in the decade after 1855. He was still in post when he
died two days short of his eighty-first birthday (October 1865). Thanks
to Palmerston, Disraeli was painfully aware that foreign policy could
be a vote-winner, and with the vexatious Viscount out of the way he
could implement his plan to seize ownership of the issue on behalf of
the Conservatives. Given Britain's record in international politics since
the Reformation, a patriotic foreign policy was a natural counterpart to
the anti-papal prejudice which Derby and Disraeli were always happy
to exploit for partisan advantage.

Not even the most attractive prospectus would sell itself, and as
Cranborne had noted the success of Disraeli's approach depended
crucially on continued "Elaborate and successful electioneering". A
National Union of Conservative and Constitutional Associations was
established in 1868, followed in 1870 by the creation of Conservative
Central Office. Disraeli (in sharp contrast to Peel) always took a close
interest in such matters, and was particularly shrewd in selecting key offi-
cials. Presidents of the National Union served one-year terms; between
1868 and 1911 the party which had supposedly betrayed the aristocracy
never had to look for a candidate from outside the ranks of the peerage
(holders of the honorific position included nine dukes). Even in death

Disraeli could inject vitality into the increasingly-efficient party organization; the Primrose League which was founded in his memory (1883) boasted more than a million members by 1891 (Pugh 1981: 27).

Disraeli is supposed to have translated Cranborne's accusations of unprincipled adventurism into an instruction ("Damn your principles! Stick to your party"). By 1933 his reputation had been comprehensively sanitized. In that year F. J. C. Hearnshaw eulogized Disraeli as the bearer of beliefs which "flowed naturally from the main stream of conservative tradition". His political creed had arisen from "*The Religious Basis of Society … The Organic Nature of the State … Solidarity of the Community …* [and the] *Balance of Powers and Interests*". As such, he was "the legitimate successor of Bolingbroke and Burke", but according to the infatuated Hearnshaw his capacious mind was also influenced by "Coleridge, the sublime mystic …. Wordsworth, Southey, Scott, Byron, Shelley, and other of the poetic crowd" (Hearnshaw 1933: 220–21). In this single, inspired individual, love for party and respect for a distinctive conservative tradition of thought were inseparable; thanks to his transcendent genius, apparently, vehement anti-Tories like Byron and Shelley could also be considered as contributors to the Conservative Party's intellectual heritage.

Conservative collectivism

In February 1868 ill-health forced Lord Derby's retirement, allowing Disraeli to reach the top of the "greasy pole", albeit as head of a government which lacked a parliamentary majority. It only survived until the end of 1868 because of a delay in compiling a register of the newly-enlarged electorate. However, it was responsible for some constructive measures, notably the Corrupt Practices Act which removed the right to adjudicate contested elections from the partisan House of Commons, and legislation which allowed the state-run Post Office to take ownership of private telegram companies. The 1868 general election brought little change in party strength in the House of Commons, leaving Gladstone's newly-renamed Liberals with a comfortable majority.

In 1872 Disraeli delivered a three-hour address to a mass rally at Manchester's Free Trade Hall. There had been mutterings against the apparent impotence of the Conservative opposition, but a brandy-fuelled

Disraeli rose to the occasion, denying any intention to make cheap political points before doing just that, comparing the government's ministerial team to "a range of extinct volcanoes". Instead of unveiling a detailed policy statement, Disraeli merely declared that "the programme of the Conservative Party is to maintain the Constitution of the country". Against those who thought that the Second Reform Act was a leap too far, he contrasted the situation in Britain, where "You could not get half a dozen men to assemble in a street and grumble", with the interminable instability of France which, in 1870, had just established its Third Republic since 1789. The 1867 extension of the franchise had merely restored balance to the constitution, unlike the Whig Reform Act of 1832 whose main effect, in Disraeli's eyes, had been to rob existing working-class voters of their rights. While tacitly praising the solid good sense of English workers, Disraeli was careful not to promise them too much. However, although he focused on specific proposals for sanitary legislation he insisted that "This is a wide subject", and that "the first consideration of a minister should be the health of the people" (Buckle 1920: 186–92).

Disraeli's short-lived first administration had abolished public executions; its successor, led by Gladstone between 1868 and 1874, introduced the secret ballot for elections. Thus, within four years two of the best excuses for the disorderly gatherings of "Merry England" had been consigned to folklore. The 1874 general election was the first such contest in Britain to be decided by voters who could make their choices without feeling undue pressure from landlords or employers. The result was a clear win for the Conservatives, who, for the first time, received more than a million votes.

Foreign policy saw the most dramatic developments during Disraeli's second premiership – which ended in electoral defeat in 1880, four years after the prime minister had been elevated to the House of Lords as Earl of Beaconsfield. In 1872 Disraeli had warned his Manchester audience that "The very phrase 'foreign affairs' makes an Englishman convinced that I am about to treat of subjects with which he has no concern". He went on to argue that such matters *should* be important to British voters, in a way which showed that he (like so many of his predecessors and successors) had been bitten by the diplomatic bug, and that his interest in foreign policy extended beyond its populist potential (Buckle 1920: 191). Apart from headline-grabbing initiatives like purchasing shares in the Suez Canal Company, and instigating the coronation of Queen Victoria as Empress of India, Beaconsfield played a starring role at the Congress of Berlin (1878), which attempted to solve the "Eastern Question" in the wake of the Russo-Ottoman war of 1877–78.

The government's activities in the field of social policy are a source of warm contestation among historians, beginning with the publication of Paul Smith's *Disraelian Conservatism and Social Reform* (1967). Smith's extensive research suggested that the party as a whole was unenthusiastic about such measures and that Disraeli's personal commitment to state intervention fell far short of his own "Young England" aspirations, not to mention the posthumous portrait of Conservative propagandists. After Margaret Thatcher's rise to the Conservative Party leadership in 1975 Smith's scholarly contribution became a useful weapon for those who sought to establish that the party had only succumbed to "collectivist" tendencies after 1945. Disraeli's reputation was a major obstacle to their revisionist endeavours. In the 1930s even the idolatrous F. J. C. Hearnshaw had to resort to verbal gymnastics when appraising this aspect of his hero's record, characterizing Disraeli as "a collectivist, in the sound non-socialist sense of the term" (Hearnshaw 1933: 233).

For W. H. Greenleaf, as we have seen, nobody can be a "collectivist" in a "sound" sense. In his account Greenleaf concedes that the 1875 Artisans' Dwelling Act was "a major attempt to tackle the problem of urban working-class housing as a whole and the first time public authorities were given the responsibility for remedying defects in privately owned dwellings by compulsory purchase if necessary". Greenleaf listed some of the Disraeli government's additional measures:

> statutes to promote Friendly Societies and secure small savings; to make labour contracts more equitable and to remove trade union activity from the operation of the conspiracy law (and incidentally to legalize secondary picketing); to improve the position of agricultural tenants in regard to "unexhausted improvements"; to protect the working conditions of merchant seamen in particular from the dangers of unseaworthy ships; to deal with the sale of food and drugs; to inspect and regulate canal boats; to extend the Truck Acts; to consolidate existing public health legislation; to codify the Factory Acts …; to prevent the enclosure of common land for private gain; to prevent

the pollution of rivers by untreated sewage and industrial water; and to improve educational facilities as by extending elementary education. (Greenleaf 1983: 213)

Despite this lengthy list, Greenleaf argues that "it would be misleading to regard the commitment and activity of Disraeli and his ministers simply as the implementation of a philosophy". This is a baffling remark in the context of Victorian politics; not even the Whig or Liberal governments whose members were influenced by utilitarianism would have claimed to be motivated simply by the hope of implementing a "philosophy".

Next, Greenleaf notes that the government's legislation reflected "an element of political expediency"; some measures were introduced "because a particular investigation and report seemed to demand action, because of the special interests of a minister or the exigencies of party politics" (Greenleaf 1983: 213–14). The idea that governments in a competitive system of representation could ever be free from "the exigencies of party politics" is particularly arresting; it is also the case that nineteenth-century governments were under no obligation to accept the findings of "a particular investigation and report" (like the Royal Commission established in 1872, whose recommendations led to the 1876 Merchant Shipping Act). When all of these attempts to debunk Disraeli's record of state intervention have failed, it is still possible to deny that Disraeli himself was the "Onlie Begetter" of the government's legislation: the credit (if such) was due to energetic underlings like the home secretary, Richard Cross (1823–1914), who (as Greenleaf reports) was privately critical of Disraeli's "lack of initiative and legislative forethought" (Greenleaf 1983: 214). At most, this would suggest that the prime minister might have been half-hearted about "collectivism" himself, but was happy to appoint senior ministers who had no such reservations.

Conservative populism

For the historian of the Conservative Party and of conservative ideology the most important point arising from this evidence is that the perceived need even for piecemeal state intervention was a reflection of failure. Governmental action was now required precisely because society could no longer be understood as an interdependent "organism"; thanks to economic change, Victorian Britain was increasingly atomistic and inherently conflictual. Among other long-term effects, this exposed the pretentions of the landed aristocracy to social leadership; even if every representative fulfilled the paternalistic role idealized in *Sibyl* and *Coningsby*, their combined efforts could not come close to addressing the complex problems of the great cities which (among other things) fostered contagious diseases against which blue blood conferred no immunity.

Imperceptibly, the old Tory idea of duty – one which focused chiefly on the management of one's estate, respect and support for one's tenants, etc – had been reinterpreted as the duty of the Conservative Party to govern the country. This notion became a crucial element of the party's attempts to drum up support from an expanding electorate; even if an incoming government had to adopt "Whig measures", it was essential that they should be implemented by "Tory men". Indeed, it was helpful for the Conservatives to imply that the nation would be utterly ruined if Whig (now Liberal) men were ever given the chance to act on their own ideas. The approach seemed to depend on an adequate supply of "Tory men", but as we shall see the party was able to find other ways to bolster its parliamentary ranks. Since the nation's future would be at stake in every election – and openly corrupt practices were being outlawed – no method of peaceful persuasion should be ruled out.

However, not even populism could ensure Conservative success without a continuation of mid-Victorian economic prosperity: in more straightened circumstances the electorate could easily turn to radical men offering desperate remedies. By 1880 Britain was suffering from the effects of a worldwide depression. Agriculture was hit particularly hard; the price of cereals slumped in the face of cheap imports from the United States, and barely revived even after the disastrous harvest of 1879. Apart from depleting the revenues of landowners, this accelerated the influx of agricultural workers into manufacturing districts. Yet Disraeli's support for agricultural protection in the 1840s had been dropped as soon as it had served his purpose of displacing Peel, and in 1880 the reimposition even of moderate tariffs to support the price of domestic agricultural produce had become unthinkable.

The *coup de grace* in the 1880 general election was delivered by Gladstone, the "extinct volcano" who had erupted out of semi-retirement in 1878 to prove that two could play at populism, especially in Disraeli's adopted theatre of foreign policy. The Liberal leader delivered lengthy moralistic monologues up until the election, excoriating Disraeli's policy of support for the Ottoman Empire. This "Midlothian Campaign" was skilfully orchestrated to maximize public attendance and media coverage. By contrast, Disraeli's health was declining, and he felt that as a member of the House of Lords he should not take part in public campaigning. In the 1880 election itself a Conservative majority of around a hundred seats was converted into a Liberal advantage of similar proportions.

On Disraeli's death in April 1881 the party's leadership was divided between Sir Stafford Northcote in the Commons and Cranborne (now Marquess of Salisbury) in the Lords. Since Northcote was an uninspiring figure, before long most Conservatives recognized Salisbury as their effective leader and "prime minister presumptive". Salisbury's willingness to serve is somewhat surprising, given his habitual pessimism about the human condition in general and the prospects for Britain in particular; the Conservative defeat of 1880 prompted him to predict that the country would soon be engulfed in "a serious war of classes" (Shannon 1992: 379). This gloomy outlook actually helps to explain his continued commitment to politics: if conflict should come, who better to lead the propertied elite than someone who had been anticipating Armageddon for the whole of his adult life? In addition, it seems that, like Derby before him and with much greater reluctance, Salisbury had fallen under Disraeli's personal influence at least to the extent of absorbing his obsession with the game of politics.

Also like Derby, Salisbury wanted to recruit political opponents – preferably moderate ones – to his own Conservative colours. In his view moderate Liberals – who continued to be designated as "Whigs" despite adopting their new name in the 1860s – were guilty of misplaced loyalty, if not of outright class treachery, in their continued attachment to a party which seemed increasingly antipathetic to the interests of landed property. In an 1883 article for the *Quarterly Review* – published anonymously, but under a title ("Disintegration") which was sufficiently glum to unmask its author – Salisbury described the Whig faction as "a mere survival, kept alive by its tradition after its true functions and significance have passed away" (Salisbury 1883: 578). This was a prime example of tribal pot-and-kettle-ism; the same gibe could have been levelled with

Lord Salisbury: the melancholy Marquess

equal justice at Conservatives like the author himself. Indeed, Salisbury was not opposed to relaunching his party with another new name – "Constitutionalist" (Salisbury 1883: 562). This would make it more congenial for Whigs who had not given up on "the Established Church, and the House of Lords, and 'our mixed form of government'"; also, Salisbury now felt that "Conservative" was a misleading label since "The object of our party is not, and ought not to be, simply to keep things as they are" (Salisbury 1883: 578, 592). Given that the party had presided over so many changes since its foundation, presumably this attempt to make a virtue out of necessity was intended to reassure any Whigs who might previously have supposed that Salisbury himself was against even limited reforms. "Constitutionalist" was a banner behind which landed gentlemen could rally to save the country from the increasingly reckless and radical Gladstone.

In 1884 Gladstone introduced proposals for a further extension of the franchise. The Bill was rejected by the House of Lords, and Salisbury withheld cooperation unless the measure was accompanied by a redistribution of seats. During the ensuing constitutional deadlock huge public meetings were held by both sides; Salisbury overcame his extreme distaste for public speaking, addressing large crowds (including one in Manchester whose attendance was estimated at 100,000). The issue was settled in true diplomatic style, with the plenipotentiaries meeting at Salisbury's house on Arlington Street. The provisions of the ensuing Third Reform Act expanded the electorate to about 5.7 million men, which was radical enough. However, the Redistribution Act represented an even clearer breach with previous practice, since it divided most of the country into single-member constituencies, whose boundaries would now be determined with reference to the size of the electorate. Salisbury's old self would have renounced politics in disgust at such innovations; two-member constituencies had been the norm ever since the introduction of representative government in the thirteenth century, and the right to return MPs had always been based on custom rather than demographics. However, the burden of party leadership in an age of reform had turned the melancholy Marquess into an enthusiastic amateur psephologist, and he had calculated that the change would increase the number of seats in areas of established Conservative strength. Partisan advantage was now more than a match for time-honoured tradition, and most of Salisbury's colleagues shared his sense of priorities; the leader managed to sell the proposed system to a party gathering at the Carlton Club.

Churchill and Chamberlain

For Salisbury in 1884, the need to unite the forces of moderation had become more urgent because of unsavoury developments within his own party. Lord Randolph Churchill, a younger son of the Duke of Marlborough who had been a member of the dissipated Bullingdon Club at Oxford, was elected to the Commons in 1874. The ageing and childless Beaconsfield seems to have regarded Churchill as a natural successor who, thanks to his aristocratic origins, might finally realize the ideal of "Tory Democracy"; certainly Beaconsfield offered no reproof despite flagrant insubordination shown by Churchill and his coterie (given the label of "the Fourth Party") towards Northcote and other senior figures, including the estimable interventionist R. A. Cross. Shortly after Beaconsfield's death, Churchill staked an explicit claim to be his legatee (or, in his own wording, to seize "Elija's Mantle"). The real implications of Beaconsfield's pledge to promote public health had not escaped Churchill, even if they have remained obscure for "Thatcherite" historians. He argued that the commitment, properly understood, justified "a scheme of social progress and reform, of dimensions so large and wide-spreading that many volumes would not suffice to explain its details" (Churchill 1883: 621).

Churchill's eager anticipation of a state-sponsored "social revolution" could hardly endear him to Salisbury, whose tolerance of such a headstrong colleague is another sign of his aptitude for sacrifices in the interests of office-holding. Churchill's obnoxious article also included belittling references to Northcote, and as such was helpful to Salisbury's own leadership ambitions at the time. But it should have been clear to him from a very early stage that Churchill was a ravenous cuckoo in the Conservative nest who would not hesitate to show the same contempt for Salisbury when a suitable occasion arose. Having quickly taken a leading role in the Primrose League, Churchill worked to ingratiate himself with the party's National Union. It looked as if Churchill was taking effective control of the party, retaining the services of the superannuated Salisbury only for as long as he served some purpose as a wizened fig-leaf of stability. Unlike Salisbury, Churchill could take the Conservative message to parts of the country which the Conservatives had not even reconnoitred. Mass audiences hung onto his every word (however vacuous), particularly the phrases which flattered the impeccable political judgement of the common people.

In April 1884, a few weeks before the introduction of the Third Reform Bill, Churchill epitomized this approach in a speech at Birmingham. He opened with a tokenistic tribute to the political role of monarchy, which he regarded as a constitutional asset for purely utilitarian reasons (in stark contrast to Disraeli's obsequious attitude). Churchill adroitly turned this argument into a defence of the hereditary principle in general, as befitted a scion of the ducal house of Marlborough. He also praised the House of Lords as a "bulwark of popular liberty and civil order" and completed the Conservative Party's bingo card by hailing the Church of England chiefly in terms of its educational role, "not only benefitting your children but saving your pockets". This fell short, by some distance, of Coleridge's exalted vision of a National Church and a clerisy which would spearhead a moral and intellectual renaissance (see Chapter 1).

Having delivered his obeisances to long-recognized Conservative Party causes, Churchill turned his attention to the present need for social reform, without specifying any policy area which required immediate attention. On such issues he would be honoured to be guided by public opinion. In a recent parliamentary debate Gladstone had used the phrase "trust the people". In his Birmingham speech Churchill reported that "I have long tried to make that my motto". Regrettably, however, "there are still a few in our party who have yet that lesson to learn". This was breath-taking insubordination; presumably Churchill knew well enough that the "few in our party" included his nominal leader, Salisbury, who in his "Disintegration" article of the previous year had attacked "the mere optimist, who solves every difficulty by an effusive profession of trust in the people" (Salisbury 1883: 571). In the same article Salisbury had acknowledged that the framers of the US constitution had improved on the British model by making it more difficult to impose radical change. Churchill retorted that "I have no fear of democracy. I do not fear for minorities … Modern checks and securities are not worth a brass farthing". There seemed to be only one point of coincidence between Salisbury and Churchill: the potential tactical advantage of further electoral reform. "Give me a fair arrangement of the constituencies", the latter declared, "and one part of England will correct and balance the other" (Churchill 1884).

When Gladstone's government was defeated in a vote on the 1885 budget, Churchill reverted to his Bullingdon Club persona, capering around the Commons' chamber in celebration (Lucy 1886: 478). Queen Victoria settled the leadership question by asking Salisbury, rather than Northcote, to form a minority administration. Churchill was given the post of Secretary of State for India which Salisbury himself had held under Disraeli. A general election at the end of the year restored the Liberals to office, but they were dependent on the parliamentary votes of Irish nationalists, whose leader, Charles Stewart Parnell, had been plotting with Churchill and had advised his English-based supporters to vote Conservative. In March 1886 Gladstone revealed plans for the introduction of Home Rule for Ireland, thus triggering the long-anticipated defection of the Whigs from the Liberal Party. Although they held back from formal identification with the Conservatives, Salisbury could now count on their support in questions concerning Ireland and benevolent neutrality, at worst, in other policy areas.

However, the Liberal split over Home Rule made Salisbury look like a fisherman who had hoped to round up a few basking sharks and ended up catching a killer whale. The Birmingham businessman and MP, Joseph Chamberlain, had been agitating with increasing confidence for domestic reforms which were too radical even for Gladstone's taste; along with land reform, free education and universal manhood suffrage, Chamberlain and his supporters envisaged the disestablishment of the Church of England. Frustrated by a lack of support from within Gladstone's cabinet for this aptly-named "unauthorized programme", Chamberlain had anticipated the government's fall by resigning from his position of president of the Board of Trade. After the 1885 general election Chamberlain accepted office as president of the Local Government Board, only to resign once again in response to Gladstone's Home Rule initiative. He spoke and voted against the Irish Government Bill, which was defeated on 8 June 1886 by a combination of Conservatives, Whigs and Chamberlain's radical followers, leading to yet another general election.

Chamberlain had been a favourite butt of Conservative attacks, returning the hostility with interest. He had, for example, denounced Salisbury personally as the representative of an aristocratic elite which was essentially parasitic rather than productive. Such insults were hardly new, but in the 1880s they were more hurtful than they had been (say) in 1846, since the functional value of the aristocracy was now open to more serious questions. Salisbury had felt compelled to hit back in terms which, in the good old days of Castlereagh and Canning, could have given rise to a duel.

The affairs of Ireland transformed Chamberlain almost overnight, from the Conservative Party's deadliest foe to an invaluable ally. Another Birmingham MP, John Bright (1811–89), also regarded the "Irish question" as sufficiently important to justify a breach with the Liberal Party. As a leading light within the Anti-Corn Law League, Bright had been an external irritant who helped to dissolve the Conservative Party into warring factions during the 1840s. His parting political shot was designed to have a similar effect on the Liberals; he delivered only one speech during the 1886 election campaign, urging the party's supporters to put aside their usual allegiance in order to save the Union.

The election gave Salisbury and his ill-assorted allies a very comfortable majority. The premier could take considerable satisfaction from this vindication of his various manoeuvres during the passage of the Third Reform Act. Evidently his party could still attract considerable support despite additional steps towards universal suffrage. If other constitutional resources failed, the House of Lords was more top-heavy with Tories than ever thanks to the Liberal schism, and retained its veto powers despite Chamberlain's recent threats of a "peers versus the people" campaign (Adonis 1993: 9). However, Salisbury had good reasons to file the 1886 election result under "Pyrrhic victories". He had no alternative but to appoint Churchill as both leader of the House of Commons and chancellor of the exchequer, with few illusions that this would exhaust his colleague's ambitions. Churchill, who had mocked Gladstone as "an old man in a hurry", was evidently hoping to travel with comparable velocity, even though he had been born after the repeal of the Corn Laws and was less than half Gladstone's age. Whatever Beaconsfield might have thought in his dotage, neither Churchill nor Chamberlain could be regarded as "Tory men", and their favoured policies certainly did not qualify as "Whig measures". While Churchill promised radical reforms as a means for self-advancement, Chamberlain was content to bide his time, on the assumption that his sincerely-held views would prevail in the end. A fully-fledged alliance between this pair was the ultimate nightmare for any politician who wished to preserve the last remnants of the old order for as long as possible. In a speech delivered at Dartford in October 1886 – prefaced by the singing of "Rule Britannia" and other demagogical devices – Chancellor Churchill, with Chamberlain's prior consent, endorsed cherry-picked elements of the latter's "unauthorized programme". With good reason, F. J. G. Hearnshaw believed that the Dartford speech was "incompatible with any form of conservatism" (Hearnshaw 1933: 229).

Within a few weeks of Churchill's insubordinate Dartford speech fate, which had rarely befriended Salisbury, offered sudden and spectacular recompense. In his first budget Churchill wanted to impose strict controls on expenditure to leave room for tax cuts. There would be no departmental exceptions, even in respect of the armed forces whose expansion would normally be a populist priority. Pre-budget negotiations with W. H. Smith at the War Office ended in deadlock, and on the same day (20 December) Smith made it clear to Salisbury that he would rather resign than submit to Churchill's demands. For his part, Churchill sent Salisbury a remarkable letter in which he accepted that his proposals were unwelcome to the whole cabinet (including Salisbury himself), "and therefore must request to give up my office and retire from the government". This gambit bore a close resemblance to Chamberlain's conduct in 1885 over his "unauthorized programme". The first draft of Salisbury's reply included an admission that the loss of Churchill would be "disastrous", but on second thoughts he simply accepted the resignation with "very profound regret" (Roberts 1999: 407–408). Salisbury was naturally concerned about the effect of Churchill's departure on the latter's extensive fan club. However, he had chosen to resign on just about the only issue where he was out of step with the jingoistic Primrose League. The government could still have been in deep trouble if Chamberlain had signalled support for Churchill, but this was not forthcoming. Far from being impaired, the government's parliamentary position was reinforced by Churchill's replacement; in January George Goschen, a respected financier who had held several cabinet posts under Gladstone, agreed to serve as chancellor and thus became the first "Liberal Unionist" recruit to a Conservative cabinet.

Salisbury's "statecraft"

Churchill's abrupt self-destruction solved an unpleasant personnel problem for Salisbury, and Chamberlain was kept busy by the protracted process of burning his boats with the Liberals, establishing a new powerbase (a "Liberal Unionist Association") and an official trip to the United States at Salisbury's suggestion, which resulted in the dapper, twice-widowed radical meeting and marrying Mrs Chamberlain III. Meanwhile the cabinet's main business was the implementation of its alternative to Home Rule in Ireland – a stick-and-carrot approach, whose repressive features earned Salisbury's nephew Arthur the sobriquet of "Bloody Balfour". The government's record in domestic matters has received scant attention and less praise (Ramsden 1978: 171). However, the Local Government Act of 1888 which established elected councils for counties and boroughs in England and Wales (including a London County Council) was a major landmark, which had been championed by Churchill and Chamberlain. Other social legislation included an Allotment Act (a measure which fell conspicuously short of Chamberlain's populist vision of "Three acres and a cow"), further limited measures to regulate working conditions in mines and shops, and a much more significant Free Education Act, which ensured that the state would cover fees for children in primary schools.

In hindsight, Salisbury's record of domestic reform could seem like a masterclass in "statecraft"; he allowed enough legislation to keep Chamberlain and his radical allies relatively content, without alienating moderate members of the informal Conservative–Liberal Unionist coalition who were concerned by the increasing scope of "collectivism" (Marsh 1978: 245). Like Disraeli, Salisbury had no principled objection to piecemeal state intervention in cases of proven need, but he felt it necessary to pay lip-service to laissez-faire, possibly to reassure himself as well as his more "libertarian" followers. Back in 1885 – before the alliance with Chamberlain – one of the latter, the former Peelite Earl of Wemyss, had attacked Salisbury's minority government in a House of Lords debate on the "Socialistic Tendency" of recent legislation. He dubbed Chamberlain a communist, and praised the aggressively anti-statist Liberty and Property Defence League (LPDL, which he had recently co-founded) as an exemplar of "true Conservatism". As well as citing the radical liberal ideologue Herbert Spencer with approval, Wemyss quoted Macaulay's attack on "the intermeddling of the omnipotent and omniscient State" (see Chapter 1). This was a remarkable instance of ideological false memory syndrome. Salisbury, who had a much clearer recollection of the issues and personalities involved in the "battle of ideas" of 1830, pointed out that Macaulay's phrase had been used to attack Robert Southey, who "was in the literary and journalistic world one of the main supports of the Tory Party …. I am following Southey, and not Lord Macaulay, and in doing so I maintain that I am not false to the principles of the political party to which I belong" (Hansard HL Deb., 31 July 1885). By clear implication, it was Wemyss and his coadjutors in the LPDL whose ideas were "unconservative".

While Salisbury could hardly hope to conceal the ideological chasms on his own side, he could at least argue that the Liberals were more disorderly and dangerous than ever. In the election campaign of July 1892 the party's "Newcastle programme" outbid Salisbury's more tentative offerings and enabled Gladstone to divert attention from the toxic issue of Irish Home Rule. However, to cobble together a parliamentary majority the Liberals were once again dependent on the votes of Irish MPs.

By this time, Gladstone was an even older man (nearing his 83rd birthday) and, for understandable reasons, in an even greater hurry. Home Rule passed through the Commons, but was poleaxed in the Lords (by 419 to 41 votes) in September 1893. Gladstone resigned for the last time in March 1894, but the Liberal-led government survived for a further year under the Earl of Rosebery – the queen's choice, a former chair of the London County Council, and the third premier in a row to have been educated at Eton and Christ Church, Oxford (where he had adorned the Bullingdon Club alongside Randolph Churchill). The Lords effectively annulled the government's domestic agenda – apart from Estate Duty, the forerunner of Inheritance Tax – and the Liberals were divided over foreign policy. In June 1895 Rosebery threw in the sponge, choosing to interpret the passage of a motion of censure on the Secretary of State for War, Henry Campbell-Bannerman, as a vote of no confidence in the whole government.

The Conservatives could enter a new general election campaign with considerable confidence, since the Liberals were demoralized under the semi-detached Rosebery. Chamberlain, who had long ago lost interest in a reunion of Liberal/Radical forces, was now committed to the Conservatives; he had even been invited to spend the Christmas of 1894 *chez* Salisbury at Hatfield House. In the previous month he had shown undiminished zeal for progressive legislation, advocating (among other things) old-age pensions and a mechanism for government arbitration in industrial disputes. During the 1895 election campaign Salisbury was studiously evasive on these subjects, promising further action to make life better for the underprivileged while showing his usual distaste for "ambitious programmes" of any kind (Ramsden 1978: 178–9).

The result of the 1895 general election was a landslide victory for the Conservatives and Liberal Unionists, who won more than 400 seats. In forming his third government, Salisbury was still enjoying the run of good luck which had commenced with the miscalculation of the now-deceased Churchill. There was never any chance that Chamberlain could become leader of the House of Commons for the government's allied forces; apart from other considerations, Salisbury was unlikely to demote his own nephew, Balfour, who had led for the Conservatives since 1891. Chamberlain rejected the post of chancellor of the exchequer, Churchill's poisoned chalice. Having been deeply impressed by the arguments of "liberal imperialist" scholars, he now felt that the political talents he had burnished in Birmingham were meant for mankind in general. In requesting the position of colonial secretary, he had no intention of ignoring domestic policy; he promoted a Workmen's Compensation Act (1897) which stipulated that employers must accept financial responsibility for workers injured in the course of their duties. The finished legislation, however, excluded agricultural workers in an unsubtle concession to the landed interest which was still reeling from the imposition of Estate Duty.

The government's record, for good and ill, was dominated by foreign policy which, in keeping with his previous practice, Salisbury continued to direct in combination with his duties as prime minister. Clashes with the USA (over the border between British Guiana and Venezuela) and France (in the Sudan) were resolved without bloodshed. The confrontation with France – the 1896 Fashoda crisis – was hailed as a major victory for British colonial interests in North and Central Africa, as well as marking a first tentative step towards rapprochement between the two historic enemies. Meanwhile Chamberlain's chief interest lay in the potential for further imperial expansion in southern Africa. This goal was nearly derailed along with his political ambitions when an attempt to effect pro-British "regime change" in the gold-rich Transvaal (the "Jameson Raid") resulted in a fiasco and an offer of resignation which Salisbury chose to decline. Nothing daunted, Chamberlain pressed on with his expansionist policy and, in October 1899, the failure of negotiations with the Dutch-speaking settlers ("Boers") in the Transvaal and the Orange Free State triggered the outbreak of war.

Boer resistance was much stiffer than expected, and their irregular but highly motivated forces won three set-piece battles as well as laying siege to the key cities of Ladysmith, Kimberley and Mafeking. In 1900 the British fought back, relieving the sieges and moving onto the offensive in the Orange Free State and Transvaal. Salisbury called an election (October 1900) at this favourable stage in the conflict; persuaded against his inclinations to issue a manifesto on behalf of his party, he ignored domestic policy and focused entirely on the war. This "Khaki" election resulted in a slight decline for the Conservative and Unionist forces from the high point of 1895, but the comfortable re-election of an incumbent government still marked a significant change from the instability of previous contests under the reformed franchise. Salisbury lightened his duties by giving up the Foreign Office, but continued as prime minister, despite failing health, until July 1902. Contrary to the expectations aroused in the 1900 election campaign, the Boers had only just accepted defeat. The protracted conflict had exposed the gulf between Britain's military capacity and its imperial ambitions, as well as the country's isolation within Europe.

One of the most pessimistic political meteorologists of all time, Salisbury would probably have muttered "*Aprés moi, le Deluge*" whatever the circumstances at the time of his departure; back in 1882 he told a friend that they would be "the 'last of the Conservatives'" (Grenville 1964: 10). If the Boer War cast a critical light on his foreign policy, the outlook was growing more unsettled on the domestic front in the early years of the new century. In 1901, led by the veteran Earl of Halsbury (1823–1921, Lord Chancellor in every Conservative government between 1885 and 1905), the Law Lords overturned a ruling in the Court of Appeal and decided that trade unions could be sued for damage to property inflicted during the course of an industrial dispute. This "Taff Vale case" was widely regarded as a reversal of the recent tendency of legislation, under both Liberal and Conservative-led governments, to address to some extent the imbalance of power between workers and employers. Whatever the merits of the judgement itself, it was not a quid pro quo for the 1897 Workmen's Compensation Act; it could be used as a precedent for claims to damages arising from the mere withdrawal of labour during a dispute, rather than the deliberate sabotage of property.

The implications of the Taff Vale case for the Conservative Party were profound. It was a serious setback to the Disraelian dream that the party could act as a vehicle of social harmony. Disraeli had stressed the natural affinity between the propertied elite and working people, and after 1867 the Conservative Party had published numerous pamphlets to underline the point. By the same token, such propaganda implied an inherent conflict of outlook and interest between the landed classes and industrialists (McKenzie & Silver 1968: 43). The Taff Vale judgement thus suggested that the Conservatives had switched sides in an ongoing "class war" (Green 1995: 15–16). The fact that the ruling was handed down by five ludicrously-antiquated legal luminaries – the most precocious was a sprightly 71-year-old – was easily overlooked by critics who cited this case as an indictment of the House of Lords as a whole and of the Conservative Party in particular. As such, the Taff Vale company which pushed its case all the way to the highest court in Britain could not have been a more effective (albeit unwitting) recruiting agent for the trade unions and their newly-formed political ally, the Labour Representative Committee. Between the Taff Vale judgement and Salisbury's death in August 1903, trade union membership more than doubled (to around 850,000). At that rate, the movement would soon boast more members than the Primrose League.

Summary

The emergence of the Conservative Party in the early 1830s reflected a general view, chiefly among adherents of the Tory Party, that a new name was needed to designate support for the existing, hierarchical political and social order in Britain. The name "Conservative" was adopted when established institutions and practices were faced with serious challenges thanks to religious and political reforms between 1828 and 1832. From the outset, supporters of the party were divided in their approaches to further reform. In 1846 many Conservative MPs abandoned their leader, Sir Robert Peel, whose willingness to compromise seemed to reflect personal sympathy with liberal principles on a range of key issues. His successors, Derby, Disraeli and Salisbury, recognized that further change was inevitable, but saw the continued political influence of the Conservative Party as the best way to prolong and alleviate the process. They showed that the party could win considerable support even from an expanded electorate: but only if it presented voters with policies which, at best, represented a caricature of conservative principles – and, at worst, met liberal positions more than half-way. In turn, this made it easier for disgruntled ideological liberals to transfer their support to the Conservatives. As a result of these developments, by the time of Salisbury's death in 1903 the initiative within the party had clearly begun to pass to ideological opponents of conservatism.

3

"Converging streams": British conservative thought from Southey to Cecil

In a debate of 31 May 1866, the Liberal MP John Stuart Mill intervened to clarify an earlier remark he had made about the Conservative Party, which, he feared, "has some appearance of being less polite than I should wish always to be". In describing the opposition as "the stupidest party", he had not meant "that Conservatives are generally stupid; I meant, that stupid persons are generally Conservative. I believe that to be so obvious and undeniable a fact that I hardly think any hon. Gentleman will question it". In fact, Conservatives should celebrate their stupidity, which helped to explain their political success: "there is a dense solid force in sheer stupidity – such, that a few able men, with that force pressing behind them, are assured of victory in many a struggle" (Hansard HC Deb., 31 May 1866).

Mill's celebrated sally might have entertained MPs on his own side of the House, but in essence it reheated an argument which had appeared in print way back in 1840. His celebrated essay on Coleridge (see Chapter 1) implied that conservatives were "bigots" who could only find intellectual and moral salvation in teachings which were infused with liberalism (Mill 1840: 300–302). Mill seemed generally bemused to find that a conservative, like Coleridge, could have written anything worth reading.

By 1866 Mill had more reason for regarding Coleridge as a freakish exception to conservative stupidity, because no thinker of comparable stature had emerged in the interim. Indeed, Coleridge's best-known intellectual disciples, like the Christian socialist F. D. Maurice, and the liberal Thomas Arnold of Rugby School fame, had incorporated elements of his work within different ideological frameworks, while W. E. Gladstone had seen the error of his ways and at the time of Mill's speech was chancellor of the exchequer in a Liberal government. In part, the lack of an obvious successor to Coleridge (or indeed to Southey) reflected the dominant role in political debate of the periodical press. The typical contribution was an extended essay dealing with contemporary issues rather than fundamental principles (McDowell 1959). This format accentuated an inherent disadvantage for conservative writers in a "battle of ideas". For understandable reasons, they tended to engage in philosophical discussion only when they perceived a significant threat to the status quo. After the repression of the radical Chartist movement in the late 1840s Britain seemed to have entered a period of relative political stability. In that context it was much easier to become a celebrated "man of letters" by telling readers that things could be even better – the typical liberal view – rather than reminding them that they had never had it so good. The absence of a new conservative star in the intellectual firmament encouraged personality cults around very unlikely figures, such as Thomas Carlyle (1795–1881) whose default prose-style was apocalyptic even when dealing with mundane matters and whose "hero-worship" of ego-driven individuals was gradually transferred, as George Orwell noted, "from successful rebels to successful scoundrels" (Orwell 1968: 34).

Ideological impurity

While Marx and Engels claimed that Europe was being stalked by the spectre of communism in 1848, by 1866 the chief ideological menace for British conservatives was Mill himself, thanks in particular to his tract *On Liberty* (1859). Mill's optimism concerning the future human condition – coupled with his style of writing, whose clarity epitomized his high estimation of the human capacity for rational thought and discussion – provoked critical reflections from a range of writers. Some of these expressed views that can be reconciled with a distinctively conservative outlook. The best-known, however, tended (like his old antagonist Macaulay) to be less "utopian" members of Mill's own liberal camp.

A case in point is Thomas Arnold's son Matthew, whose *Culture and Anarchy* appeared in instalments of the *Cornhill Magazine* in 1867–68 before being published in book form. Although Arnold barely mentioned Mill by name in *Culture and Anarchy*, *On Liberty* haunts many of his pages. Against Mill's view that human conduct should be free from the constraints of the law or of public opinion – provided that it did not result in harm to others – Arnold argued that the contemporary under-standing of liberty amounted to little more than claims to "Do As One Likes". He depicted a society which was divided between "Barbarians" (aristocrats), "Philistines" (the middle class) and "the Populace" (work-ing class). Each group had its own ideas about liberty which, unchecked, would undoubtedly cause "harm to others". In contrast to Mill, Arnold believed that an enlightened state could promote a more rounded view of freedom. He foresaw revolutionary changes in the aftermath of the second (1867) Reform Act, but insisted that this should be an orderly process overseen by the "organ of our collective best self, of our national right reason" – i.e., the state (Collini 1993: 100–101).

Arnold considered himself to be a liberal, but that his views had been "tempered by experience". Certainly no orthodox liberal could have pre-sented the bleak vision of Arnold's poem "Dover Beach" (published in 1867 but apparently written much earlier). Arnold's exalted view of the state is reminiscent of Coleridge and the Edmund Burke of *Reflections*; indeed, he regarded Burke as "our greatest political thinker" (Collini 1993: xxiii–iv). However, he was no apologist for the "Barbarians"; like Mill he regarded aristocracies as "by the very nature of things inacces-sible to ideas", and asked "whether upon the earth there is anything so unintelligent, so unapt to perceive how the world is really going, as an ordinary young Englishman of our upper class" (Collini 1993: 90–91).

Another contestable case is that of Sir James Fitzjames Stephen (1829–94). In 1881 the ailing Beaconsfield regretted that Stephen had pursued a legal rather than a political career, because he would have made an excellent leader of the Conservative Party. In fact, Stephen did stand for parliament, in 1873 – but as one of three Liberal candidates in a by-election to fill a vacant seat at Dundee. According to Russell Kirk, Stephen's defeat had a formative effect: he "had been eclipsed by one of the new-style collectivist Liberals, and had come to realize that he was a conservative through and through" (Kirk 1954: 304). The prob-lem with this breezy account is that Stephen was a candidate for the Liberal Party *after* the publication of *Liberty, Equality, Fraternity*, which first appeared as a series of articles in the *Pall Mall Gazette* (1872–73) and is regarded as the best evidence of his *conservative* credentials. In fact, while Stephen did learn at Dundee that his views put him at odds with current developments within the Liberal Party, he regarded the Conservatives as "not much, if at all, better than the radicals". Rather than converting Stephen to conservatism, the episode inspired him with "deep-rooted disgust at the whole system of elections and government by constituencies like this" (Stephen 1895: 345). This emotion was no doubt accentuated by the extent of his defeat. In the three-cornered contest he barely mustered 10 per cent of the vote, a particularly dismal showing since he was acknowledged to be the Gladstone government's favoured candidate, and while he devoted considerable energy to speeches and canvassing, he was easily outpolled by the aforementioned "new-style collectivist" who had spent the whole campaign in the United States.

According to his campaign literature, "Mr Stephen's liberalism is the liberalism of self-help, of individualism, of every form of conscious industry and energy". This would seem to settle the issue of ideological identification. However, Stephen's thought was more complicated than that. A utilitarian who was capable of defending Pontius Pilate on the grounds that the preservation of public peace was more important than the life of an innocent man, his view of human nature was heavily influenced by Thomas Hobbes (Stephen 1993: 63). From this perspective, the extended critique of Mill in *Liberty, Equality, Fraternity* is little more than a one-sided shouting match; all Stephen really proves is that he does not share Mill's optimism about the human condition. Thus Mill's concept of "liberty" is better understood as "licence"; "equality", in economic terms, is just a slogan used by envious people who want to despoil the rich; and "fraternity" is pernicious humbug: "Why there should be wicked men in the world is like the question, Why should there be poisonous snakes in the world? Though no men are absolutely good or absolutely bad, yet if and in so far as men are good and bad they are not brothers but enemies" (Stephen 1993: 200).

As applied to politics, the notion of equality leads inexorably to universal (manhood) suffrage. Stephen denies that he is trying to hold back the tide of democracy: "The waters are out and no human force can turn them back". However, he did not "see why as we go with the stream we need sing Hallelujah to the river god" (Stephen 1993: 156).

True to his word, Stephen proceeds to blow a series of raspberries in the direction of the democratic "river god". In his view, democracy will tend to "invert what I should have regarded as the true and natural relation between wisdom and folly" (Stephen 1993: 156). Echoing almost exactly a phrase used by Carlyle in his unpleasant rant against the second Reform Act, *Shooting Niagara – And After?* (1867), Stephen believed that "wise and good men ought to rule those who are foolish and bad". All institutions – even trade unions – are in fact ruled by elites, so dreams of real political equality are futile at best. Having said that democracy was inevitable, Stephen absolves himself from the task of offering an alternative means of selecting the elite. However, he criticizes the existing representative system because even without full democracy policy-makers are "obliged to be constantly stopping to obtain the popular consent at every step". The House of Commons has too much power, ensuring that "Nothing can be done at all till the importance of doing it has been made obvious to the very lowest capacity" (Stephen 1993: 159). The worst effects of the system are seen in the conduct of foreign policy: "There is no department of public affairs … in which the general level of knowledge is so low. There is none in which popular passions are so violent, so ill-instructed, or so likely to produce incalculable mischief". After this blistering assault, Stephen concedes tamely that "I do not for a moment suggest that we can be governed otherwise than we are" (Stephen 1993: 160–61).

Overall, the decision of the voters of Dundee to stymie Stephen's parliamentary ambitions was probably in the best interest of constituents and candidate alike. Stephen could be categorized alongside Arnold as a liberal "tempered by experience". In his case, a relevant "experience" was his service (1869–72) as a judge in India, but this seems to have made little difference to a disposition which was already pugilistic (the inoffensive Arnold was, indeed, one of his favourite targets). Perhaps Stephen's most valuable contribution to ideological literature was an essay on "Liberalism", published in the *Cornhill Magazine* in 1862. Discussing political terminology, he argued that careful attention should be given to "party names which aim not merely at identifying political parties, but at describing their principles". This was particularly true of "the words Liberal, Radical, Conservative, and their strange compounds Liberal-Conservative and Conservative-Liberal, which are so constantly in use amongst us at the present day" (Stephen 1862: 70). These "strange compounds", of course, were not party names; rather, they were being used "so constantly" in mid-Victorian Britain because they were regarded as the most informative short-hand designations of the beliefs of many senior politicians in both of the main parties (see Chapter 2). It might have become rare to find "pure" examples of ideological thinking; but these abstract models were recognized, long before ideology became a subject of academic study, as reference points against which the beliefs of real political actors could be evaluated. This approach seems particularly appropriate in the cases of Arnold and of Stephen himself. Although the most suitable of the "strange compounds" in either instance is open to endless dispute, "conservative liberal" seems more appropriate.

Later writers present fewer complications. Stephen was a close friend of Sir Henry Maine (1822–88), who had also served the British Raj in a judicial capacity. Maine's major work, *Ancient Law* (1861) advanced the argument that relationships in the premodern world were based on "status", from which mankind had progressed to voluntary bonds arising from "contract". In itself, this highly influential generalization indicated a significant deviation from the position of conservatives like Coleridge and Southey, who had argued that the relationship between employer and worker in manufacturing industry was no better than slavery.

Maine's only book directly concerned with politics, *Popular Government* (1883), was based on articles initially published in the *Quarterly Review*. Maine rivalled Stephen in his dread of democracy, without sharing his friend's view that its victory was inevitable. More astute in his constitutional observations than Stephen, Maine noted the growing tendency of the executive branch of government to dominate the legislature. Indeed, "Democracy is monarchy inverted", since the cabinet "has succeeded to all the powers of the Crown, has drawn to itself all, and more than all, of the royal power over legislation" (Maine 1977: 94, 125). If the monarchy no longer provides an adequate check on the House of Commons, the role of the Lords becomes crucial. However, Maine feared that the hereditary principle no longer enjoyed its previous authority – no doubt at least partly thanks to the shift from "status" to "contract". It was even possible that "We are drifting towards a type of government associated with terrible events – a single Assembly, armed with full power over the Constitution, which it may exercise at pleasure" (Maine 1977: 135–6).

The latter prophecy recalls the anti-revolutionary panic of the 1790s, and echoes of Burke are also evident in Maine's extensive critique of Rousseau. Superficially, he seems to share Burke's sceptical view of human nature. However, there are important differences. Maine divides human beings into two categories: the fortunate "Few" who constitute an "intellectual aristocracy", and the masses who are too stupid even to understand their own interests. Most people (especially women) are averse to change. For Burke this was an invaluable bulwark against revolution in a country like Britain, but for Maine it means that democracy would put an end to human progress:

> It seems to me quite certain that, if for four centuries there had been a very widely extended franchise and a very large electoral body in this country, there would have been no reformation of religion, no change of dynasty, no toleration of Dissent, not even an accurate Calendar. The threshing-machine, the power-loom, the spinning-jenny, and possibly the steam engine, would have been prohibited. Even in our day, vaccination is in the utmost danger. (Maine 1977: 112)

The prospect that individuals with few educational opportunities might soon exercise direct political influence provoked a significant departure from Burke on the subject of "prejudice". "The prejudices of the people", Maine stormed, "are far stronger than those of the privileged classes; they are far more vulgar; and they are far more dangerous, because they are apt to run counter to scientific conclusions" (Maine 1977: 87). Maine's preoccupation with the material advances associated with science is a further indication of his distance from distinctive conservative ideology. The threshing-machine and the spinning jenny were the kind of modern innovations which Coleridge and Southey had regarded either with mixed feelings or unalloyed abhorrence, making a mockery of the notion that the move from "status" to "contract" held out the promise of personal liberation and self-development.

Initially Maine had been a Peelite; whether or not he followed the majority of Peel's followers in transferring his support to the Liberal Party is not known for certain, but it would have been consistent with his views, especially since he detested Disraeli. However, by the 1880s his sympathy for the Conservative Party was sufficiently well known for him to be invited (in more than one election) to stand for a safe Cambridge University seat. A key argument in *Popular Government* reflected current developments within the party (see Chapter 2). Maine asserted that attacks on the hereditary ownership of land could easily be extended into "objections to all private property" (Maine 1977: 189). Thus Maine's book provided intellectual cover for those who thought that the political battle lines in Britain had been transformed by the extension of the franchise: Arnold's "Barbarians" and "Philistines" should put aside their differences and join forces against the "Populace". This, as we have seen, was a reversal of Disraeli's rationale for Conservative adoption of parliamentary reform in 1867; it also entailed a shift of emphasis among defenders of economic inequality, from the Burkean notion of the duties of property-ownership to a liberal discourse of "rights".

There is less uncertainty about the partisan affiliations of the constitutional theorist Arthur Venn Dicey (1835–1922). Another friend of Henry Maine, and a cousin of Fitzjames Stephen, Dicey had been much more explicit in his identification with liberal individualism, showing particular admiration for Jeremy Bentham who, he argued, had inspired Peelites as well as reformers within the Liberal Party (Dicey 1905: 180). He also differed from his friends and relatives in finding little to fear in democracy as such. His concern was aroused by a general trend towards "collectivism", and his *Law and Opinion in England* (1905) anticipates W. H. Greenleaf's work on the British political tradition (see Chapter 1).

In 1885 Dicey's brother Edward contributed "A Plea of a Malcontent Liberal" to the *Fortnightly Review*. A. V. Dicey, who shared Edward's disillusion with the party's "collectivism", found a convenient bridge to the Conservative Party in the Liberal Unionist Party, founded in 1886. Dicey was a leading figure in the movement, along with the historian William Lecky (1838–1903), an Irish landowner who was alienated by Gladstone's policies as well as a fear of democracy which he expressed in a substantial volume, *Democracy and Liberty* (1896). In the previous year, Lecky had been elected as a Liberal Unionist candidate for Dublin University, which he represented in tandem with Sir Edward Carson until his death. Another avenue was provided by the Liberty and Property Defence League (LPDL), which had been established in 1882 with the backing of several prominent Conservatives, such as the Peelite Lord Elcho (later Earl of Wemyss: see Chapter 2).

The LPDL's most celebrated supporter was the libertarian exponent of pseudo-science, Herbert Spencer (1820–1903). Spencer published his most explicit intervention in the political controversies of his time, *The*

Man Versus the State, in 1884. Like his near-contemporary (and now his neighbour in Highgate Cemetery) Karl Marx (1818–83), Spencer appreciated the value of a punchy first sentence. *The Man Versus the State* opens with the claim that "Most of those who now pass as Liberals, are Tories of a new type" (Spencer 1969: 63). With his customary disregard for historical evidence, Spencer argued that "Tories" and "Whigs" had originally represented "two opposed types of social organization, broadly distinguishable as the militant and the industrial", representing the kind of socio-economic relationships explored by Henry Maine in *Ancient Law*. "Toryism" could thus be associated with "status", and by extension with an authoritarian state, while "Whiggism" or "Liberalism" favoured "contract" and freedom. Spencer was hoping to detach fellow-libertarians from their allegiance to the Liberal Party, which in his view had betrayed its Whiggish principles. It would be an exaggeration, he thought, to argue "that Liberals and Tories have changed places", but he did think that such an evolution might be under way and that the "Tories" could turn out to be the best "defenders of liberties which the Liberals, in pursuit of what they think popular welfare, trample under foot" (Spencer 1969: 81). Spencer, in short, was an advocate of the ideological "entryism" within the Conservative Party which was already taking place.

The "malcontent liberals" wrote clearly – not for them the airy abstractions of a Coleridge – and were anxious to spread their message far beyond the "intelligentsia". However, they were consciously addressing an audience of property owners who had a vested interest in turning back the tide of collectivism and needed little persuasion about the thoroughly bad motives of its advocates. It was one thing to preach to the readily convertible, but such work needed to be supplemented by appeals to workers who might otherwise be tempted to misuse their newly-granted voting rights. An eager volunteer for this task was William Mallock (1849–1923) an affluent freelance man of letters whose wide-ranging publications included *Is Life Worth Living?* (1875). Even before the Liberal split over Irish land policy and Home Rule, Mallock had identified the Conservative Party as the most likely source of effective opposition to collectivist ideas, and had seriously considered an invitation to stand for parliament on behalf of the party. His cousin, Richard Mallock, did become a Conservative MP (for Torquay, 1886–95), and William's role in his campaigns convinced him that the party was in grave danger of losing the battle of ideas by default, "because the Conservatives as a whole were so ignorant that they did not know, or so timorous or apathetic that they did not dare to use, the true facts, figures, or principles by the promulgation of which alone the false might be systematically discredited" (Mallock 1920: 159). Or, as he had put it more charitably in a much earlier publication, their beliefs "have been regarded as things so sacred and self-evident that it would be as idle to prove their truth as it would be wicked to question it" (Mallock 1882: 23–4). Now that the party seemed ready to adopt Mallock's own liberal ideology, it should take pride in its principles.

A member of the LPDL's council, Mallock was active in other anti-collectivist societies as well as lending practical assistance to the Conservative Party as a kind of one-man think tank and a coach for budding orators. He identified socialism as a specific tradition of thought which had to be contested, giving the impression of having read the works of relevant authors (including Marx), and attempting to engage with their arguments (notably the labour theory of value) rather than dismissing them out of hand. His characteristic approach was to bury socialist idealism under an avalanche of "facts". Thus, for example, he argued that the land-reformer Henry George had greatly exaggerated the proportion of national income owned by "our titled and untitled aristocracy". If landed proprietors were expropriated and their revenues equally divided, Mallock insisted, the benefits would be minuscule – and unlike Burke in 1795 he produced statistical evidence to prove the point.

Having demonstrated the relative unimportance of "unearned" income in contemporary Britain, Mallock moved effortlessly to a justification of economic inequality in other respects, on the basis of generalizations about human nature. It is natural for people to want a guaranteed basic income; but some individuals hope to do better than this, and if the state controls the distribution of wealth their creative impulses will be crushed. Thus for Mallock, "greed is good": or, in his more verbose formulation, "Cupidity is in itself the most general and legitimate desire to which any politician or political party can aspire" (Mallock 1894: 12). Like Maine, Mallock assumed that most people are passive – Burke's cud-chewing cattle again – so that progress depends on the ultra-talented, dynamic few. Such individuals will always rise to positions of power and impose their wills, whether or not a political system follows democratic procedures. Thus social, economic and political inequality are entirely natural and attempts to prevent them, however well-intentioned, will be worse than fruitless. Mallock is reticent about his own preferred system, but by implication the best forms of government are those which present the fewest obstacles to the ascendancy of the natural elite.

In *The Conservative Mind* Russell Kirk claimed that at the time of his death Mallock was "half-forgotten", but deserved "great credit for being the author of a reasoned conservative apologetic". Indeed, "for bulk and thoroughness, quite aside from Mallock's gifts of wit and style, his work is unexcelled among the body of conservative writings in any country" (Kirk 1954: 397, 416). In part, like Sir Ernest Barker's estimation of Stephen's *Liberty, Equality, Fraternity* as "the finest exposition of conservative thought in the latter half of the nineteenth century", this compliment is diminished by an absence of serious competition (Barker 1928: 172). It required very considerable ingenuity for Kirk to reconcile Mallock's unflinching individualism with his own "organic" conception of conservative thought. Mallock's "wit and style" are a matter of taste; for example, in a lecture delivered by invitation in the US, he sneered at "people who now call themselves socialists", claiming that they chiefly consisted of "academic students, professors, clergymen, and also of emotional ladies, who enjoy the attention of footmen in faultless liveries" (Mallock 1908: 4–5).

Self-conscious "conservatism"

In a conversation of 1882 with Henry Maine the liberal historian Lord Acton had been "much struck to find a philosopher, entirely outside party politics, who does not think Toryism a reproach" (quoted in Kirk 1954: 315). Mallock was certainly not ashamed of association with "the stupidest party", feeling rather that Conservatives would be far more self-confident if only they would make proper use of the intellectual "weapons of precision" which he had provided.

Remaining inhibitions were shed in the years between 1903 and 1914, which as Ewen Green has written, "saw a host of books and pamphlets published that engaged with the whole gamut of questions the party faced", ranging far beyond the obvious topics of tariff reform and Home Rule (Green 2004: 5). Several of these (notably F. E. Smith's *Unionist Policy and Other Essays* (1913), *Tory Democracy* (1914) by the historian Keith Feiling, and *The Tory Tradition* (1914) by the academic and MP Sir Geoffrey Butler), were serious attempts to characterize a conservative position.

The publication from these years which has attracted the most subsequent attention is Lord Hugh Cecil's *Conservatism* (1912). In part, its status as an authoritative statement of conservative beliefs reflects the author's prominence within the Conservative Party. Cecil (later Baron Quickswood, 1869–1956) was the youngest son of the Marquess of Salisbury and the cousin of Arthur Balfour, who had only recently stepped down as party leader (see Chapter 4). Cecil was regarded as an appropriate contributor to a prestigious series of studies published by the "Home University Library of Modern Knowledge"; the volumes on liberalism, socialism and communism were composed respectively by L. T. Hobhouse, Ramsay MacDonald and Harold Laski. One commentator duly praised Cecil's book as a "careful and temperate statement of Conservative principles", noting the frequent allusions to Burke (Buck 1975: 6). However, Cecil's reading of Burke testifies to his personal predilections; for him, the primary point of *Reflections* was "the importance of religion and the value of its recognition by the State" (Cecil 1912: 48).

In fact, the central place accorded to religion is one of the few features which distinguish Cecil's take on "conservatism" from Mallock's secular output. For good reason, a study of *Contemporary Political Thought in England* published a few years later included a chapter which bracketed Cecil and Mallock as "Individualists", without mentioning conservatism at all (Rockrow 1925). Both writers believed that the role of the state should be strictly circumscribed; both were elitists who were anxious to justify inherited wealth as well as the proceeds of personal initiative, deploring attempts at redistribution beyond a basic minimum. For both, as for Maine and other recent authors, inequality was thus natural and the most effective engine of progress.

Cecil is therefore best understood as another of Fitzjames Stephen's hybrid cases, with liberal ideas outweighing any residual "conservatism". As such it is not surprising that he presents "Political Conservatism" "as an amalgam. Or rather it may be compared to a river, the waters of which come from many converging streams" (Cecil 1912: 23). It was due chiefly to biographical accident that Cecil's own "stream" was still babbling along within the Conservative Party. His fierce attachment to free trade set him at odds with the majority of his party, and was the issue which had persuaded his close friend Winston Churchill to defect to the Liberals (See Chapter 1). Family connections acted as a curb on Cecil, unlike Churchill who claimed to be acting out of principled loyalty to his long-dead father, Lord Randolph.

A similar move was also problematic for Cecil because, as a vehement anti-Catholic, he shared the Conservative Party's opposition to Irish Home Rule. In 1912, Cecil wrote that "natural conservatism" was "deeply seated in almost all minds" and was by no means restricted to supporters of the Conservative Party; its features included a "distrust of the unknown, and preference for experience over theory". Far from being incompatible with progress, it provided an element of security without which "progress may be if not destructive at least futile". "Restraint", he wrote in this context, "is not only essential to hinder what is foolish, but also to guide and control what is wisely intended and save movement from being vague, wild and mischievous" (Cecil 1912: 9, 8, 14). His father would have grunted gravely and approvingly. However, Cecil's endorsement of "natural conservatism" did not guarantee that he would obey its precepts. Soon after his father's death his conduct in parliament had earned for his Conservative cronies (including Churchill) the apposite nickname of "Hughligans". By the time his book went to press he had gone much further, gesticulating wildly and screaming "Traitor!" while the prime minister, Asquith, was speaking in the Commons. His conduct provoked a Labour MP to observe that "Many a man has been certified as insane for less than half of what [Cecil] has done this afternoon" (Dangerfield 1961: 56; Hansard HC Deb., 25 July 1911). Later Cecil addressed a Unionist demonstration at Enniskillen, affirming the right of Ulster to act in defiance of the law. While the "careful and temperate" *Conservatism* awaited publication, its author joined in cries of "To hell with the pope!". In these antics Cecil was abetted by F. E. Smith (later Lord Birkenhead, 1872–1930), who in the same year wrote that those who loved "an old and highly civilised country" should be guided by "the spirit of Burke". Perhaps Smith was thinking of the dagger-wielding Burke rather than the author of *Reflections* (Smith 1913: 3). In his most celebrated speech, delivered after the First World War, the bibulous Birkenhead outraged members of his own party (notably Stanley Baldwin) by praising self-interest and claiming that life's "glittering prizes" were awarded to "those who have stout hearts and sharp swords" (Taylor 1931: 232–3).

It is unremarkable, but unhelpful, that the contestable nature of conservative thought became more apparent when the subject had attracted interest from so many writers with personal axes to grind. Cecil's book can be seen as, in part, an attempt to incorporate the ideological refugees from the Liberal Party into the "conservative" tradition, apparently confirming his claim about "converging streams" as well as his own liberal leanings. The brief bibliography of *Conservatism* (just eight authors) included Stephen and Maine; no rationale is presented in Cecil's text for their inclusion alongside Bolingbroke, Burke and Coleridge. Cecil did allow that the Conservative Party had been more willing than its rivals to extend the scope of state activity, particularly in relieving poverty, but in his discussion of this issue he made no secret of his own dislike of collectivism, echoing the LDPL with laudatory references to Herbert Spencer (Cecil 1912: 169). For his part, Sir Geoffrey Butler – father of "Rab" Butler who played a very prominent intellectual role in the Conservative Party after 1945 – placed much more emphasis on the "Burkean" themes of an organic society and the duties associated with property; but he side-stepped the difficulties of definition by confining his discussion to just four uncontentious figures (Bolingbroke, Burke, Disraeli and Salisbury).

Whether or not Cecil was justified in portraying "Political Conservatism" as a river composed of many streams, in the years before the First World War it seemed in danger of bursting its banks. Pessimistic observers of the human condition could find ample confirmation in the events of the Great War. Even before the carnage commenced the novelist Thomas Hardy wrote that the temper of the times "simply makes one sit in an apathy and watch the clock spinning backwards". In a similar mood, William Inge ("the gloomy Dean", 1860–1954) announced in his Romanes Lecture of 1920 that "the idea of progress" had been disproved, at least as an inexorable "law of nature" His only tangible suggestion for "progress" was a reversal of the industrial revolution: the disappearance of "great manufacturing towns" would "be no great loss" (Inge 1920: 30). While the logical response of ideological conservatives was disengagement from practical affairs, two young politicians claimed that the wartime spirit offered a "Great Opportunity" for national renewal (Lloyd & Wood 1919). Such well-intentioned wishful thinking had been exposed long before the outbreak of a fully-mechanized and even more bestial war; one of the optimistic authors, Richard Wood (later Lord Halifax) ended his career as the Conservative foreign secretary who tried to strike a deal with Adolf Hitler.

Summary

After the political and religious reforms between 1828 and 1832, distinctive conservative views continued to be expressed, particularly in periodical journals like the *Quarterly*. But such writers, whose leitmotif was the prophecy of doom, seemed far less *relevant* than their ideological opponents like John Stuart Mill, or more ambiguous figures such as Matthew Arnold and James Fitzjames Stephen who expressed unease, rather than mortification, at the prospect of additional reform. Fear of democracy was widespread among the propertied classes in the later nineteenth century, and the most effective counterattacks were launched by ideological liberals like Sir Henry Maine. As such, the first "authoritative" attempt to construct a "conservative" tradition – Lord Hugh Cecil's study, published in 1912 – cited Maine and other liberal figures. According to Cecil, political conservatism was not a distinctive ideological position, but rather a blend of Burkean sentiments with liberal dogma on key issues like economics and the role of the state. As an ideological liberal himself, Cecil's chief objective was to rationalize and justify his personal view that the Conservative Party, rather than the Liberals, had become the most promising electoral vehicle for defence of the propertied classes.

4

The Conservative Party, 1902–45

At least the succession to Salisbury was seamless. Arthur Balfour was the obvious choice, partly thanks to the accident of consanguity but also because his political career (since joining the Commons in 1874) suggested real political ability. At the time of his elevation to the premiership, Balfour had been piloting through parliament an Education Bill which began to extend previous provision of elementary schooling to the secondary level, entrusting responsibility to county and borough councils. Generally regarded nowadays as a sensible measure, at the time it aroused furious opposition from Protestant dissenters who, through compulsory local taxation, would have to cover the costs of teaching in Anglican (or Catholic) schools. Nonconformist objections to the proposal had been overridden by well-placed Anglican lobbyists, notably Salisbury's eldest son (who in 1903 was promoted to the cabinet alongside two cousins – Balfour and his brother Gerald – and his brother-in-law the Earl of Selborne). Equal opportunities were still a distant dream for progressive educationalists, but no-one could deny their existence within the Salisbury clan.

The terms of the Act were deeply unsettling to Joseph Chamberlain – a unitarian who owed his Birmingham powerbase to his identification with Protestant dissent as well as his charisma and business acumen. In its dealings with Chamberlain, the Conservative Party was not well served by the substitution of the dilettante Balfour for the Delphic Salisbury. If the succession had been determined on the grounds of political ability and seniority rather than the nepotism immortalized at the time by the phrase "Bob's your uncle", Chamberlain would almost certainly have been the choice. As the Boer War came to its inglorious close, Chamberlain might not have been an ageing man in a hurry; but he was always a man with a plan. After dining with a group of young

Conservative MPs in the spring of 1902, he confided that tariffs "are the politics of the future" (Gilbert 1991: 148).

Chamberlain was referring to a project that had been canvassed, particularly in imperialist circles, for many years, under various names – "tariff reform", "fair trade", "imperial preference", etc. At its most basic, the idea envisaged protection of British products by means of import duties, which would be reduced (or waived entirely) in relation to trade within the empire. For Chamberlain, tariffs had two main attractions: they would strengthen the economic bonds of empire, while providing a source of revenue for the state which could be applied to his favourite "collectivist" purposes.

Chamberlain believed that the Boer War highlighted the advantages which tariff reform could produce for Britain in both of these respects. In an era of intensified imperialist competition, the formation of an economic bloc centred on London would give British colonies a material incentive for loyalty, while the need for greater state promotion of the health and education of the domestic population had been proved by the unfitness of many would-be volunteers for active service in Britain's armed forces. No stranger to "unauthorized" policy initiatives, Chamberlain gave the first public exposition of his ideas on 15 May 1903. Frustrated by Balfour's lukewarm response, he resigned from the government in September 1903 in order to take his case to the country.

Balfour's position – i.e., that the question of protective tariffs should be decided by pragmatic considerations rather than forming part of a grandiose scheme of imperial unity and social reform – was perfectly defensible, particularly from the Burkean perspective of incremental change. However, Chamberlain's crusade provided a plausible pretext for a general outbreak of hostilities between the incongruous elements of Salisbury's "Conservative" coalition. The problem was, if anything, more acute because divisions cut across previous allegiances: some zealots for tariff reform had always considered themselves to be Conservatives, while the ideological advocates of "free trade" included many of the "Unionists" who had recently abandoned the Liberal Party over Home Rule and now found themselves confronted by an equally divisive issue within their new party.

This particular aspect of the "Crisis of Conservatism" is exemplified by the case of one of the young MPs who had been dining with Chamberlain when he dropped his heavy hint about tariffs. When first elected in 1900 Winston Churchill was already a national celebrity, thanks to his buccaneering exploits before and during the Boer War. It was natural for him to accept nomination as a Conservative candidate (at Oldham). However, almost as soon as he took his seat he began to reconsider his party affiliation. Partly this arose from unreflective fealty to his late father – Lord Randolph had come a cropper over defence spending, therefore Winston had to take up the same cause regardless of the official Conservative position (or the national interest). However, even in his maiden speech Winston showed that he was not simply a "chip off the old block", showing a degree of empathy towards the (still undefeated) Boers which Randolph had never extended to his numerous adversaries.

Just two years after becoming a Conservative MP Churchill was hankering after a realignment that would create a "centrist" party equipped to halt the forward march of the Labour movement. In his view, as an organized political entity Labour was "anti-national & irreligious and perhaps communistic" – a view which he never entirely discarded. His proposed centrist party would be "free at once from the sordid selfishness and callousness of Toryism on the one hand & the blind appetites of the Radical masses on the other" (Gilbert 1991: 151–2). From this perspective Churchill lost no time in signalling opposition to Chamberlain's tariff initiative, predicting that its adoption would mean that "The old Conservative Party, with its religious convictions and constitutional principles, will disappear, and a new Party will arise like perhaps the Republican Party of the United States of America – rich, materialist, and secular" (Hansard HC Deb., 28 May 1903). Churchill's objections to the Conservative Party were both ideological and institutional: as he told his friend Hugh Cecil, "I am an English Liberal. I hate the Tory party, their men, their words and their methods" (Gilbert 1991: 158; note the reversion to the word "Tory" in this negative context). At the end of May 1904 Churchill "crossed the floor", part of an exodus of Conservative free traders into the Liberal ranks.

Balfour's attempts to keep the show on the road after Chamberlain's resignation had only exposed the futility of his balancing act. He engineered the departure of three cabinet free traders, including the chancellor of the exchequer, C. T. Ritchie. Evidently in Balfour's calculations the weight of one Chamberlain equated to three run-of-the-mill ministers from the opposite camp. But any illusion of even-handedness between the factions was dissipated by his decision to replace Ritchie with Chamberlain's son Austen. The three departing free traders became four when the nominal leader of the Liberal Unionists, the Duke of Devonshire, also decided to quit. In October 1904 Balfour called a truce, announcing that nothing would be done until the voters had delivered their verdict on tariffs at the next general election. This bought his government more time to introduce populist measures such as the anti-semitic 1905 Aliens Act. Churchill opposed this legislation at every stage, recording his "contempt at the spectacle of a great Party trying to retrieve its shattered reputation by exploiting and aggravating the miseries of some of the weakest and poorest of mankind". Apart from demonstrating Churchill's humanitarian streak, his stance exposed his ignorance of the fact that the "great party" he had joined had rarely hesitated to exploit religious prejudice (Hansard HC Deb., 3 July 1905). In December 1905 the beleaguered Balfour resorted to his last tactical weapon, submitting the resignation of his government in the hope that the Liberals would be too disunited to assemble a cabinet of their own. True to form, he had miscalculated and Henry Campbell-Bannerman was able to put a team together before parliament was dissolved for a January election. In the campaign, opponents of the Conservative Party suffered from an embarrassment of riches; apart from continuing resentment against the 1902 Education Act, allegations that the government had allowed the savage mistreatment of indentured Chinese labourers in South Africa dismayed Balfour himself (Ramsden 1978: 16–17). By contrast, the Conservatives could not even make much of the Home Rule issue, since Campbell-Bannerman played down the prospect of early legislation. A limited non-aggression pact between the Liberals and the Labour Representation Committee helped to give the latter its first healthy parliamentary contingent (24 of its 29 MPs were not opposed by Liberal candidates). In 1900, 402 MPs had been elected on the Conservative and Unionist ticket; six years later the tally was reduced to 156.

At least the rout had settled the issue of tariffs within the party, since more than a hundred of its surviving MPs supported reform. Balfour had lost his Manchester seat on a swing to the Liberals of more than 20 percentage points, and it took a few weeks to contrive his return via a convenient by-election. In the meantime Chamberlain acted as leader in the Commons, but resisted the obvious temptation to put that arrangement on a permanent footing. Instead, he secured Balfour's public agreement that "imperial preference" was now the party's chief policy priority. However, in July 1906 Chamberlain suffered a devastating stroke, days after celebrations of his 70th birthday, effectively ending his extraordinary career.

The mantle of tariff reform passed to Austen Chamberlain, who resembled Joseph physically but lacked the political brutality of his self-made father. Although Balfour's capitulation over tariffs had disarmed potential critics at a party meeting in February 1906, he proved an ineffective opposition leader. In the Commons, of course, the Conservatives were hopelessly outnumbered, but Balfour was unwilling or unable to offer constructive alternative policies, relying instead on the House of Lords to obstruct the government's agenda. At least in this isolated instance Balfour had lived up (or down) to a promise; as the extent of his party's electoral defeat became evident in 1906, he had reassured a Nottingham audience that Unionists "should still control, whether in power or opposition, the destinies of this great Empire" (Adams 2013: 233).

The stand-off between Lords and Commons came to a head in 1909, when David Lloyd George proposed a budget which increased imposts on unearned income (including the proceeds of landownership), as well as introducing a new "super-tax". The purpose was to pay not only for the Liberal government's welfare policies (including old-age pensions, introduced in 1909) but also to appease public demands for increased expenditure to maintain Britain's naval advantage over Germany. According to Roy Jenkins, the package was "as a whole hardly revolutionary" and the sums involved were "modest" (Jenkins 1998: 166). However, the social and political implications were momentous. In effect, the propertied classes were being asked to assume additional burdens in order to finance policies which were intended to benefit the less well-off – and to underwrite a bellicose foreign policy which enjoyed considerable support from the "masses". For the Conservatives in their present mood, the budget represented an additional provocation because, if accepted, it threatened to undermine the argument that only tariff reform could provide adequate revenue for an interventionist state. At the same time, if they used the House of Lords to veto the budget the Liberals would be able to call an election on the cry of "Peers versus the People".

Thanks to the opposition of the Lords, it took a year for the budget to come into effect. By that time "the people" had been given a chance (in January 1910) to express their views on Lloyd George's measures, and before the end of the year a further election had been called as the government sought a mandate for reform of the upper chamber. Neither contest produced an overall majority; although on both occasions the Conservatives and Unionists won the largest share of the vote, the Liberals remained in office thanks to support from Labour and the Irish Parliamentary Party. The king, George V, was forced to follow the example of William IV and promise the mass-creation of peers in case of further resistance from the Lords. Also like William, George was spared from this unpalatable duty by the Lords themselves, who voted by 131 to 114 to replace their veto rights over legislation with a power to delay bills by a maximum of two years (money bills could only be delayed for a month). Although the Act contained a pledge to replace the Lords with "a Second Chamber constituted on a popular instead of a hereditary basis", it accepted that this "could not immediately be brought into operation". In this case, "not immediately" turned out to mean "not for at least another century".

Balfour had continued to lead the party throughout a process which Uncle Salisbury would not have hesitated to describe as "Disintegration". During the December 1910 election campaign he had proposed that the future of the Lords and the issue of tariff reform should both be decided by referendums – a clever ploy, but an unusual one to emanate from the leader of a party which was associated with defence of the traditional constitution. In November 1911 Balfour finally stepped aside to pursue his passion for golf, which he preferred to the compulsory Conservative pastime of fox hunting.

The succession was determined in a fashion which is barely explicable to those who think that leadership contests should be decided by ordinary party members. The main contenders were Austen Chamberlain and Walter Long, another advocate of tariff reform and a fervent supporter of the Union. Superficially, it might seem that the result would have no effect on the party's future direction, but tribal allegiances died hard and Long, a bucolic Conservative, had once described Joseph Chamberlain as "a bloody radical" who could never lead the party (Ramsden 1998: 188). Apparently support for the pair was roughly equal, and party managers prepared for the unseemly device of a secret ballot as a tiebreaker. There were, however, two other candidates – Sir Edward Carson, the Dublin-born barrister who had succeeded Long as leader of the Irish Unionists, and Andrew Bonar Law, another MP with Irish connections, who had inherited a fortune from relatives with interests in the steel industry. Carson realized he could not win and withdrew, but Bonar Law, whose support was even more meagre, refused to follow suit. Chamberlain quixotically offered to renounce his candidature provided that Long did the same. As John Ramsden put it, "once that offer was made, Long could hardly refuse"; whereupon Law, who would probably have attracted the least votes in a secret ballot, was acclaimed as the new leader of the Conservative Party, to general satisfaction (Ramsden 1978: 65–6). Far from being a candidate of sufficient stature to heal party divisions, Bonar Law's only conceivable advantage over Austen Chamberlain and even Walter Long was that nobody had ever heard of him. Whatever he would have thought about the elevation of a Glasgow-based merchant banker to the leadership of one of Britain's major parties, the ghost of Edmund Burke would have smiled at this new testament to human irrationality.

The new leader had certainly not been plucked from relative obscurity because of his charisma; Roy Jenkins characterized his life as "almost aggressively joyless" (Jenkins 1998: 147). As a young man he had given a talk on the topic "Is Life Worth Living?", possibly inspired by W. H. Mallock's 1871 book of that title (see Chapter 3). According to his first biographer, Robert Blake, "He came to the comforting conclusion that on the whole it is", but this was emphatically untrue of a life devoted entirely to the accumulation of wealth. Anyone cursed with that pre-occupation, Bonar Law admonished, "spends his days like a mole in grubbing with blinded eyes in the mouldy earth, but unlike the mole his grubbing is altogether aimless" (Blake 1955: 28). By 1911, when Bonar Law became leader, there were plenty of "moles" at every level of the Conservative Party.

Bonar Law's chief attraction for a party in the doldrums was a dogged partisanship which, as he explained to the prime minister, Asquith, before their first front-bench encounter, laid him under a regrettable obligation to be "very vicious" (Ramsden 1998: 209, 207). While he was prepared to apologise in advance for parliamentary pugilism, Bonar Law was less punctilious when it came to oratory "out of doors", such as a speech at Blenheim Palace in July 1912 in which he promised unquestioning support for Ulster in its resistance to Home Rule. He had no hesitation in warning of impending civil war, while using rhetoric which was likely to foment it. George V was drawn into the search for a possible compromise over Ulster, as around 2 million of his subjects swore, through a Solemn League and Covenant, to "use all means necessary to defeat the present conspiracy to set up a Home Rule parliament in Ireland". Protestant paramilitary groups prepared for violence, and there was good reason to anticipate mass mutiny if the British Army was asked to repress a rebellion in Ulster. But the war which broke out in August 1914 was not a conflict near the very heart of the British empire, pitting Anglophile imperialists of all parties against the advocates of national self-determination in Ireland and elsewhere. Rather, it was a European conflict whose effects extended throughout the world. Within a year, the British cabinet, still led by Asquith but now representing a coalition, included not only Lloyd George and Churchill but also all four of the candidates for the Conservative leadership in 1911, along with Balfour himself and Labour's Arthur Henderson.

Stanley Baldwin and his party

According to J. M. Keynes, Stanley Baldwin characterized the newly-elected MPs of 1918 as "a lot of hard-faced men who look as if they have done very well out of the war" (Skidelsky 1983: 383). Most of the flinty new faces belonged to Conservatives, who in terms purely of domestic politics had done very well indeed out of the war. The Conservatives fought the 1918 (or "Coupon") election in alliance with David Lloyd George's Coalition Liberals. The bitter contest between Lloyd George's supporters and former colleagues who remained loyal to H. H. Asquith (who had been replaced as prime minister in December 1916) consolidated the breach in party ranks into a lasting split which was not repaired until the Liberals had been destroyed as a potential party of government.

The American historian George Dangerfield thought that "The Strange Death of Liberal England" could be foretold on the basis of pre-war developments (the rise of militant trade unionism and the suffragette movement, the Home Rule crisis and attempts to reform the House of Lords). Despite his vivid character sketches and colourful accounts of key events, from the perspective of ideological history Dangerfield's title promises more than the author delivers. Did a particular approach to government (or, indeed, a set of values which encompassed the whole English nation) perish in these years? The situation is not clarified by Dangerfield's elegiac final chapter, in which he laments the poets of the pre-war "Romantic Revival" as "the last victims and the last heroes of Liberal England" (Dangerfield 1961: 430). Yet the central figure of the chapter, Rupert Brooke, fancied himself as a socialist rather than a liberal. A more suitable symbol for the death of Liberal England would have been Asquith's talented son Raymond, who died in battle rather than succumbing to disease like Brooke; but Raymond Asquith is not even mentioned by Dangerfield.

In truth, although the events chronicled by Dangerfield exposed serious dilemmas for liberalism – and on the outbreak of war the question of conscription compounded the ideological challenges – the situation was even less propitious for what remained of "Conservative England" after the momentous economic, social and political changes of the previous century. The financial position of the landed interest had been sapped further by Lloyd George's 1909 budget, and the removal of the Lords' veto was a crushing political blow. However, if Conservative England was dead circumstances conspired to reprieve the Conservative *Party*. The 1916–22 coalition which inflicted lasting damage on the Liberal Party was helpful to the Conservatives in several ways. It dealt with issues – a further extension of the franchise, and (especially) the partition of Ireland – which might have caused more trouble if they had been handled by the Conservatives governing alone. Less tangibly, a party which had entered the war after a series of defeats ended it as the dominant member of a winning team, satisfying the conceit that "Conservative men" were the only reliable custodians of the national interest whose sense of patriotic duty would overcome any petty political divisions in the hour of need. The question remained whether the party was still composed of Conservative men, or whether (as one MP put it), since Salisbury's death it had become little more than "a dumping ground for disgruntled Liberals" and a vehicle for "sectional" rather than "national" interests (Bentinck 1918: 78, 45).

In October 1922 Conservative MPs decided that Lloyd George had outlived his (considerable) usefulness. Bonar Law took office at the head of a single-party administration, and although the Conservatives lost seats in a general election held in November they still enjoyed a comfortable parliamentary majority. However, Bonar Law was already mortally ill and he resigned in May 1923. Baldwin, his replacement, was no evangelical in the cause of tariff reform but was persuaded that the case for protection was now unanswerable. Since the party had abandoned Balfour's idea of settling the question through a referendum, Baldwin followed constitutional propriety by calling a "snap" general election. The result, for the Conservatives, was a net loss of more than 80 seats; they remained the largest party at Westminster, but could not govern without Liberal support. This was withheld by Asquith, whose preference was for a minority Labour government which (hopefully) would quickly discredit itself.

Thanks to Asquith's tactical ruse, Baldwin's apparent blunder in calling an early election soon began to look far-sighted. Although the minority Labour government disappointed both its radical supporters and its reactionary detractors by working within accepted constitutional parameters, the idea that Asquith had been willing to risk a Bolshevik-style reign of terror was yet another reason for property-owners to regard the Liberals as unduly soft on socialism. To consolidate their new *raison d'être* as defenders of property against organized Labour, the Conservatives and their media sidekicks harried Ramsay MacDonald's government with constant slurs and distortions, culminating in the 1924 general election campaign in which the party joined forces with the *Daily Mail* to exploit a brazen forgery – the "Zinoviev Letter", which implied that Labour policies were helping the Bolshevik cause in Britain. The Liberals were reduced to just 40 seats; the Conservatives won 412 (out of 615). Baldwin was back. Apparently he believed that the fake Zinoviev Letter was genuine; certainly on this occasion he attacked Labour as if it really was sympathetic to the Soviet Union (Young *et al.* 1967).

Among those who deserted the Liberals after the 1923 election was Winston Churchill. Back in 1904 Churchill had expressed concern that "the Liberal Party will be smashed to pieces between organized capital on the one hand and organized labour on the other" (Glibert 1991: 160). Thus he accurately predicted the developments which, 20 years later, had persuaded him to earn his ticket of readmission into the Conservative parliamentary ranks (standing initially, however, as a Constitutionalist – the alternative party label Salisbury had suggested in 1883). Churchill had convinced himself that Baldwin was "setting country before Party" and that since there was no longer any place for an independent Liberal Party his former colleagues (including Lloyd George) should join with the Conservatives on "a broad progressive platform", hopefully to keep Labour out forever (Gilbert 1991: 160, 461, 462).

Apart from quashing any chance of a Liberal revival, Baldwin's main partisan objective during his 14-year leadership was to divert Labour from a revolutionary path – as he put it, "to see our Labour movement free from alien and foreign heresy" (Baldwin 1928: 169). His failure in May 1926 to negotiate a compromise between trade unions and employers which could have averted a General Strike was thus a serious personal and political blow. Thankfully, though, "We were saved by common sense and the good temper of our own people". Baldwin retained his faith in the British system of government, which ensured that "Our people are not going to throw over Parliament to set up divine right either of the capitalist or of the trade unionist, and we are not going to bow down to a dictatorship of either" (Baldwin 1928: 168, 169). However, this did not mean equality in the workplace; employers should be conciliatory, but from a position of strength. It is generally thought that, had he so wished, Baldwin could have modified the terms of the vengeful Trade Disputes Act (1927), which outlawed "sympathetic" strikes and mass picketing, as well as hitting Labour's finances by replacing the previous "political levy" on the income of trade unionists into a voluntary payment. His inaction strongly suggests that, whatever his personal views, he could not afford to displease the "hard-faced" supporters of his party.

Conservative "pragmatism"

Baldwin's most famous speech – delivered early in his leadership – has often been diagnosed as a symptom of hopeless nostalgia. He evoked "The sounds of England, the tinkle of hammer on anvil in the country smithy, the corncrake on a dewy morning, the sound of the scythe against the whetstone, and the sight of a plough team coming over the brow of a hill, the sight that has been in England since England was a land". However, Baldwin was no reactionary; he knew that his ideal of "Conservative England" was long gone, if it had ever existed. He went on to acknowledge, with regret, that such sights and sounds were no longer "the childish inheritance of the majority of people to-day in our country" (Baldwin 1926: 7). Elsewhere, Baldwin neatly summarized the reasons why state intervention had supplanted aristocratic paternalism, and also why liberal individualism was outmoded: "You cannot go back to the rule of the country gentleman … Urban populations and mass provision of services are inseparable" (Baldwin 1935: 69–70).

The titles given to Baldwin's collected speeches (e.g., *Our Inheritance* and *Service of our Lives*) suggest a Burkean veneration for the past and an emphasis on duty rather than rights – on an understanding of liberty which was compatible with, rather than subversive of, a sense of order. The exception – the liberal-sounding *This Torch of Freedom* (1935) – included the text of a speech delivered at Old Sarum (see Chapter 1). The occasion could easily have been the cue for a volley of democratic clichés ("This place should be a lasting memorial to those who fought and suffered for the right to vote", etc). Instead, Baldwin told his audience that "I sometimes think the time may come when our enlightened posterity may think it just as inconceivable that men should be returned to parliament by making promises they know they can never fulfil, as we regard it impossible that men should be returned for rotten boroughs" (Baldwin 1935: 132).

In a July 1936 speech to the City of London Conservative and Unionist Association, Baldwin reflected that "If I have achieved anything during these last fourteen or fifteen years I have tried so far as I can to lead this country into the way of evolutionary progress, but I have tried to warn it against revolutionary progress, and I have tried to bring about a unity of spirit in the nation" (Baldwin 1937: 43). In relation to the British constitution, Baldwin's approach to reform was not so much "evolutionary" as "glacial"; although he felt compelled to engineer the abdication of Edward VIII, he lost an excellent opportunity to revise the composition and powers of the House of Lords. Much more to his credit, he faced down a challenge to his leadership from the "press barons", Beaverbrook and Rothermere, accusing them of seeking "power without responsibility". He was also modern-minded enough to realize the potential of radio as a means of appealing to the people, but as a medium of pacification rather than populism. The evolutionary approach was on display – far too much so for the taste of die-hards like Churchill – in respect of the empire, where Baldwin's government tacitly accepted the case for Indian self-government and foreshadowed a new relationship with the colonies through the 1926 Balfour Declaration.

It was fully in keeping with Baldwin's approach that, for his party's slogan in the 1929 general election campaign, he approved "Safety First". The headline result of the election – a loss of more than 150 Conservative seats, leaving Labour for the first time as Britain's largest parliamentary party – was bad enough, but concealed even worse news for Baldwin since the Liberals, now reunited under Lloyd George, won almost a quarter of the popular vote. Baldwin showed little appetite for opposition against a second minority Labour government, presumably hoping that it would succumb to "events". When the government duly collapsed amidst the economic crisis of August 1931 Baldwin was deeply reluctant to commit to a new coalition, but was left with no alternative by the advocacy of the king and the fact that Herbert Samuel, who was deputizing as Liberal leader while Lloyd George was unwell, had already agreed to serve if Ramsay MacDonald could be persuaded to stay on as head of a broadly based "National Government". Naturally the vast majority of MacDonald's parliamentary colleagues refused to join him, and at the ensuing general election (October 1931) only 59 Labour MPs were returned, 46 of whom were passionately opposed to the man who had led the party (in two instalments) for more than a decade. MacDonald remained as prime minister but, of the 556 MPs who now supported the National Government, 472 were Conservatives – an unprecedented tally, albeit in unusual times.

Back in 1835, Disraeli had claimed that "The Tory Party in this country is the national party; it is the really democratic party in England" (Hutcheon 1913: 216). A hundred years later – in June 1935 – Baldwin succeeded the increasingly-decrepit MacDonald as prime minister. Although the government was still nominally "National", the Conservatives had been the dominant force from the outset. After the 1935 election there were still 387 Conservatives – more than the number returned in the "Coupon" election of 1918 when the House had contained 707 MPs. Since then, the final step towards universal adult suffrage had been taken with the 1928 Equal Franchise Act. The Conservatives, it seemed, had fulfilled Disraeli's improbable boast. Baldwin's avuncular persona, accessible to the British public as Disraeli's had never been thanks to technological developments, was ideally suited to cement the party's national status. Like Disraeli, Baldwin thought that the stability of the political system required a viable opposition, and in this respect the 1935 election was also helpful since Labour under Clement Attlee won more than 150 seats, making the remaining Liberals look like an increasingly eccentric rump which would soon fall to the gravitational pull of the dominant parties of left and right.

Yet the supposedly "national" party was far from united within its own ranks. Baldwin might reassure the voters, but he was an enduring source of frustration to colleagues who were not satisfied with "Safety First". Austen Chamberlain's half-brother Neville, who served as chancellor of the exchequer from 1931 to 1937 and was seen (not least by himself) as Baldwin's heir-apparent, provided the main evidence for those who regarded the party as a "progressive" force. He had been a hyperactive minister of health (1924–29), famously embarking on the role with a list of 25 policy proposals, only four of which awaited enactment when he left office. As chancellor (1931–37 – his second stint, after a brief apprenticeship in 1923), Chamberlain made his influence felt far beyond the Treasury, associating himself with familiar measures to improve housing and limit factory working hours, but also taking a more interventionist approach to public health through the Physical Training and Recreation Act (1937). Chamberlain earned Professor Greenleaf's "collectivist" black spot by encouraging the reorganization of the iron and steel industry, demonstrating his "corporatist" belief in cooperation between state and industry (Greenleaf 1983: 244).

As chancellor, however, Chamberlain resisted Keynesian ideas about deficit financing and ambitious schemes of public works. His preferred remedy to the blight of unemployment was to stimulate private enterprise, by alleviating some of the burden of taxation in approved laissez-faire style but also through selective state subsidies. His approach, and that of his late father, was accepted as wholly compatible with the Conservative Party's traditions: indeed, in 1938 the partisan historian Sir Charles Petrie hailed Joseph Chamberlain for having "saved Conservatism by compelling it to return to the true sources of its faith, the preaching of Mr. Disraeli and the practice of Mr. Pitt" (Petrie 1938: 91). Neville Chamberlain himself had no interest in such matters – indeed, far from regarding his father as the saviour of "Conservatism" he greatly disliked the word and preferred to see himself in terms of "Radical Joe's" Liberal Unionism. His proudest achievement was the introduction, in 1932, of a modified version of the latter's tariff reform programme; the emotional high generated by this achievement seems to have distracted him from its cool reception at the British Empire Economic Conference, held in Ottawa, where the leaders of the imperial colonies and dominions showed an alarming awareness of Britain's relative decline (and an equally troubling taste for Keynesian ideas). A "good hater", whose antipathies extended to President Roosevelt as well as Lloyd George, Chamberlain seemed anxious to distance himself as far as possible from the Baldwinian/Disraelian approach, losing no opportunity to advertise his contempt for the parliamentary Labour Party (and, by implication, the benighted members of the public who voted for them). This trait was to cost him dearly in 1940 (Jenkins 1998: 353).

Some of Chamberlain's parliamentary colleagues were more sensitive to accusations that the party had become a vehicle for laissez-faire liberalism. Lord Eustace Percy (1887–1958), who had been an education minister in the 1920s and served briefly in the National Government, opened his contribution to a collection of essays on *Conservatism and the Future* by claiming that conservatives "emphatically do not seek to conserve the present social system or the present distribution of wealth", and decrying the "selfish worship of 'private enterprise'" (Percy 1935: 1, 24). In 1927 a small but energetic group of young Conservative MPs had published an edited book, *Industry and the State – A Conservative View*, which advanced several interventionist ideas including the formation of "an economic General Staff" to address "the present chaotic condition of the great industries". The proposals were welcomed by serious commentators, and duly denounced by the *Daily Mail* as the work of "Socialists in Conservative disguise". For the party's liberal individualists, this allegation was the more unsettling because one of the authors, Robert (later Lord) Boothby (1900–86), was attached to the Treasury at the time as private parliamentary secretary (PPS) to the chancellor, Winston Churchill (Rhodes James 1991: 87). Boothby, who combined a colourful private life with a penchant for progressive thinking, had tried to persuade Baldwin to drop the punitive elements of the 1927 Trade Disputes Act. Other contributors included Oliver Stanley (1896–1950), from the illustrious Derby dynasty, and an obscure backbencher, Harold Macmillan. Their domestic approach was heavily influenced by another Tory MP, Noel Skelton, who in 1924 had coined the phrase "property-owning democracy" to emphasize his preference for state-supervised capitalism as opposed to socialism. Awarded the derisive nickname "the YMCAs" by less innovative Conservatives, the informal group tended to be associated in the 1930s with Churchill's campaign for rearmament against a resurgent, totalitarian Germany. This was a further source of inter-party division which, despite their party's huge majority, Baldwin and Chamberlain could easily do without as the war clouds regathered over Europe.

Until quite recently, when historians such as Philip Williamson, Stuart Ball and Robert Self have introduced a proper sense of balance to our understanding of the 1930s, commentary on the governments of Baldwin and Chamberlain was dominated by discussions of foreign affairs. For example, in one history of the Conservative Party since 1918, the chapter on "Conservative Policy in the 1930s" dispensed with domestic issues in four pages, while devoting nearly ten to the party's inadequate response to the rising forces of fascism. For good reasons, the authors did not pile personal guilt on Baldwin and Chamberlain, the usual suspects. However, their verdict – that "Britain's fundamental problem in the 1930s was that her commitments, Imperial and European, far outstripped her actual or potential power" implies a heavy indictment of the party's record since the days of Disraeli (Lindsay & Harrington 1974: 116–29, 123). If the British empire had been forged in a "fit of absence of mind", it had knowingly been exploited by the Conservatives for electoral purposes, without serious attention to the question of its likely fate if the "mother country" should ever find itself preoccupied by a life-or-death struggle with a European antagonist. In such a conflict, the empire on which "the sun never set" would provide relatively easy pickings for any extra-European power (i.e., Japan) which was far less absent-minded in its quest for territorial expansion. From this perspective, it hardly mattered that Baldwin was all too eloquent in his public exposure of fears about the consequences of war ("the bomber will always get through"), or unduly receptive to expressions of anti-war feeling (e.g., the 1933 Fulham East by-election and the 1935 Peace Ballot), or that Chamberlain took his desire for "appeasement" to the lengths of flying to Germany three times in the hope that personal diplomacy would deter Herr Hitler. If Churchill – who had no alternative political home to go to, having used up his allowance of "ratting and re-ratting" – had been heeded, a rearmed Britain would have been in a much better position to defend itself against Nazi Germany. But, given Hitler's intentions, Britain would still have found itself engaged in a conflict which exposed the vulnerabilities of the empire, inflicting the same kind of economic damage which, after 1945, stripped the country of "Great Power" status. The policy of appeasement was far from being the isolated miscalculation of a single generation of Conservative "Guilty Men"; but it was clear where the responsibility should lie when the wartime suspension of party conflict came to an end.

Summary

In the first half of the twentieth century a series of developments ensured that the Conservative Party, rather than its Liberal rivals, would provide the main opposition to a Labour Party which was guaranteed to be a major political force under the conditions of universal (manhood) suffrage established by 1918. The Conservatives owed their continued prominence to their new readiness to defend property in general, rather than the privileged status of the landed classes. However, apart from marking a decisive shift from the party's original purpose, this position overturned the Disraelian claim that the Conservatives stood for national unity. In 1923, through a chapter of accidents the party stumbled upon a leader, Stanley Baldwin, whose personal views were distinctively conservative. After the 1926 General Strike Baldwin was unable to prevent his party from demonstrating its transformation since the days of Disraeli. Although in general his appeals for national unity were successful in papering over the ideological cracks, these became more apparent under his successor, Neville Chamberlain, who disliked the word "conservative" in any sense and combined a pragmatic brand of liberalism in his approach to political issues with a class-based disdain for the Labour Party.

5

"We must have an ideology": conservatism since the First World War

In the opening paragraph of his meticulous study of the Conservative Party between 1902 and 1940, John Ramsden noted that "The book does not delve into the philosophy of conservatism as such" (Ramsden 1978: ix). In justification of this approach, he related an anecdote concerning Stanley Baldwin, who led the party for around a third of the period in question. Asked about his intellectual influences by an enthusiastic young Conservative (Frank Pakenham, later, as Lord Longford, a controversial Labour peer), Baldwin paused for a moment before nominating Sir Henry Maine: "I never ceased to be grateful for all I learned from him". Pakenham asked Baldwin what he considered to be Maine's most important insight. After a longer pause, Baldwin mentioned that Maine had established "once and for all" that human progress depended on the movement from status to contract: "He paused again and this time for quite a while, and suddenly a look of dawning horror, but at the same time of immense humanity and confederacy stole across his face. 'Or was it', he said leaning a little towards me, 'or was it the other way round!'" (Ramsden 1978: ix–x).

The most likely explanation of Baldwin's behaviour is that he was teasing his visitor – an alumnus of Eton who had obtained a first-class degree in PPE from Oxford despite the distractions of the Bullingdon Club. Nobody who had ever heard of Sir Henry Maine could fail to regurgitate his most celebrated catchphrase: "from status to contract" tripped off the tongue as readily as "from Alpha to Omega". Baldwin's pregnant pause (no doubt accompanied by a pull on his ever-present pipe) probably arose from appreciation of his own anti-intellectual intellectual joke, which conveyed a suggestion that he was wiser than Sir Henry Maine himself. Maybe Coleridge and Southey had been right, and the movement from status to contract had actually been a regressive step?

Much as Baldwin enjoyed playing up to his bluff persona, he could not always maintain the pretence. For example, in a House of Commons tribute to Bonar Law he remarked that his dead colleague's character reminded him of a passage in Plato's *Phaedo* – not the kind of analogy that would have occurred to an unlettered leader. In the following year, 1924, he addressed the London Teachers' Association, confessing that he appeared "not as an educational expert, nor – God forbid! – as an intellectual". Before the end of his brief talk he had quoted H. G. Wells and Bertrand Russell (Baldwin 1926: 173, 160–67).

In 1927 the Conservative MP Walter Elliot (1888–1958) published a book entitled *Toryism and the Future*. Baldwin contributed a Preface, which was unremarkable in itself since Elliot was a junior minister in his government at the time. However, Elliot's intellectual influences were eclectic to an extent which bordered on the surreal; seemingly it was pure chance which persuaded him to settle on the main thesis of his book, i.e., that politicians should take their cue from the common sense "of a great mass of people held for hundreds of years" rather than "*a priori* reasoning", leading to "a humility of the intellect and therefore a trust in continuity: a conviction that whatever has worked once may work again; and finally a certain optimism, believing that external affairs are on balance friendly to mankind, that they are good, albeit good and irrational" (Elliot 1927: 4).

Elliot's education (at the University of Glasgow) had been scientific, and it was only towards the end of his book (in an over-long "Chapter of Speculation") that he could really air his personal views, which he summarized by claiming that "the key to all this thought is biology, and that biology squares rather with the creed of the Right than with the creed of the Left" (Elliot 1927: 136). Any normal person, asked to endorse a rambling disquisition of this kind, would have laid it aside as soon as it became unreadably esoteric. Baldwin's preface does include one ambiguous reference to his feelings on reaching "the last page of the essay", but this is followed by the unlikely claim that he had found the book "thoroughly exhilarating". He goes on to assert that "there is here much more than a defence of loyalty, tradition, and continuity in our national life", and that Britain's political parties should harness "the new truth vouchsafed to us by modern science" (Elliot 1927: ix–x). Unless the task was delegated to one of Baldwin's underlings, it is possible that the prime minister really did read most of Elliot's book, and made a serious attempt (against all odds) to make it seem relevant to the politics of the late 1920s. Thus, not only was Baldwin far more cerebral than he pretended; he was also keenly interested in the potential political impact of ideas on others.

As we have seen (Chapter 4), the domestic ramifications of the First World War greatly benefited the Conservative Party and despite the best efforts of Lloyd George it emerged as the most potent electoral challenger to Labour. However, Baldwin continued to worry that Conservatives were disadvantaged in the battle of ideas – against the Liberals (amply supplied with eggheads like John Maynard Keynes) as well as Labour. There was no Conservative equivalent of the Fabian Society – a think tank affiliated to Labour – nor was there a nursery for the right-wing intelligentsia approximating to the London School of Economics (LSE). In 1923 the party established the Philip Stott College in a Northamptonshire stately home donated by a designer of cotton mills. The purpose was to provide "a permanent centre for working men [sic] who want to study economics and Constitutional History" (Spectator 1923). Baldwin offered enthusiastic support, delivering more than one set-piece speech at the college. However, the venture was not a success, partly because its initial plan of fortnight-long courses demanded too much from its students who, by definition, depended on regular work for their livelihoods (Lexden 2020).

The party soon hatched an even more ambitious project for intellectual outreach. After a fundraising effort instigated by Baldwin's friend and advisor J. C. C. Davidson, it took possession of an extensive estate, Ashridge in Hertfordshire. To allay any hint of serious intellectual pretensions, the Ashridge college was named in memory of the bovine Bonar Law. It had a permanent and well-remunerated teaching staff and attracted an illustrious list of speakers, including Baldwin, Neville Chamberlain and Anthony Eden, as well as academics and civil servants. The popular novelist John Buchan was closely involved in the work of the college and served on its board of governors (Berthezene 2015: 66–70). Also in 1929, the party established a new body (the Conservative Research Department, CRD) to provide relevant information for its parliamentary speakers.

Thus by the end of the 1920s Baldwin's party had provided itself with promising institutional remedies for its perceived intellectual weakness in the fight against Labour (and to guard against a potential

Liberal revival). However, following on from Hugh Cecil's misleading but influential book, these initiatives raised additional obstacles to an objective understanding of the conservative tradition. The party leadership, essentially, had launched a bid to appropriate "conservatism" for its own purposes. It was unlikely (wittingly, at least) to patronise intellectuals who felt serious misgivings about the party's current direction. Writers associated with Ashridge would find it difficult to resist an impulse to rationalize the conservative tradition in a way which fitted the outlook of existing party leaders. Their interpretations were unlikely to be challenged by academics, or by other intellectuals lacking a vested interest in the fortunes of the party, since scholarly attention to conservatism (unlike socialism and liberalism) tended to be confined to card-carrying partisans. In these circumstances, even though accounts of conservatism almost invariably began with the Whig Burke, it was all too easy even for people with a serious appreciation of political ideas to suppose that "conservatism" was whatever the Conservative Party chose to make of it rather than a distinctive and coherent ideological position.

This problem is illustrated by *The Spirit of Conservatism* (1929), a volume written by the popular historian Arthur Bryant, a friend of Baldwin who was also a part-time director of Ashridge. If asked about his own influences, Bryant would not have made an obscure joke about Henry Maine; the dominant figures in his account are Burke and Disraeli. The authority of Burke is claimed in support of Bryant's preference for gradual rather than radical change. Disraeli is presented as the genius who saved the Conservative Party from another deadly enemy – laissez-faire. This dogma, according to Bryant, was "a thing utterly unlike the ancient and ordered liberty of England" and promotes "a return to the savage law of the jungle, out of which man had so slowly and painfully climbed" (Bryant 1929: 19). This, perhaps, was more outspoken than Baldwin would allow himself to be; but Bryant's book clearly enjoyed approval in high quarters and, with a preface by John Buchan, it was published on the eve of the 1929 general election.

Key elements of Bryant's message were rehearsed by another historian, Keith Feiling, in a very brief answer to the question *What is Conservatism?* (1930). Feiling did include the subversive observation that "English conservatism and the Conservative party, though often confused, are just as often rivals ... The official party merely unites for its limited objects some men who in other things are endlessly divided, and does not include many others whose whole outlook is as conservative as their own" (Feiling 1930: 6). However, this train of thought is overshadowed by a condemnation of laissez-faire which is even more angry than Bryant's, recalling Southey's assault on manufacturing industry: the latter "dehumanizes our life by leaving hundreds of thousands to struggle on the margin of employment, and at the mercy of outside forces which England cannot control … it must be the duty of anything calling itself a society to keep the balance between its members, and this must include both security of employment and pecuniary reward" (Feiling 1930: 16).

According to Feiling, "the controversy of State versus Individual is, for the next half century, decided. The remedies applied by any party will be what old-fashioned gentlemen call 'Socialistic'". For Feiling, however, there remained a crucial difference between socialism and the conservative approach: "The one bases the State on equality, the other on the lasting value of life itself; it is the difference between unity and levelling" (Feiling 1930: 32). The "controversy of State versus individual" reopened in earnest almost exactly in line with Feiling's 50-year schedule, thanks to Margaret Thatcher and her ideological allies.

Bryant and Feiling were not simply seeking to furnish an intellectual gloss for the leadership's position; their published views were sincerely held. However, the knowledge that their understanding of the conservative tradition was broadly congruent with that of the leadership allowed them to advance their interpretation with more confidence. Baldwin had no wish to reopen the pre-war debate about the scope of government intervention; the welfare reforms of the Liberal government elected in 1906 were acceptable to him and his senior colleagues, and there were other ways in which the state could help the economy to recover from the ravages of global conflict. Equally, while hard-line liberals like Mallock had implied that the Left in Britain and elsewhere was led either by affluent fellow-travellers or sinister "agitators", Bryant preferred to characterize Labour's leaders as "Radicals", whose "instinct is, in its origin, a fine one" (Bryant 1929: 2).

While authors like Bryant and Feiling could interpret the conservative tradition in a way that lent intellectual support to Baldwin's hopes of social and political harmony, it was natural for many members of the Conservative Party to hanker after a more confrontational approach towards socialism. The argument of the "malcontent liberals" – i.e., that the battle lines now lay between "the masses" and property-owners in general – seemed even more persuasive after Labour replaced the Liberal Party as the chief electoral threat to the Conservatives. Growing antagonism in the workplace, culminating in the 1926 General Strike, suggested that Britain was vulnerable to the "Bolshevism" which had destroyed the established order in Russia. While Bryant and Feiling sought to remind party supporters that laissez-faire was the real ideological enemy of the conservative tradition, there was an obvious rejoinder. The kind of "C/conservatism" celebrated by Baldwin's allies had been useful in the previous century, when the main threat to the established order emanated from radical liberals. However, the danger now came from a different direction – not from excessive individualism, but rather from creeping collectivism. Laissez-faire was the obvious ideological antidote; and since the Liberals had abandoned it, there was nothing to stop the Conservatives from deploying it in their battle with Labour. This argument was perfectly consistent with the "converging streams" of Hugh Cecil (whose book had by now been accepted as a "conservative" classic); it also suggested that Herbert Spencer's hopes had not been misplaced, and that there was no reason why "the Tories" should not emerge as the true champions of (economic) freedom.

These new "diverging streams" – the imperative to follow the leadership's line, and the temptation to promote the cause of laissez-faire liberalism – are painfully apparent in the work of another Ashridge teacher, F. J. C. Hearnshaw (1869–1946: see Chapter 2). In 1933 he published a book based on his lectures, entitled *Conservatism in England*. As we have seen, Hearnshaw was unstinting in his praise of Disraeli – the most plausible model for Baldwin's approach – and he showed considerable respect for overt anti-liberals like Coleridge and Southey. However, readers expecting a scholarly exposition of conservative thought – written by a professor of medieval history – would have been surprised to discover that Hearnshaw's introductory chapter opened with an attack on "The Menace of Socialism". This was followed by a section on "Conservatism as the Alternative to Socialism", in which Hearnshaw looked forward to the day when "Socialist-labour" would "free itself from the insanity of its socialism". Conservatism was the only force which could bring it to its senses, since the Liberal Party's days were clearly numbered. In a telling passage, Hearnshaw lamented that "If only it had remained faithful to its old cries of individualism, laissez-faire, personal freedom, and national economy, it might have continued to form a party around which could gather those sections of the community who desire to limit the functions of the all-encroaching state" (Hearnshaw 1933: 5, 4). Despite his long and devoted service to the Conservative Party, Hearnshaw was hankering after his natural political home – the Liberal Party. However, that avenue was no longer open: "The small remnant of genuine liberals who remain true to the principles of Gladstone and Rosebery find their natural affinities in the large and sympathetic conservatism of Mr Baldwin" (Hearnshaw 1933: 4). This passage was clearly inserted to keep the author onside with his patrons at Ashridge College, since the overall message of his book actually implies that Baldwin's outlook was much *too* "large and sympathetic".

The reference to "the principles of Gladstone and Rosebery" is puzzling, since it was under those leaders that the Liberal Party began to shed its "malcontent liberals", because of Ireland as well as its desertion of laissez-faire. Although Hearnshaw was of a later generation, he was still old enough in the mid-1880s to feel keenly this twin betrayal. His analysis of the Home Rule crisis is highly instructive; far from criticizing Bonar Law for inciting mutiny in Ireland, Hearnshaw claims that the latter "distinguished himself by his resistance to the government's Home Rule Bill, and by the support that he had given to Ulster's determination not to surrender herself to her remorseless and merciless enemies". While Bonar Law's attempts to subvert the rule of law were heroic, the General Strike was "a direct and deadly... challenge to constitutional government" (Hearnshaw 1933: 261, 279). Apart from being wildly inconsistent even by normal partisan standards, these judgements are difficult to reconcile with Hearnshaw's insistence that "It has been, and is, the historic task of English conservatism to maintain the organic unity of the nation and the living continuity of its institutions, together with the kindly and genial English spirit" (Hearnshaw 1933: 37). No doubt Hearnshaw would have been prepared to argue that "Bloody Balfour's" policy of coercion in Ireland was conducted in a "kindly and genial English spirit".

Macmillan and "the Middle Way"

It was perhaps unfortunate for the Conservative Party that it should start cultivating intellectuals in the interwar years, when dangerous ideas were in the air. Ashridge had more than a sprinkling of fascist fellow-travellers; even Baldwin's friend Arthur Bryant seemed to think that support for Hitler was compatible with "The Spirit of Conservatism" (Berthezene 2015: 110–13). The liberal Hearnshaw could scarcely sympathize with Hitler's methods, but he was sympathetic to his motives, seeing "hope in eugenic reform; in the segregation of the unfit; in the purification of the race; in the growth of temperance and self-control". Communism, Hearnshaw felt, had been "generated by Jewish atheism in the morass of German economics" (Hearnshaw 1933: 288, 303, 297).

Another discordant visitor to Ashridge was the war veteran Harold Macmillan (later Lord Stockton, 1894–1986) who had first been elected to parliament in 1924 and co-wrote the interventionist *Industry and the State* (1927: see Chapter 4). Although emphatically unfriendly towards fascist ideology, Macmillan was briefly attracted by Oswald Mosley's challenge to "mainstream" economic thinking. He would almost certainly have joined the Liberals had it not been for their fading postwar fortunes; as a Conservative MP he quickly established a reputation for recalcitrance, showing scant regard for the party whips. He continued to associate with the Liberal economist John Maynard Keynes, whose books were published by Macmillan's family firm. Macmillan's own output was prolific during the 1930s; he offered proposals for economic recovery in such works as *Reconstruction: A Plea for National Unity* (1933) and, more famously, *The Middle Way* (1938).

Following Keynes, Macmillan argued that prudent state intervention could be a guarantor of human freedom, rather than a threat. "Let us make human liberty the first objective of our plans", he declaimed, "– that is, liberty from the humiliation and restraints of unnecessary poverty, liberty from any unnecessary burden of toil, liberty from the haunting fear of insecurity". Against any advocate of laissez-faire who tried to pin Britain's current economic woes on excessive state intervention, Macmillan argued that the difficulties had in fact arisen from "the incomplete and limited application of the principles of planning". To rescue Britain from its economic plight, "we must advance, more rapidly and still further, upon the road of conscious regulation" (Macmillan 1966: 14, 11). Macmillan was not interested in justifying his views by referring to a conservative ideological tradition; he did not even mention Disraeli, whose interventionist authority could easily have been cited. Instead, his closing appeal reads like a deliberate attempt to draw opposite conclusions from the liberal premises of Sir Henry Maine:

> The fate of democracy is linked up with the problem of economic progress ... Without tolerance there is no freedom. In the absence of freedom, every form of cultural progress is stultified, distorted and destroyed. The defence of Democracy is not merely for the preservation of political liberty, it is for the preservation of the conditions of freedom in which alone the highly individualistic efforts of men [sic] in the intellectual and cultural sphere are made possible (Macmillan 1966: 375–6).

The Conservative MP Cuthbert Headlam recorded in his diary that *The Middle Way* was "terribly dull"; he found it "almost impossible to read – let alone digest" (Ball 1999: 141). However, Headlam evidently thought that the book was sufficiently important to make the effort worthwhile, even though the author was only a backbench MP with a rebellious reputation. In the context of the late 1930s, the eye-catching title of Macmillan's book was certainly a misnomer; like Joseph Chamberlain, Macmillan was careful to deny that his advocacy of state intervention amounted to "socialism", but at best his approach split the difference between Baldwin's centrist government and the programme of the "left-wing" Labour Party. Effectively, despite the attempts of Baldwin's allies to show the continued relevance of a distinctive conservative tradition, ideological debate within the Conservative Party had become a shoot-out between rival schools of *liberalism* – against those who followed Herbert Spencer in thinking that the state was a threat to individual liberty, Macmillan (who had studied at the headquarters of "new" liberalism, T. H. Green's Balliol College), argued that freedom was meaningless unless the state provided the resources necessary for self-development, and secured the individual against the effects of economic depression, ill-health and old age.

A non-ideological ideology

Macmillan's message – or his ministerial prospects, which had been transformed by the war from miserable to meteoric – could not save his seat of Stockton-on-Tees in the 1945 general election. The unexpected landslide defeat prompted a reconsideration of the party's approach, including an attempt to explain to voters what "conservatism" meant in the postwar world. By far the best-known response was *The Case for Conservatism*, by Quintin Hogg, later Lord Hailsham (1907–2001). Like Hugh Cecil's *Conservatism*, this volume was bound to enjoy considerable attention, appearing as part of the popular "Penguin specials" series. As the publisher explained apologetically, the counterpart Labour book (*Labour Marches On*, by John Parker MP) was less expensive because the author had stuck to the agreed word-limit, while Hogg's effort "had run to about double the size we had anticipated".

The author – a Conservative loyalist from central casting, who had entered parliament after a hotly-contested 1938 by-election, helped to topple Neville Chamberlain and then defended the party's interwar record against its Labour critics – certainly had plenty of ground to cover. He proposed to outline his interpretation of Conservative principles; to criticize the socialist alternative; and to discuss various pressing policy questions. The result, in literary terms, was undoubtedly a success. Was Conservatism "A depressing creed? A negative creed?". Hogg answered with a resounding "No!". However, "Conservatives do not expect to found a society wherein a perfected human nature will function contentedly". For the Conservative, "it is every bit as important to combat evil as to create good". Conservatives "see nothing inconsistent in having opposed Whiggery in the interests of the Crown, Liberalism in the name of Authority, Socialism in the name of Liberty". The party's "eternal and indispensable role is to criticize and mould the latest heresy of the moment in the name of tradition" (Hogg 1947: 13, 12). Thus, for example, it was not odd that, having opposed laissez-faire in the nineteenth century, "Conservatives should now very largely be engaged in fighting the battle of Liberalism against the Socialists" (Hogg 1947: 53).

This did not mean, however, that Hogg was seriously interested in the defence of laissez-faire; after all, a key claim for Labour in the1945 campaign was that the Conservative Party had ignored mass unemployment and associated social evils in the 1930s because of its addiction to economic liberalism. Hogg, perhaps, could have borrowed from Harold Macmillan and stated a "libertarian" case for state intervention. Rather, as he explained towards the end of his book, the party should adopt "a Conservative social and industrial policy based on social democracy, equality of opportunity and a planned economy without state monopoly or the abolition of private enterprise". This suggestion reflected Hogg's hunch that "while the vast majority of our fellow countrymen favour social democracy they remain fundamentally opposed to Socialism" (Hogg 1947: 306).

If a book by a maverick like Hugh Cecil could command almost universal respect as an authoritative statement of conservative principles, it is easy to understand the influence of Hogg's account, which was far better written and emanated from the mainstream of the party in the immediate aftermath of the Second World War. *The Case for Conservatism* – which was reissued in slightly modified form as *The Conservative Case* before the 1959 general election – was quickly established as a template for moderate postwar Conservative writers. Conservatism, according to Hogg, is not an ideology; it is "not so much a philosophy as an attitude". This did not prevent the author from referring to "Conservative philosophy" when the occasion seemed to demand this (Hogg 1947: 33). What he meant, presumably, was that the conservative approach was not "doctrinaire", and that this was a recommendation rather than a defect, since ideologues are political obsessives who worship false "new religions". Sensible conservatives, by contrast, keep politics in proportion: "The simplest among them prefer fox-hunting – the wisest religion" (Hogg 1947: 13, 10). This phrase – the most-quoted in Hogg's eminently-quotable book – was revealing in more ways than one. Apart from claiming continuity between the postwar party and eighteenth-century Tories, it betrayed its continuing class alignment: few "simple, conservative" members of the urban-dwelling working class could indulge a preference for fox hunting. More seriously, Hogg himself had advised Conservatives to support policies deriving from an ideological position – social democracy – which was difficult to reconcile with his Burkean view that "man is an imperfect creature with a streak of evil as well as good in his inmost nature", imposing "inherent limitations on what might be achieved by political means" (Hogg 1947: 11). Finally, Hogg's conceit of a Conservative Party which threw its weight *against* the prevailing heresies of the time might have been a plausible rationalization of its early history, when (as we have seen) it was almost always throwing its weight on the losing side. However, in the political context of 1947 Hogg's advocacy of a "social democratic" approach was more like an invitation for Conservatives to board a rolling bandwagon than to impede its progress. Despite ritual references to "socialism" in the speeches and publicity of Attlee's ruling Labour Party, overall its policy decisions are best understood in social democratic terms.

Hogg's depiction of his party's historic mission did have a precedent of sorts: it echoed the approach of Viscount Halifax, the "Trimmer" (1633–95), a brilliant early-modern sceptic who was beginning to feature more regularly in accounts of the conservative tradition. However, Halifax had been writing in pre-democratic days. For a modern mass political party his reduction of political action to tactical manoeuvres left something to be desired; it implied that "conservatism" was only a way of responding to the ideas of others, rather than in itself providing a vision of human nature and society which might inform a truly distinctive policy programme. Hogg's Conservative Party could never make the political weather, merely supplying an umbrella or sunscreen as conditions required.

After the war, the party established a Conservative Political Centre (CPC), which produced a steady stream of publications including David Clark's *A Conservative Faith* (1947). This persuasive and well-researched tract also featured some nakedly partisan language, such as "Socialism is a belief based on greed and tyranny". However, even Clarke portrayed conservatism as a compromise, between "the anarchy of extreme individualism" and "doctrinaire collectivism" (Clarke 1947: 41, 7). It was not surprising that the most ardent young Conservatives should have hankered after some real blue meat, even if it savoured slightly of anarchism. Thus an Oxford undergraduate, Margaret Roberts, had been thrilled by *The Road to Serfdom* (1944), by the Austrian-born economist Friedrich von Hayek. From Hayek's more bracing perspective, Britain would have been much better off if the Conservative-dominated governments of the 1930s had really earned their unfounded reputation for laissez-faire. Hayek's ideas also inspired Ralph Harris (later Lord Harris of High Cross, 1924–2006), who worked for the CPC before taking an academic position and becoming in 1957 general director of the Institute of Economic Affairs (IEA). A dynamic organization on the model of the IEA – with its own sources of funding and hence a licence to canvass ideas without having to defer to the "official" party line – would arguably have served the Conservative Party better than Ashridge College. However, the IEA's contributors were almost invariably aggressive purveyors of laissez-faire, who (like Harris, who had stood more than once as a Conservative candidate) might have some sympathy for the party, but were looking to make converts among influential people regardless of political affiliations. Indeed, they felt limited respect for politicians in general, regarding them with the mixture of pity and contempt which earlier "political economists" had shown towards Coleridge and Southey. In turn, rather than welcoming the IEA as a potential source of creative ideas, the Conservative "establishment" tended to treat it as a subversive force, the haunt of awkward customers like Enoch Powell (see Chapter 6).

"Being Conservative"

Within academia, the shortage of celebrity conservatives persisted after the 1945 general election. A tremor of excitement was generated by the appointment of Michael Oakeshott (1901–90) to the LSE's Chair of Political Science: his predecessor, Harold Laski, had taken an active role in Labour Party politics (to the considerable displeasure of Clement Attlee). In 1956 Oakeshott wrote an essay ("On being Conservative") which characterized conservatism in Hogg-like terms as "not a creed or a doctrine, but a disposition". For Oakeshott, being conservative meant "to prefer the familiar to the unknown, to prefer the tried to the untried, fact to mystery, the actual to the possible, the limited to the unbounded, the near to the distant, the sufficient to the superabundant, the convenient to the perfect, present laughter to utopian bliss". This lyrical passage implies that conservatism "is pretty deeply rooted in what is called 'human nature'", but Oakeshott shied away from a conclusion which would have suggested that it was "a creed or a doctrine" after all (Oakeshott 1962: 173–4).

With a prose style which is equally elegant and elusive, Oakeshott somehow contrived to persuade his readers to attribute any remaining ambiguities to their own inattention or intellectual inadequacy. Despite his denial that conservatism is a doctrine, he claimed that "detail might be elaborated to show, for example .... Why [the conservative] believes that the main (perhaps the only) specifically economic activity appropriate to government is the maintenance of a stable currency" (Oakeshott 1962: 191). This sounds suspiciously like a recommendation of the "doctrine" of liberal laissez-faire, but Oakeshott contented himself with the tantalizing hint and left the reader to work out the "details" which might have been "elaborated". In the context of 1956, an "Oakeshottian" would have been hoping (although presumably not actively campaigning) for radical reforms; the prevailing Keynesian economic approach would certainly have to be ditched, and the state would reverse the nationalizations of the Attlee governments. Oakeshott only alludes to *economic* policy; presumably his "Conservative" would also be looking for sharp reductions in the scope and cost of welfare provision. Government, he argues, should "preserve peace ... not by imposing substantive uniformity, but by enforcing general rules of procedure upon all subjects alike" (Oakeshott 1962: 188). This seems congruent with the laissez-faire ideal of a "nightwatchman state", but since the author is Oakeshott it is difficult to be sure. In other writings he provided a more sustained critique of "collectivism", arguing that the state should be regarded as a "civil association" in which citizens can follow their freely-chosen goals, rather than an "enterprise association" where they are forced to serve collective purposes.

In terms of personal conduct, in the 1956 essay Oakeshott claimed that "it is not at all inconsistent to be conservative in respect of government and radical in respect of almost every other activity" (Oakeshott 1962: 195). On that reckoning, a "Conservative" would feel at liberty to take hedonistic impulses a lot further than fox hunting. Whatever else he had done, Oakeshott had certainly managed to make it seem cool to be a conservative. In a review of *Rationalism in Politics* Oakeshott's exasperated LSE colleague Bernard Crick summarized the formula for "being conservative" as: "whenever so-and-so sensible is preferred to such-and-such silly, that is what I mean by being conservative" (Crick 1972: 129). Oakeshott – the co-author of a *Guide to the Classics* (1936) which was actually a system for identifying Derby winners – had a quirky sense of humour and it is even possible that "On being Conservative" was another of his pranks. If so, it was a remarkable success, putting "conservatism" back on the academic map in Britain and spawning an "Oakeshottian" sect in the US. Among his coterie of British-based disciples was W. H. Greenleaf, who celebrated his work in a 1966 book. Oakeshott's self-identification with a "conservative" outlook tempted Greenleaf into an infringement of his own rule about ideological categories. Not even the besotted Greenleaf could find evidence to support Oakeshott's claim to be conservative, preferring to designate him as "a libertarian Whig" (Greenleaf 1966: 81–2).

The most illuminating studies of conservative ideology at this time tended to emanate from America. In addition to Russell Kirk's *The Conservative Mind* (1953), which included sympathetic commentaries on the work of numerous British theorists, Clinton Rossiter's *Conservatism in America* (1955) is more informative about conservative ideology in *Britain* than most other books published in these years (its subtitle, "The Thankless Persuasion", was particularly apposite on either side of the Atlantic). In Britain, intellectual opponents of the Conservative Party could only respond to its electoral success by denying it "the oxygen of publicity"; they were chiefly concerned with attempts to explain the failures of the left. Until 1974, when Andrew Gamble published *The Conservative Nation*, students of the Conservative Party would have searched in vain for a serious analysis of its postwar ideas (Gamble 1974). The few scholars who took a more detached view of the party tended to be historians who focused on its election-winning machinery, while accepting at face value the self-serving claims that it was a pragmatic organization whose flexible approach derived from the fortunate fact that "conservatism" was not an ideology.

However, serious debate about the nature of conservatism in Britain was sure to re-emerge after the party lost office (1964), and to become more searching after it suffered a second defeat (1966). Enoch Powell's direct ideological challenge, culminating in the "Rivers of Blood" speech of 1968 (see Chapter 6) actually diverted attention from more considered contributions. Angus Maude – a friend of Powell but a more sophisticated (and interesting) thinker, published *The Common Problem* in 1969. Maude made the usual noises about conservative respect for established practices, but argued that by the 1960s "the tradition in which politics have worked has been seriously weakened and compromised" (Maude 1969: 108). Quite unlike the "authorized" Conservative Party literature since the 1945 defeat, whose social analysis rarely strayed beyond flattery of target voters and an indictment of "socialism" for any malignant developments, Maude wanted to investigate the spiritual malaise which he sensed beneath the superficial hedonism of the 1960s. Although his conclusions were open to varied interpretations, the main theme came over very clearly: no political party could hope to address the issues facing contemporary Britain unless it came into office armed with *ideas*.

A blunter book-length message of dissent was delivered in 1970 by Lord Coleraine (1901–80), the son of Andrew Bonar Law. The true tendency of Coleraine's thoughts can be gauged from an earlier book (*Return from Utopia*, 1950, when he was plain Richard Law), whose penultimate sentence announced that "Lucifer is the Prince of Darkness, and he is amassing all the reserves of night to overwhelm us". "I have built much upon the goodness of man", Law lamented somewhat improbably, "and I understand at last that I have been building on sand" (Law 1950: 200, 199). Democracy had turned out to be as bad as Salisbury, Lecky and the rest had feared.

Coleraine's 1970 volume, *For Conservatives Only*, marked a positive mood-shift from "apocalyptic" to "exceptionally gloomy". Coleraine echoed some of the key problems of postwar "conservatism" which are highlighted in the present chapter. For example, he traced the Conservative Party's problems beyond 1945 and back to the Baldwin era. Even in those days the party "lacked any clear convictions". It adopted policies "deliberately designed to attract the widest possible measure of support from men of goodwill of all parties". Far from implying that the Conservative Party was no place for "men of goodwill", Coleraine was arguing that it had mistakenly pursued the mythical "middle ground" which, according to psephologists, was key to winning elections. Since the Second World War the party had continued this tactical approach, and for far too long it had merely offered "a reformulation of the fashions of the day" (Coleraine 1970: 58, 54, 63). In short, the party's electoral success – the aspect of its activity which attracted most attention from academic observers – was also the reason for the paucity of its distinctive principles.

Despite his ingrained pessimism, in 1950 Coleraine had found some ideological solace in Hayek's inspirational writings, and he remained equally enthusiastic in 1970 despite the fact that his hero had, in the interim, added a postscript to his *The Constitution of Liberty* (1960), explaining very persuasively why he was "not a conservative" (Hayek 1960). In particular, Coleraine was attracted by Hayek's concept of "spontaneous order" arising from free economic activity. This, he asserted, "is more efficient than an imposed order, and need not be much less humane" – a somewhat lukewarm endorsement for most people, but a glowing encomium coming from Coleraine. The notion of "spontaneous order" sounds like Oakeshott, but Coleraine's darker view of human nature placed limits on his own libertarianism. While governments have interfered far too much in economic matters there are some tasks they ought to perform beyond the nightwatchman role envisaged by Oakeshott and Hayek. They could, for example, take action to protect the environment (although Coleraine grossly underestimated the potential scope for state action in this respect). The grudging acceptance of a positive role for the state is reinforced by respectful references to Burke, who did not figure in *Return from Utopia* but is now hailed as not only "the greatest of Conservatives: he is the most modern, too" (Coleraine 1970: 127–8, 23). However, Coleraine's most significant difference from Oakeshott lies in his approach to moral questions. Far from embracing Oakeshott's "anything goes", he deplored the Conservative Party's acquiescence in "the abolition of the death penalty, the abolition of censorship in the theatre, the relaxation of the law on obscenity, [and] the reform of laws relating to sexual offences and abortion" (Coleraine 1970: 74).

Unlike Maude, Coleraine did not examine the underlying causes of this "spontaneous disorder". In this respect, and others, his work anticipated some of the key debates within the Conservative Party in the era of "Thatcherism" (see Chapter 6). A central figure in the story of Thatcherism owed a great deal to the half-forgotten Coleraine. When Sir Keith Joseph embarked on a series of soul-searching lectures in the wake of the Conservative defeat of February 1974, one of his strongest arguments was that his party had found itself "stranded in the middle ground", which as Coleraine had argued was actually a psephological myth. Not himself an original thinker, Joseph was able to popularize Coleraine's case (with a few additions contributed by the economic liberal think tanks) partly because of his high profile as a former cabinet minister, but also thanks to his born again zeal. This inspired him to take the "battle of ideas" into the heart of enemy territory – Britain's universities.

While Joseph was sure to encounter hostility from students (and their irredeemably leftist lecturers), his arguments were scarcely more acceptable to the majority of his colleagues in Edward Heath's shadow cabinet. In 1975, Joseph published some of his speeches, along with a foreword which proclaimed that "It was only in April 1974 that I was converted to Conservatism" (Joseph 1975: 4). This was an arresting claim, not least since the overall message of Joseph's recent speeches was broadly similar to his public utterances before the 1970 general election. At that time, Labour's Harold Wilson had exploited Joseph's affirmations of economic liberalism to conjure the horrid figure of "Selsdon Man" – an atavistic free-marketeer, whose ideas had inspired the Conservative Party to plan "a wanton, calculated and deliberate return to greater inequality" (Denham & Garnett 2001: 186). Whether consciously or not, Wilson's diatribe was an uncanny echo of an attack on laissez-faire launched by the conservative historian Keith Feiling back in 1930 (see Chapter 5). To his Conservative critics, the precise nature of Joseph's ideological odyssey was less important than the impression he had given that "Conservatism" was akin to a faith, and that true believers were readily distinguishable from heretics. In *The Case for Conservatism* Hogg (still, as Lord Hailsham, a senior Conservative politician in 1975) had written that "the last thing Conservatives believe is that they have the monopoly of the truth. They do not even claim the monopoly of Conservatism" (Hogg 1947: 13). Thus, on Hailsham's terms, by claiming suddenly to have stumbled upon the party's true creed, Joseph had actually proved that he was *not* a Conservative. The same could be said of Coleraine, whose provocative title *For Conservatives Only* suggested an ability to distinguish the ideological elect from the lieutenants of Lucifer.

Almost certainly, Coleraine had written *For Conservatives Only* in the expectation that the Conservatives would deservedly lose the next election – their third in a row – so his strictures seemed irrelevant when the party won in 1970. However, two electoral defeats in 1974, combined with Joseph's ideological assault, the advent of Margaret Thatcher in February 1975 and the failure of moderate Labour leaders (Wilson and Callaghan) to assuage fears that Britain was becoming ungovernable, alerted Conservative supporters of centrist (or "consensus") politics to their vulnerability. In 1976 Hailsham himself accepted that the time-honoured flexibility of the British constitution no longer offered adequate protection for the rights of the citizen. Without a codified constitution, Hailsham argued, citizens were effectively defenceless even against a government lacking a parliamentary majority (let alone a resounding "mandate" from the electorate).

Hailsham's proposal – delivered in a televised lecture – cut both ways in partisan terms; if adopted, it would restrain the radical purpose of a future Thatcher-led government, as well as the existing Labour administration. However, it marked a significant update on the same author's *Case for Conservatism*, where he had boasted that "we have evolved a type of democracy in which the executive is still sufficiently powerful to govern without yet achieving sufficient independence to be absolute or free of control" (Hailsham 1976: 34). In 1947, Hailsham had argued that Conservatives should support social democratic policies; three decades later he felt compelled to endorse a long-standing liberal campaign for radical constitutional reform. Back in 1883, Lord Salisbury had ruminated wistfully on the advantages of the US constitution, Hailsham was now equally convinced of the need for "checks and balances". When, in 1947, he had written that "the doctrinaire application of a political theory inevitably involves the statesman in extremes", he had never imagined that his dictum could be directed against the leader of his own party (Hogg 1947: 53). However, by the late 1970s his chief ambition was to protect the legal profession from radical change, and he had no wish to jeopardize his chances of serving for a second time as lord chancellor. As a result, he kept his reservations concerning Thatcher largely to himself, even after he finally retired from her government in 1987. Other senior Conservatives who shared Hailsham's scepticism – William Whitelaw, home secretary in the first Thatcher government, and Lord Carrington (foreign secretary) – were equally reticent, hoping that the prime minister's actions would not be as radical as her rhetoric.

Since Edward Heath was unlikely to change the habit of a lifetime and show a belated interest in ideas, the intellectual fightback against Thatcherism was entrusted to a less senior figure, Sir Ian Gilmour, an MP since 1962, who published *Inside Right: A Study of Conservatism* in 1976. Gilmour (later Lord Gilmour of Craigmillar, 1926–2007) was chiefly concerned to rebut Joseph's equation of "Conservatism" with economic liberalism (although he prudently used Hayek and Enoch Powell as surrogates in his attack on the Joseph/Thatcher position). Gilmour did expound some conservative themes, on the basis of brief accounts of leading figures "who were undoubtedly Tory or Conservative in their views". But he denied that Conservatism was an ideology, in terms broadly similar to those employed by his friend Lord Hailsham. This self-denying ordinance forced him to concentrate on "what Conservatism is not", rather than offering a distinctive rationale for his party's postwar record. The Conservatives had made mistakes, but to imply that "almost the whole Tory Party has been marching in the wrong direction for thirty years" entailed the supposition that "Churchill, Eden, Macmillan, Butler, Douglas-Home, Heath and Macleod were all either grossly misguided or were not true Tories"

(Gilmour 1976: 12). This, however, was exactly what the logic of Keith Joseph's position implied, and Gilmour's eloquent riposte would have been more effective if he had allowed himself to present a more positive account of his own views.

At around the time that Gilmour was denying the ideological nature of "Conservatism", the party's leader Margaret Thatcher was reported to have exclaimed: "We must have an ideology; the other side have got an ideology they can test their policies against. We must have one as well" (Young 1989: 406). Thatcher's challenge was delivered at a meeting of the Conservative Philosophy Group, whose regular attendees included journalists, businesspeople, and more than one convert to the Conservative cause from the far left. Hayek and Oakeshott were amongst the academic gurus invited to impart their wisdom in person. According to one account, Thatcher held up a copy of Hayek's *Constitution of Liberty* during a meeting with political advisers and announced, "*This* is what we believe", before slamming the book on the table. It was a dramatic incident which would have been even more memorable if the book had fallen open at the bit where Hayek denied being a conservative.

In 1978 several members of the group contributed to a volume of *Conservative Essays*. In his concluding editorial remarks, the Cambridge historian Maurice Cowling (1926–2005) claimed that the various contributors had "laid out a form of Conservatism", as if the contents of the volume had met Mrs Thatcher's challenge and furnished the party with a coherent ideology. However, apart from their shared tendency to express views which were "rather different from the consensus Conservatism which was associated with the Conservative Party in the 1950s and 1960s", and their predictable hope that Thatcher would become prime minister after the next general election, the essayists were sharply divided. Some contributors (especially the American-born Shirley Letwin (1924–93) and the New Zealander Kenneth Minogue (1930–2013), both of whom had strong connections with Hayek, Oakeshott and the LSE) were not afraid to use words like "rationality" and "individualism" while insisting that these key liberal concepts could also be understood in a "Conservative" sense. In a phrase which would have made Edmund Burke choke on his cornflakes, Letwin mused that "If democratic government is taken to mean responsible government under law, then the Conservative individualist is a democrat". While the libertarian Letwin had no wish to undermine the authority of the state in its proper sphere, she insisted that "the conservative individualist refuses to endow the state with the glamour of an omniscient guardian" (Cowling 1978: 67–8). For Minogue, "Liberalism and Conservatism [are] but different emphases within the same tradition of political prudence", implying that an incoming Conservative government could draw freely on both in a more explicit update of Cecil's metaphor of "converging streams". In an earlier chapter, however, the Cambridge-based literary scholar John Casey had insisted that "The conservative position … differs profoundly from liberalism" (Cowling 1978: 124, 96)

A very different, but equally jarring, perspective was offered by Peregrine Worsthorne (1923–2020), an outspoken "traditionalist" who in 1978 commanded considerable authority in Conservative circles as Associate Editor of the *Sunday Telegraph* newspaper. Worsthorne asserted that "The urgent need today is for the State to regain control over 'the people', to re-exert its authority, and it is useless to imagine that this will be helped by some libertarian mish-mash drawn from the writings of Adam Smith, John Stuart Mill, and the warmed up milk of nineteenth-century liberalism". Having singled out and destroyed the ideological objectives of his fellow contributors, he argued (and lamented) that "a great majority of British citizens today feel much freer, much less coerced, than their grandfathers did" (Cowling 1978: 145). "What is the sense, then", he asked, "of Mrs Thatcher keeping on about Socialism as the threat to freedom, when so many of her listeners must inevitably feel that this is wholly at variance with their experience?". According to Worsthorne, Hailsham's fears about the prospect of a British "elective dictatorship" were wholly wrong-headed: "the real charge against the Labour Party is that it has helped to bring about a state of affairs where government is too weak to govern" (Cowling 1978: 149, 145, 147). Worsthorne was often described as a "High Tory" (Bates 2020). This was not because of any predilection for mood-enhancing chemicals, although his contribution suggested that those who continued to hold distinctive conservative views could experience a similar sense of detachment from the realities of contemporary Britain.

Michael Oakeshott's *Rationalism in Politics* had included a typically abstruse "retelling" of the biblical story about the Tower of Babel. The authors of *Conservative Essays* had produced an ideological cacophony to rival the multilingual misunderstandings in the original myth. The journalist T. E. Utley (1921–88) claimed that the Conservative Party was "gratuitously magnifying its divisions". Echoing Hogg/Hailsham, Utley preached pragmatic "Trimming", arguing that the party "feels itself called on at some moments in history to emphasize the importance of authority and at others to emphasize the importance of liberty" (Cowling 1978: 46). In the present circumstances, he argued, it could and should do both. Thankfully, in his view, the party's new leader agreed: "She speaks the language of liberty, not of libertarianism. She is an instinctive and wholly English Conservative. Her belief in individual freedom is firmly set in the context of respect for institutions". She was far too wise to heed her more excitable followers (like Joseph), who had launched "a general attack on the whole concept of moderation as a political virtue" (Cowling 1978: 50, 47).

If Utley's assessment was accurate, the contributors to *Conservative Essays* could have employed their time more usefully (or, as the economic liberals in their midst would have put it, more profitably). Perhaps the Conservative Party did need an "ideology" to fight socialism; in this respect Thatcher was renewing the mission of W. H. Mallock, whose works she is unlikely to have read. However, the current political situation in Britain was best understood as a more melodramatic version of "business as usual"; the opponents of the Conservatives were failing horribly, so the electorate would turn towards "the natural party of government" without any need to fight a battle of ideas. At best, the explicit adoption of an ideology could help to create the impression that the Conservatives had wrested back the intellectual initiative from socialism. At worst, it could make the party look extreme and thus unelectable. Certainly, if Thatcher really had been seeking ideological support for her instinctive position, the overall evidence of *Conservative Essays* showed a preference for a dogmatic adherence to laissez-faire liberalism. In the year after the appearance of the volume, the Conservatives duly reclaimed their "natural" position in government and the British people would be in a position to judge Thatcher on her practical decisions rather than the conflicting opinions of her intellectual camp-followers.

Summary

Contrary to his non-intellectual public persona, Stanley Baldwin was acutely conscious of the importance of ideas and made a concerted attempt to win recognition for his pragmatic approach to politics as an authoritative interpretation of a long-established tradition of conservative thought. This was presented as a sharp contrast to the position of the Labour Party, which (whatever the actual views of its senior policy-makers) was invariably stigmatized as a movement in thrall to rigid socialist ideology. Conservative leaders like Baldwin genuinely thought of themselves as pragmatic and non-ideological, despite their party's ingrained obedience to the presumed interests of property-owners and the influx of ideological liberals since the 1880s. Until 1945, Baldwin's formula succeeded in its aim of preventing Labour from forming a majority government. However, the election of the radical Attlee administration lent credence to the charge – which had always appealed to a vehement minority of party members – that Baldwin, his allies and their successors had allowed "socialists" to win the battle of ideas by default. Pragmatism, on this view, was not enough: rather than denouncing ideological politics of all kinds, Conservatives should have been offering British voters an approach based on distinctive principles which offered a clear contrast to Labour's "collectivism". Laissez-faire liberalism provided the most cogent response to socialism, and became increasingly attractive to grass-roots Conservative Party members who deplored the tendency of postwar governments of both main parties to accept policies such as the state ownership of major public utilities. Since the party had retained the "Conservative" label, it proved necessary for laissez-faire liberals like Margaret Thatcher and her key ally Sir Keith Joseph to claim that their beliefs represented a revival of "true conservatism". Their remarkable success in this improbable undertaking was helped by a continuing lack of academic interest in the subject, which had previously allowed the philosopher Michael Oakeshott to gain international repute as a "conservative" sage merely by equating his libertarian outlook on life in general with "Being Conservative".

6

The Conservative Party since 1945

In hindsight, the only surprising thing about the 1945 general election result was that it surprised so many observers. Almost all of the opinion polls before the campaign suggested a Labour victory, and by common consent the Conservatives performed poorly in a contest which its leaders had not wanted. In part, this was because the Conservative organization was depleted by continuing military commitments, giving rise to the alarming thought that the party would have fared better if its members had taken less interest in the nation's defence.

However, the inevitable inquest covered the product itself as well as the marketing. Writing immediately after the defeat, Quintin Hogg argued that it arose from "a long pent-up and deep-seated revulsion against the principles, practice and membership of the Conservative Party". Other post-mortems noted "the decline over several decades, of Conservative thought", and the fact that the party "lacked a doctrine", having been "be-devilled for years by pseudo-Conservatism" (Hoffman 1964: 27–8). The party's war-winning leader proved worse than useless in rebutting these allegations. Churchill exposed the main reason for his final choice of partisan allegiance in a notorious election broadcast, alleging that socialism could only be imposed on Britain by means of "some kind of Gestapo". In his own mind this allegation made perfect sense: existing Labour politicians might be patriotic and talented public servants, but if their party won office they would instantly be swept aside by "Bolsheviks". The MP Cuthbert Headlam, the only one of four Newcastle Conservatives to retain his seat in 1945, shared Churchill's view, even persuading himself that the new foreign secretary Ernest Bevin would seek to appease the Soviet Union. Before the election Headlam had expected his party to fare badly at the hands of "a new electorate which has been brought up on left wing nonsense without any kind of contradiction for five years". When the Commons reassembled, he found that Baldwin's "hard-faced" contingent of 1918 had been replaced by "half baked young men", many of whom had risked their lives during the war rather than simply profiting from it (Ball 2000: 472, 460, 470).

Even Headlam's curmudgeonly comments suggested that the party was unlikely to recover electoral ground without a thorough review of its policy stance. While the revival of the party organization was entrusted to Lord Woolton (1883–1964), a popular (and initially non-political) wartime minister of food, new machinery (including a revamped publicity arm, the Conservative Political Centre (CPC)) was introduced, overseen by R. A. Butler who had chaired the party's Post-War Problems Central Committee (PWPCC) and headed the Conservative Research Department from 1945. In the proposed intellectual fight-back Churchill was an obstacle rather than an asset; he would probably have been content if the party had kept its vague principles and changed its name (his suggestion of something like "the Union Party" understandably won little support (Ramsden 1998: 317)). He envisaged a limited role for the CRD with a less intellectual supremo, but this was another losing battle and Butler was soon identified as the main source of postwar thinking (Cooke & Parkinson 2009: 29).

At the 1946 Conservative conference Churchill listed eight objectives for the party. Far from setting any new direction, the principles could have characterized any Conservative government of the interwar years; indeed, his inspiration seemed to lie even further back, because (like his old friend Hugh Cecil) he made his top priority "To uphold the Christian religion and to resist attack upon it" (Hoffman 1964: 142–3). Assuming that Labour had seized the intellectual initiative, Churchill's senior colleagues insisted on a more explicit mission-statement. After the conference the leader bowed to the inevitable and agreed to the appointment of a high-powered Industrial Policy Committee, chaired by Butler and including such prophets of Conservative "collectivism" as Harold Macmillan and Oliver Stanley. The ensuing document (*The Industrial Charter*) was a genuine attempt to find a "middle way" in the postwar context; it sought "to free industry from unnecessary controls and restrictions", envisaging "a system of free enterprise ... which reconciles the need for central direction with the encouragement of individual effort". While accepting much of Labour's programme of nationalization, it expressed opposition to state ownership as a general principle, rejecting its extension to road haulage and iron and steel. Without containing much detail, it indicated Conservative hopes for a more cooperative relationship between workers and employers – the interwar aspiration of Macmillan, Stanley and the "YMCAs" (Hoffman 1964: 148–52).

The charter could not be adopted as party policy without an expression of support from the 1947 conference. Butler and his allies embarked on a series of speeches and meetings in order to engineer consent from the rank and file. Success was no foregone conclusion, and elements of the press predicted that it would "split the Tory Party as it has not been divided for half a century" (Hoffman 1964: 153). In 1944, Headlam had described the interventionist Town and Country Planning Bill as a measure "which all Conservatives dislike and disapprove of" and marvelled at the fact that his colleagues had persuaded themselves to vote for it (Ball 2000: 427). The sponsors of the industrial charter were hoping to pull off a similar feat, with at best lukewarm support from the party leader. Reginald Maudling, one of Butler's young lieutenants, was asked by Churchill to provide a few lines explaining the charter for his closing conference speech. "He read it with care, and then said, 'But I do not agree with a word of this'" (Maudling 1978: 45). Maudling had moved the conference motion in support of the charter, which passed with only three objections. The document was fortunate in its laissez-faire opponents, notably Sir Waldron Smithers (1880–1954) who, apparently, was "not insensitive to the consoling effects of alcohol" and whose parents seemed to have baptised him in anticipation of a reactionary outlook (Boyd-Carpenter 1980: 79).

Even John Ramsden – a historian not given to hyperbole – has argued that the establishment of the Industrial Policy Committee can be compared to the production of the Tamworth Manifesto as "one of the key moments of Conservative Party history" – indeed, Butler and his colleagues themselves drew the same parallel while drafting the charter (Ramsden 1991: 321). The notion that it liberated the party from the unmerited stigma of laissez-faire was lent unwitting support by Smithers, who denied that there could be any compromise with socialism and claimed that "the existence of the Conservative Party, therefore of Britain" depended upon its rejection (Hoffman 1964: 165). In fact the charter did nothing to prevent the party from deploying the rhetoric of freedom against its Labour opponents. Even Smithers should have been content with the 1951 party manifesto, which denounced "The attempt to impose a doctrinaire Socialism upon an Island which has grown great and famous by free enterprise": the campaign slogan was "Set the People Free!". The charter resembled the Tamworth Manifesto in its aim of allaying the fears of moderate, uncommitted voters. It would steady the nerves of "National" Liberal MPs who had supported Churchill's coalition and were already gravitating towards the Conservatives. In turn, with the Liberals apparently on the verge of extinction, aspiring politicians who might have been attracted to that party if it had been a going concern could now regard the Conservatives as a tolerable alternative.

The Conservative Party's success in its long-running campaign to mop up talented would-be Liberals is impossible to quantify and can easily be exaggerated. Thus, for example, according to his biographer Iain Macleod (1913–70) was encouraged in his political ambitions by the enlightened policy of the wartime coalition, particularly the Beveridge Report (1942). There was never any chance that Macleod would side with Labour: "His comfortable, country-town, middle-class background predisposed him towards the Tories" and indeed his unbridled baiting of "the Socialists" later made him a darling of Conservative conferences (Shepherd 1994: 38). But this does not exclude the possibility that he would have offered his considerable talents to a viable Liberal Party; the author of the Beveridge Report was, after all, a Liberal like Keynes. A similar case was that of another Conservative who, like Macleod, was first elected in 1950. Robert Carr (later Lord Carr of Hadley 1916–2012) had a business background and a science degree. Like Macleod, Carr was committed to the Conservatives before the industrial charter, but he had been inspired by publications of the Tory Reform Committee (TRC), a group of backbenchers whose members included Quintin Hogg. The views of the TRC foreshadowed the message of the industrial charter; before coming across their literature Carr had not considered a political career, feeling more inclined to vote for Labour (private information; Love 2020).

Macleod and Carr both joined the One Nation Group (ONG), formed soon after the 1950 general election which saw a strong Conservative recovery (a net gain of 98 seats, leaving Labour with a precarious 5-seat majority). The emergence of such ginger groups within the parliamentary party was becoming customary; the ONG could be regarded as an attempt to assume the title of "young men in a hurry", once held by the

YMCAs and which the middle-aged members of the TRC had relinquished by 1947. The legendary status of the ONG is chiefly attributable to the calibre of its original members. Apart from Macleod and Carr, they included two notable former members of Butler's CRD, Angus Maude and Enoch Powell, as well as Edward Heath. The group's eponymous pamphlet was researched, written and published with impressive speed. As well as its punchy, Disraelian title its content did mark an advance from the TRC's output, having a specific policy focus (the social services) and a consistent timbre of constructive reformism. The overall message was that the basic framework of Labour's post-1945 welfare reforms should be retained, but that the Conservatives could make the system work more efficiently. Notoriously, the group's initial cohesion was eroded over the years, so that after Heath became party leader in 1965 his earliest critics were ONG founder-members, Maude and Powell. As such, it is easy to argue that there never really was any such thing as "One Nation Conservatism". More pertinent for the present purpose is that even when the group *did* seem united, at the outset, it was difficult to reconcile its approach with distinctive "conservative" ideology (beyond the argument that the welfare state was a guarantor of social stability). If the underlying tendency of the first "One Nation" pamphlet fell within any ideological tradition, it was the "new" liberalism of T. H. Green (1836–82), who had studied and taught at Heath's Oxford alma mater, Balliol College.

In part, the formation of the ONG arose from a feeling among its members that the party should provide more vigorous opposition, in every sense, to the ailing Attlee government. The 1951 general election saw a small but sufficient upswing in Conservative support, giving the party a workable parliamentary majority. The fact that Labour had attracted more votes, after six years of office in unpropitious circumstances, suggested that on balance the British people wanted to be "set free", but preferably in modest instalments. The Conservative Party thus embarked on 13 years in government with no mandate for radical change, even if its leading figures had been so inclined. In the years between 1951 and the party's return to opposition in 1964 there were few significant ideological developments, although from the Greenleaf standpoint it was possible to detect a further drift in a collectivist direction. Churchill, who clung onto office until 1955, was chiefly concerned with defence and foreign policy in the new Cold War environment. His successor Anthony Eden had the same preoccupations; he was a persistent pesterer of his cabinet colleagues, but this was probably a symptom of the chronic illness which destroyed any chance that he would leave a positive legacy. In domestic matters, according to Greenleaf, Eden had spoken with "the genuine accents of orthodox Tory collectivism" at the 1947 party conference, when he had insisted that "we are not the political children of the laissez-faire school" (Greenleaf 1983: 259). Yet in his speech of the previous year Eden had asserted that "We base ourselves upon the individual, upon the need to develop the individual personality". While "State Socialism will be fatal to individual liberty and responsibility", government had a duty "to see that out of the fruits of your labour you can build a life of your own, for yourself and your family". It would fulfil this task by providing essential services like medical care, but also by fostering a more cooperative environment in the workplace, not least by widening share ownership to include employees. Eden used this 1946 speech to revive Noel Skelton's idea of a "property-owning democracy" (Eden 1947: 419–24).

Eden's ailments contributed to the 1956 Suez disaster – a graphic illustration of Britain's relative decline which effaced memories of his previous diplomatic achievements as well as his eloquent advocacy of a coherent alternative to both socialism and laissez-faire. He was replaced by Harold Macmillan, the leading interwar proponent of "Tory collectivism". Through a variety of accidental biographical quirks (including a renewed zest for the political game as a means of escape from his unhappy marriage), by the time he took over from Eden in 1957 the fearless champion of the "middle way" had adapted Disraeli's famous adage to "Damn your principles! Stick to your personal ambition!". Some instincts, however, were unchanged. Thus in January 1958 he forced the resignation of the chancellor, Peter Thorneycroft, when the latter, along with two junior Treasury ministers, argued for cuts in government spending. In prioritizing economic growth, rather than responding to the threat of price inflation, Macmillan could claim that he was staying true to the economic teaching of Keynes whose ideas had become entrenched within the Treasury. However, Keynes had never argued that governments should ignore inflationary pressures. As such, Macmillan's determination to face down Thorneycroft is best interpreted as a sign that he wanted "most of our people" to keep thinking that they had "never had it so good" at least until the next time they cast their votes.

Apart from the Treasury kerfuffle, which with considerable brio Macmillan dismissed as "little local difficulties", the main problem for the Conservative Party in these years was its attempt to adapt to Britain's reduced status in a world dominated by genuine "superpowers", the United States and the Soviet Union, without alerting the British public to the need for such an adjustment. Churchill had continued to hanker after the days of empire, even though he had been a signatory to the 1941 Atlantic Charter which, along with some anodyne aspirations that he could readily accept, included an anti-imperialist commitment to national self-determination. The process of decolonization, which commenced under Labour but continued after the Conservatives returned to office, provoked the formation in 1953 of the party's Suez Group to agitate against the withdrawal of British forces from their base on the Suez Canal. Members of the Suez Group included Lord Hinchingbrooke, who had been a leading figure in the TRC, and Enoch Powell – the founder-member of the ONG who later helped Thorneycroft (ex-TRC) to cause Macmillan's "little local difficulties" with the Treasury. Assumptions of Britain's lofty global status had helped to keep the party's ideological factions together before the war, and they were exposed by the abrupt removal of that adhesive.

Angus Maude was another Suez Groupie, who was sufficiently disillusioned with developments at home and abroad to resign his seat in 1958. While Maude was far from being a stereotypical right-winger, most of the party's troubles came from more predictable sources. The League of Empire Loyalists (LEL), founded in 1954, was regarded by Conservative Central Office as a potential threat but was riddled with antisemitism and other views which even right-wing members of the party found unpalatable. As such, the LEL effectively siphoned off people who might have caused serious embarrassment if, for example, they had been selected as electoral candidates. A greater danger came not from people who left the party in disgust at its moderation, but rather from "entryists" who joined in the hope of making it extreme. The most notorious case was that of Edward Martell (1909–89), initially a Liberal who in 1956 founded the People's League for the Defence of Freedom (PLDF). This organization, which published a newspaper as well as holding rallies, anticipated UKIP by combining libertarian economic ideas with an authoritarian, populist outlook which appealed to disgruntled Conservatives. The party's ideological watchdogs could not prevent Martell becoming a member (and even a constituency branch secretary) (Pitchford 2011: 97–108).

Most worrying of all for the leadership was the possible emergence of a more broadly-based variant of the Suez Group, capable of attracting prominent party figures who cherished a variety of grudges. The Monday Club, founded in 1961, was such an organization. While decolonization (and immigration) were key issues, the club catered for Conservatives (including several MPs) who were out of sympathy with the party's general direction under Macmillan. The first president of the club was the 5th Marquess of Salisbury, who had resigned as leader of the House of Lords in 1957 over colonial policy and was wholly dedicated to the task of removing Macmillan. For this purpose his main vehicle was a shadowy "Watching Committee", formed in December 1960 and including some very seasoned dissidents like Hinchingbrooke and Richard Law (later Lord Coleraine; see Chapter 3) (Ball 2004: 351–69).

This was not the most auspicious context in which to persuade the Conservative Party that Britain should join the European Economic Community (EEC). That crucial postwar question, which Conservative leaders had tried to ignore in the 1950s, promised to add new dimensions to the party's divisions over imperial questions; for example, EEC entry was opposed by the National Farmers' Union (NFU) which influenced around 80 Tory MPs from "safe" rural constituencies (Gilmour & Garnett 1997: 161). Macmillan was able to win agreement from his cabinet colleagues and received a respectful hearing from the backbench 1922 Committee (with the exception of a hostile question from the ubiquitous Lord Hinchingbrooke who, Macmillan confided to his diary, "is *mad*" (Catterall 2011: 399)). Having surmounted the most awkward obstacles, the prime minister revealed his intentions to the Commons in a studiously dull speech of 31 July 1961. For the time being, Macmillan was only asking MPs to approve the application; considerable difficulties might have arisen if, after the initial negotiations, the government had asked parliament to accept terms of membership. In September 1962 the prime minister reported that two cabinet colleagues (one pro-Europe, the other lukewarm at best) had warned him "of the trouble which the 'sovereignty' argument was going to cause in the Party. It is being put about that I am determined to abandon the Queen and promote a federal Europe at the expense of the national identity" (Catterall 2011: 503). General de Gaulle's veto in January 1963 spared Macmillan from further exposure to this early instalment of Europhobic distortion and fearmongering.

While the EEC application was pending, Macmillan took a further "collectivist" step by establishing a National Economic Development Council (NEDC). In this long-forgotten forum, representatives of government, employers and trade unions could discuss long-term economic priorities. Modelled loosely on the existing French General Planning Commission – whose initial driving force had been Jean Monnet, a key instigator of European cooperation – the NEDC was far from being the instrument of centralized economic dictation which was feared by its laissez-faire opponents. In a prolonged cabinet discussion of September 1961 Macmillan had discovered that his current team included some of the latter (Catterall 2011: 412–3). Earlier he had quipped to his chancellor, Selwyn Lloyd, that on this subject "I shall be able to claim, like Disraeli, that I have educated my party". For the time being, at least, the lessons were lost on many financial journalists; at a meeting to explain the proposals, Lloyd found himself accused of having "abandoned free enterprise and the use of market forces" (Dorey 2009: 135–6). The very existence of the NEDC was offensive in the eyes of economic liberals who were heavily represented in the financial press as well as Conservative-supporting businesspeople; the involvement of the trade unions agitated others, who thought that the government's general approach to industrial relations smacked of appeasement.

In September 1962, Macmillan's voracious bedtime reading included a biography of Peel, featuring "the destruction of the Tory Party in 1846 (wh[ich] I may be about to repeat" (Catterall 2011: 494). In July he had sacked a third of the cabinet, including Chancellor Lloyd, in the hope of giving his top team a more youthful, vigorous image. Unfortunately, the secretary of state for war (not a full cabinet member), the Oxford and Bullingdon Club graduate John Profumo, had been displaying an excess of vigour and an absence of judgement in his amatory activities. Macmillan's mishandling of the ensuing scandal was the beginning of the end for his premiership, although his departure in October 1963 was prompted by a health scare which afflicted him just as he was preparing to tell the cabinet that he would stay on to fight the next general election.

Once Macmillan realized that his life was not in immediate danger, he began to regret his decision. However, with the assistance of the party's business managers he could still engineer the selection of his successor. The most logical candidate was Butler who had been acting as an unofficial deputy; but Macmillan's ascent within the party had been accomplished mainly by stepping over (and on) Butler, and he was not prepared to give his old rival a last leg-up. Lord Hailsham was more than willing to sacrifice his hereditary peerage (under recently passed legislation) to take the top job. Hailsham reminded Macmillan of his younger self, which was not necessarily a recommendation for Hailsham since Macmillan's younger self had almost joined forces with Oswald Mosley. Hailsham's chances were finally forfeited when, at the Blackpool party conference which coincided with the leadership crisis, he behaved in a fashion which could be presented to Macmillan, on his sick bed, as distastefully populist. Iain Macleod, the most interesting possibility, was not seriously considered since his liberal views on racial questions made him odious to the right wing of the party. Finding (and exaggerating) objections to all the sensible contenders, Macmillan gambled on an unconsidered outsider who had never been a rival; was unlikely to be accused of populism; and was certainly not objectionable to the party's imperialist wing. Unfortunately these negative factors were almost the only things which favoured Macmillan's new fancy, the foreign secretary Lord Home.

Macmillan's conduct has attracted considerable, and varied, speculation. Some have even tried to clear him of race-fixing allegations, arguing that he faithfully reported the outcome of deliberations held behind closed doors within the party's "magic circle" of key decision-makers. He provided a rationale of sorts in a memorandum drafted two days before the decision was finalized. Home, Macmillan wrote, "represents the old governing class at its best". This was an arresting remark from a politician whose party now claimed to reflect a more "meritocratic" society. As Ian Gilmour (a prominent Hailsham supporter) subsequently pointed out, while the sentiment might have been true in itself, "it scarcely addressed the main question: was Alec Home a suitable man to lead the Conservative Party and govern the country in 1963?". The answer might have been "Yes" if the year in question had been 1863. Shortly after becoming prime minister, Home was asked to explain his personal philosophy as a guide for speechwriters. Amidst a welter of sporting allusions, Home expressed his admiration for "countrymen who living close to nature have a sixth sense of what is possible or impossible" (Gilmour & Garnett 1997: 197, 210). Given a free hand, he would probably have chosen his cabinet team from among tenants of his estate in the Scottish borders.

A possible explanation for Macmillan's choice is that he saw Home as a figurehead rather than a leader in the sense which British voters were coming to expect. With limited interest in, and knowledge of, domestic policy, Home could be expected to focus on foreign affairs while leaving more talented colleagues to "govern the country". Thus the team Macmillan was leaving would remain unchanged with the exception of his (deeply regretted) absence; and the party would be more united since Home would provide some reassurance to the right-wingers who had been making Macmillan's life a misery.

If these were Macmillan's calculations, they were flawed. Two gifted members of the team – the old One Nation colleagues, Macleod and Powell – promptly resigned, outraged by the secretive process and even more so by its outcome. Although Hailsham and Butler agreed to stay in place, both had been diminished by Macmillan's machinations. Macmillan also forgot that his nominee would be confronted in the Commons by Labour's Harold Wilson – a representative of a new meritocratic governing elite at its most cunning. In his message to the fateful Blackpool conference – read out by Home himself, as honorary president for 1963 – Macmillan claimed that "Since 1945 I have lived to see the Party of our dreams come into being ... I have seen our policies develop into that pragmatic and sensible compromise between the extremes of collectivism and individualism for which the Party has stood in its great periods" (Gilmour & Garnett 1997: 202). The ghost of Baldwin might have muttered, "Been there, done that". As his leaving present to the party of his dreams, Macmillan had landed it with a leader who fulfilled Labour's wildest fantasies.

"A meaningless irrelevance"

The Conservatives duly lost the general election, held in October 1964, but they polled well enough to restrict Labour's overall majority to just four seats. Home (who had demoted himself from the peerage in order to secure a seat in the Commons) stayed on as leader until July 1965, and even then his departure was involuntary. The opaque method of leadership selection had been abandoned, so his successor, Edward Heath, became the first person to occupy his position after a formal ballot. Although Heath won more than half the votes his margin of victory was insufficient under the party's new rules. However, his main challenger, Reginald Maudling, conceded defeat (the other candidate, Powell, received only 15 of the 298 votes), after which Heath was declared as the outright winner.

Heath was known within the party as a tough and able operator, a successful chief whip before winning praise for his unavailing conduct of the EEC negotiations. Home had appointed him president of the Board of Trade, where he lived up to his abrasive reputation by adopting and forcing through parliament the abolition of the system of resale price maintenance (RPM), which prevented price-cutting by large retailers (e.g., supermarkets) to the detriment of smaller outlets. This reform had been advocated by Heath's department for many years, and it was probably overdue. However, while consumers were likely to benefit the chief losers would be small businesspeople (the descendants of entrepreneurs like Margaret Thatcher's grocer father) who played a crucial role in many Conservative constituency organizations and could be considered as core party supporters.

Superficially, RPM abolition looked like a big ideological gesture from a politician who was prepared to take on vested interests in the name of the free market. In reality, Heath stood for precisely the kind of "pragmatic and sensible compromise" which Macmillan had dreamed about. Enoch Powell once claimed that if Heath was confronted with an idea he would "go red in the face" (Campbell 1993: 239). This was the mischievous exaggeration of a jealous rival, but not a wild one. A grammar-school boy who won an Oxford scholarship and had been a very efficient officer during the war, Heath was another of those Conservatives who could easily have joined a resurgent Liberal Party. The same could be said with even more confidence about Harold Wilson, who had joined the Liberal Club at Oxford and had acted as research assistant to the Liberal William Beveridge. Heath had been preferred to Maudling among Conservative MPs (contrary to expectations) not just because his campaign was better organized, but also due to the feeling that he was a more aggressive parliamentary performer and thus a more suitable adversary for the wily Wilson. As it turned out, Heath rarely worsted Wilson in debate because they shared the same broad policy objectives, and Wilson was much more quick-witted.

Heath was appointed by Home after the 1964 election as shadow chancellor; he was also the director of a wide-ranging policy review, which was organized with his usual efficiency. Many of the proposals were included in the party's 1966 manifesto whose title (*Action not Words*) was a neat encapsulation of the leader's empirical approach. As Ian Gilmour put it years later, "The manifesto read less like a political document than a commander-in-chief's staccato orders for a massive offensive on all conceivable fronts". Even Home (now Heath's shadow foreign secretary) suggested that it might benefit from some ideas. The hint was not taken (Gilmour & Garnett 1997: 225).

Heath, indeed, had already encountered criticism for his unimaginative prospectus. In January 1966 – while Wilson was starting to prepare for an election which would secure a bigger majority for his party – Heath's former One Nation comrade Angus Maude, now back in the Commons and a member of the frontbench team, levelled the astonishing accusation that the Conservatives had become "a meaningless irrelevance", and that "For Tories to simply talk like technocrats will get us nowhere". Writing in the *Spectator* magazine – still owned, ironically, by the Conservative moderate Ian Gilmour – Maude appended an unfeasible list of policy aspirations, including "a substantial reduction of crime at all costs" and the hope that the party would "say firmly that ugliness is a sign of a bad society" (Maude 1966).

No formal disciplinary code applied to the conduct of shadow spokespeople, but Maude had ridden roughshod over any rational rules and the only wonder is that Heath hesitated before relieving him of his frontbench duties. It is doubtful that Maude made much difference to the result of the general election which Wilson called a few weeks later, to be held in March 1966. However, there were ominous signs that Maude had been working in tandem with a more formidable figure – Enoch Powell, who had returned to the frontbench after the 1964 election and had opted to shadow defence when offered a choice of roles by Heath. In their discussions Powell had gained the impression that Heath broadly accepted his assessment of Britain's future role, especially that "we were a European power without obligations to or dependence upon the United States" (Heffer 1998: 386–7). However, this did not mean that Heath would welcome a public expression of views which would startle most grass-roots party members as well as alarming Britain's most important international ally. In fact, Powell had already made his position clear in one of three articles (published in *The Times* under the pseudonym "A Conservative") in April 1964, including the brutal judgement that the Commonwealth was "a gigantic farce" rather than a respectable cover for Britain's relative decline. The articles advertised Powell's general disagreement with the party's direction since 1945, and particularly with developments under Macmillan, who was accused of embracing change in the name of "modernization" without providing a coherent rationale.

Conservative demagoguery

At the 1965 party conference Powell hinted at a radical curtailment of Britain's global commitments, but (perhaps fortunately for himself) his real message eluded the audience (Heffer 1998: 391). There were no controversial comments about Britain's world role in the 1966 party manifesto, which instead included positive remarks about the Commonwealth, suggesting a continuation of the prevailing postwar approach. Equally, the resounding Conservative defeat in the 1966 election seemed to confirm Powell's view that a radical change of approach was needed across the board, and that, like a latter-day Joseph Chamberlain, he was serving the party (as well as his personal ambitions) by offering tangible alternatives. In April 1968 Powell told the *Sunday Times* that he deliberately included provocative material in his speeches in order to "build a power base" within the party which would make him unsackable (Gilmour & Garnett 1997: 236). On 20 April he staked his future on a speech which warned that endemic racial violence in America could be replicated on this side of the Atlantic – "Like the Roman, I seem to see 'the River Tiber foaming with much blood'". Presumably Powell was unaware that, with its blood-soaked imagery and classical quotation, this notorious phrase was constructed on almost identical lines to a passage in Edmund Burke's unhinged "dagger" speech of 1792 (see Chapter 1; Burke had quoted the poet Horace rather than Powell's Virgil).

By circulating the text of his speech in advance, Powell ensured the widest publicity for views which many Conservatives shared, but which few MPs were prepared to support in public. By contrast, Iain Macleod had testified in 1961 (in words which would have nauseated

James Fitzjames Stephen) to his belief in "the brotherhood of man". The colleagues consulted by Heath agreed with his view that Powell should be sacked; indeed, Macleod (now shadow chancellor), Carr and Hogg would have resigned rather than continue to serve alongside Powell. Their outrage against the inflammatory speech was compounded by the fact that, in Powell's presence, they had just been trying to develop a demeaning compromise approach to Labour's pending Race Relations Bill, signalling approval of the general principles while dissenting from the details.

Despite his careful preparations, not even Powell could have anticipated the public reaction to his speech. He received an avalanche of supportive letters, and racist agitators orchestrated a strike among East End dockworkers, who marched on Westminster in support of "Enoch". As we have seen, the Conservative Party has spawned its share of populist orators, and even prominent figures have sometimes felt unconstrained by cant about "freedom within the law" on issues such as Irish Home Rule. However, Lord Randolph Churchill, Bonar Law and the rest could claim that they were using violent rhetoric in order to *prevent* their Liberal Party opponents from persevering with a policy which would lead to bloodshed. By contrast, in 1968 Powell delivered a speech which was very likely to incite an immediate rash of violent attacks against innocent people settled in Britain, merely on account of their physical appearance.

Powell preferred to think of himself as a "Tory" rather than a Conservative in the hope that this (along with his compulsory penchant for fox hunting) would endear him to the party's traditionalists. However, luminaries like Lord Eldon and the Duke of Wellington would have deprecated his tactic of using the purported opinions of low-born individuals in support of his argument. For example, Powell divulged a conversation with "a quite ordinary, working class man". This "decent, ordinary fellow Englishman" had claimed that he would leave the country if he had enough money, and would encourage his children to escape from Britain because "In this country in 15 or 20 years' time the black man will have the whip hand over the white man". After quoting this testimony as if the witness was credible, Powell continued: "I can already hear the chorus of execration. How dare I say such a horrible thing? How dare I stir up trouble and inflame feelings by repeating such a conversation? The answer is that I do not have the right not to do so" (Berkeley 1977: 129–30). Sir Henry Maine would have provided an alternative response: "The prejudices of the people are far stronger than those of the privileged classes; they are far more vulgar; and they are far more dangerous" (see Chapter 3).

At the 1968 party conference Powell received a rock-star's reception and repeated his views on immigration in much more measured language. He was answered by Hogg, the party's spokesperson on home affairs, whose own ovation was capped by a technical victory because the leadership's approved motion was passed. However, Powell dominated the headlines, and hoped to outshine the party leader's closing speech to the Blackpool conference with another bravura performance at a rival Lancashire seaside resort. Powell's "Morecambe Budget" proposed a virtual halving of income tax, funded by selling off nationalized industries and slashing a wide range of interventionist bodies (including, inevitably, the NEDC) as well as cutting subsidies to industry and agriculture. Overseas aid would be abolished (Heffer 1998: 484–7).

However, Powell discovered that in the very different context of the 1960s a Conservative demagogue could no longer emulate the impact of speeches on economic policy by the likes of Joseph Chamberlain and Randolph Churchill. Compared with "Rivers of Blood" the Morecambe speech produced a miserable trickle of publicity; much of the press comment was negative, if not scathing. Powell's failure to hit the headlines with his latest intervention probably saved him from a more serious setback; as Peregrine Worsthorne wrote at the time, his working-class worshippers would have been alienated by many of Powell's laissez-faire ideas, particularly his anathema against housing subsidies (Heffer 1998: 487).

Although the leadership managed to dampen down Conservative divisions before the 1970 general election, the lasting ramifications of the Powell episode were unlikely to help the party's prospects. Given his irreconcilable differences with his former frontbench colleagues, Powell the man of principle could scarcely offer a whole-hearted pre-election endorsement; but Powell the tactician prevailed. Like most observers he thought that the Conservatives would lose anyway, and his chances of succeeding Heath would be scuppered if his enemies could accuse him of having delivered the *coup de grace* by sounding less than wholly loyal. Ironically, according to some estimates the supportive noises he decided to make two days before the election effectively saved Heath's leadership, by delivering crucial votes for his party in marginal West Midlands constituencies. The Conservatives won the 1970 election with an overall majority of 30 seats.

Lame ducks

At the ensuing party conference, the victorious Heath uncharacteristically alighted upon a telling phrase – "we will have to embark on a change so radical, a revolution so quiet and yet so total, that it will go far beyond the programme of a parliament". With his baleful eye on the Powellites, Heath littered his speech with references to "freedom". For him, "The question now that we are in office is not what kind of government, but how much government. The answer, with which I know you agree, is that there must be less government, and of a better quality" (Heath 1970).

Unfortunately for Heath, another senior Conservative arrived at the 1970 conference armed with an even more memorable soundbite. John Davies, a businessman who had been fast-tracked into the cabinet after winning a seat at the 1970 election, announced that the government would no longer cushion companies from the effects of their own incompetence – it would not, in short, bail out "lame ducks". Unfortunately for the Heath government, thanks to adverse economic circumstances it soon found itself having to contradict its own hardline rhetoric. In the case of Rolls-Royce – a leading global manufacturer of aircraft engines as well as luxury motor-cars – it could argue that the national interest dictated a drastic rescue operation, amounting to a nationalization which was always designed to be temporary. But other "lame ducks" were rescued for partisan purposes – the Conservatives, given their history, could not be seen to allow companies to fail in areas which had suffered during the 1930s.

Bad luck dogged the Heath government almost from the outset; within a month, the most gifted member of the cabinet, the chancellor Iain Macleod, had succumbed to a heart attack. But in most other respects the government was the architect of its own ill-fortune. In particular, its economic strategy depended upon reform of industrial relations – an issue which the preceding Wilson government had tried to tackle, only to fail for lack of political will. Heath thought he would fare better, through an Industrial Relations Bill which radiated "fair play" between workers and employers. However, having faced down the proposed reforms of a Labour government, the unions were unlikely to accept a broadly similar measure from the hands of Conservatives – particularly when the "carrot and stick" approach was entrusted to Robert Carr, who was all carrot and no stick. Loopholes in the 1971 Industrial Relations Act enabled the trade unions effectively to nullify the legislation, allowing those who brazenly breached a sensible compromise to present themselves as heroic descendants of the Tolpuddle Martyrs. From the perspective of the 1980s, when the Thatcher governments introduced far more sweeping reforms, the militants who had opposed Heath looked more like turkeys striking for an early Christmas.

In practice, the government's radicalism was only revealed in ways which left its natural supporters baffled at best. Some significant reforms which offended British "exceptionalists" (like the decimalization of the currency which was completed in February 1971) were already in train before the 1970 election. Others, like local government reform which transformed traditional administrative boundaries and erased tiny Rutland from the map, were Conservative versions of policies which had been planned under Labour. However, Heath's government seemed oblivious to the genuine concerns of people who felt disorientated by the disappearance of familiar landmarks – a mood which coincided with, and was fatefully fostered by, the prospect of joining the EEC (on 1 January 1973).

Matters under the government's control, like the future structure of local government and even its approach to a fast-changing world, were to be determined by the application of cool reasoning, rather than emotion. When unexpected challenges cropped up Heath and his colleagues remained imprisoned by the same outlook, whether or not this persuaded them to change their policies. It should have been apparent to the government after the confrontation over the Industrial Relations Act that the trade unions took a very different view of decision-making. Yet in the face of rising inflation Heath engaged in intensive consultations with the unions, confident to the bitter end that reason would prevail and that they would sign up to his attempt to control incomes as well as prices. Similarly, despite the wartime experiences of several senior ministers, the government attempted to assuage the murderous passions on both sides of the Northern Ireland conflict with proposals based on the assumption that the various factions were rational actors *au fond*. The impression of an earnestly liberal government working at cross-purposes with human nature is best illustrated by the decision of the anarchist Angry Brigade to launch a bomb attack in January 1971 on the home of the most emollient of all the ministers, Robert Carr.

The circumstances of the government's downfall epitomized its career. For good reasons, Dominic Sandbrook's vivid chronicle of these years was entitled *State of Emergency*. In October 1973 war broke out in the Middle East, and when the US started supplying the Israeli side Arab producers retaliated by raising the price of oil by 70 per cent, punishing America's allies even if (like Britain) they protested their neutrality. The National Union of Mineworkers (NUM) exploited the situation by calling an overtime ban, plunging Britain into a period of power-cuts and a three-day week. While most of Heath's closest allies urged him to call a snap election to demonstrate and reinforce the government's authority, the prime minister himself was hesitant at the prospect of a contest which was likely to accentuate existing social and political divisions. As Sandbrook put it, Heath continued to "hope that if he held firm, if the country rallied and the three-day week worked, the miners would see sense" (Sandbrook 2011: 603). But when the NUM voted for an all-out strike, on 4 February 1974, even Heath had to accept that an election was unavoidable. The Conservatives actually won the greatest share of votes (almost 40 per cent), but Labour was the largest parliamentary party and Heath was unable to attract enough support from other parties to keep the Conservatives in office.

After the defeat of February 1974 the scene is shrouded by a host of counterfactuals. In hindsight, Heath should have stepped down either after the February election, or a subsequent narrow defeat in October. As part of the team assisting with his memoirs (*The Course of My Life*, 1998), the present author asked Heath why he had decided to stay on. He replied that he wanted to stop "the Right" from taking over the party, which merely prompted the further question of why he thought that he was best placed to prevent that eventuality. The obvious alternative to Heath was the party's deputy leader, William Whitelaw. Perhaps Heath suspected that Whitelaw – a "consensus" man *par excellence*, but known for his instinctive approach to politics rather than a mastery of policy detail – would try to reach an accommodation with the party's Powellite wing instead of resisting them. If so, Heath's suspicions would have been borne out by Whitelaw's subsequent record; but meeting the critics of the 1970–74 government halfway would have been preferable to helping one of their number to seize the leadership, which is what Heath effectively did by refusing to create a vacancy at the most propitious time for a (relatively) smooth transition to Whitelaw.

Another "what if?" concerns Enoch Powell, who decided to sit out the February 1974 election (presumably expecting that the Conservatives would win, handing Heath a renewed "mandate"). He rationalized this decision on constitutional grounds which resembled those which Heath had brooded over before calling the snap election; a poll was unnecessary since the government already enjoyed a clear parliamentary majority. However, as Powell knew very well, Baldwin had dissolved parliament in 1923 to seek a mandate for tariff reform, even though his party had received an overwhelming endorsement in the previous year. Powell went on to recommend a vote for Labour because of its promise to hold a referendum on EEC membership. Yet this had been official Labour policy since April 1972, after which time Powell had continued to sit as an elected representative of a party which overwhelmingly supported Britain's application (as he had done himself until a timely "conversion" after his ejection from the shadow cabinet). In October 1974 Powell returned to parliament as a candidate for the Ulster Unionist Party (UUP), which had just decided to break its long association with the Conservatives in protest against Heath's attempts to put an end to violence in the north of Ireland. As a result, when the Conservatives revised their procedures to allow challenges to incumbent leaders, Powell could not be a candidate. Yet his behaviour since February 1974 testified to an execrable political judgement which would have convinced anyone except his most starry-eyed supporters that he was unsuited to leadership.

If Powell had ever become leader – or even if he had come close to winning a leadership contest – he could easily have triggered a realignment of parties, since Labour had been exhibiting equally fissiparous tendencies thanks not least to "Europe" (Dick Taverne won Lincoln as an Independent in March 1973, having been deselected as a Labour candidate because of his support for EEC membership). When the new Conservative leadership rules were formalized in January 1975 they raised the barrier for a successful candidate: now he (or she) would have to beat the runner-up by a margin of 15 per cent of *all* Conservative

MPs, not just those who voted. This provision proved fatal to Margaret Thatcher in 1990. In January 1975, although Heath was offended by the transparent purpose of the rule-changes, the stipulated conditions for victory seemed less important than the fact that incumbent leaders could now be subjected to annual challenges (Fisher 1977: 156–7). Heath immediately called a contest, in order to smoke out his potential opponents.

One of these had already ruled himself out. Despite his expression of Powellite economic views before the 1970 general election, Sir Keith Joseph had proved a loyal (and high-spending) secretary of state for health and social services in Heath's government. However, Joseph's leadership bandwagon had barely begun to roll when he was felled by his own intellectual curiosity. Speaking on 19 October 1974 in Powell's Birmingham heartland, and possibly hoping to make a comparable impact to "Rivers of Blood" amidst feverish speculation about the leadership, Joseph plunged into a morass of muddled moralizing, claiming that "The balance of our population, our human stock is threatened" by unmarried mothers. Plagiarizing the Powell approach to prophesy, he claimed that "If we do nothing, the nation moves towards degeneration" thanks to unsuitable mothers some of whom were "of low intelligence, most of low educational attainment". If the speech showed anything, it was that a woeful lack of common sense was no obstacle to winning a fellowship at All Souls College (Denham & Garnett 2001: 265–71).

In the apocalyptic atmosphere of the mid-1970s some panic-stricken Conservatives were ready to acclaim Joseph's speech. Yet even they could hardly overlook the fact that Joseph himself had been the responsible minister in the relevant field (social services) between 1970 and 1974, so that if any single individual could be blamed for national "degeneration" it was the self-flagellating orator himself. At least Joseph, unlike Powell, had no reason to fear dismissal; the second electoral defeat of 1974 had left Heath far too weak to exercise discipline over his frontbenchers (another good reason why he should have stepped aside straight after his third defeat in four general elections as leader). But as soon as it became apparent (in November 1974) that the rules would be changed to allow leadership challenges, Joseph let it be known that he was out of the running. For a while the spotlight fell on Edward du Cann, the chairman of the backbench 1922 Committee whose chief claim to the crown, apparently, arose from Heath's personal animosity towards him.

However, du Cann also dropped out, citing family reasons, even though a campaign team headed by the astute tactician (and Colditz escapee) Airey Neave had been assembled on his behalf.

Thatcherism and after

Reflecting on the 1975 Conservative leadership contest, Enoch Powell said that Margaret Thatcher was "opposite the spot on the roulette wheel at the right time, and she didn't flunk it" (Shepherd 1996: 462). As usual, Powell's judgement of other people's decisions was astute. Thatcher's ascent to the leadership owed a good deal to luck – not least because, by the time that she embarked on her insurgency, she was able to inherit a well-established network of anti-Heath activists who were only too happy to have *someone* to unite behind. In early 1975 Thatcher was less well-known than either Joseph or du Cann; she had attracted publicity mainly for negative reasons, particularly the decision to limit free milk for schoolchildren which had earned her the undeserved nickname "Thatcher the Milk-Snatcher". In fact, as education secretary she had found herself compelled to implement policies she opposed on principle, notably the closure of many grammar schools in accordance with the drive for comprehensive education which the Conservatives had inherited from Labour. But in sharp contrast to Joseph she was never over-burdened by a sense of personal responsibility for past mistakes. Powell's comment about the "roulette wheel" captures the element of fortune in Thatcher's rise to the party leadership, but it does not explain why she was present in the casino, and thus in a position to place a winning bet. This was due to a mixture of courage and conviction.

Unlike Joseph, Margaret Thatcher had been a convinced economic liberal throughout her political career. Reading Hayek's *Road to Serfdom* only confirmed what she already believed, thanks largely to her beloved father. According to Hugo Young, Thatcher made only "small and tentative" contributions to discussions of the party's principles in the 1960s (Young 1989: 56). However, in 1967 as a Treasury spokesperson she had expressed regret that "We cannot immediately denationalize everything" and outlined "the philosophical reasons behind our policies today, why we are opposed to nationalization, and why we stand for private enterprise" (Thatcher 1967). This represented a marked contrast with the relevant section of the 1966 party manifesto, which offered little more than pledges "to run this country's affairs efficiently and realistically" and for "a new drive to put the customer first in the nationalized industries". The word "freedom" featured only once in that document – in relation to the activities of local government rather than individuals or economic policy.

At a fringe meeting with the CPC during the 1968 Conservative conference Thatcher took the opportunity to express her views at greater length. Under the title "What's Wrong with Politics?", she traced contemporary dissatisfaction to "The great mistake – too much government". The mistake was not confined to Labour; choosing her words carefully, Thatcher argued that the problem began in "the early 1960s. At about that time 'growth' became the key political word". Although government was increasingly intrusive in people's lives, at the same time it had become more "remote". To illustrate her point she quoted the words of an enthusiastic ministerial "planner" – not Harold Wilson, but Enoch Powell, speaking as minister of health in the Macmillan government. What was needed now, she claimed, was "a far greater degree of personal responsibility and decision, far more independence from the government, and a comparative reduction in the role of government". There was "nothing laissez-faire" or "old-fashioned" about her views, she insisted. However, "No great party can survive except on the basis of firm beliefs about what it wants to do". It should not simply adhere to a "consensus", which "could be an attempt to satisfy people holding no particular views about anything. It seems more important to have a philosophy and policy which because they are good appeal to sufficient people to secure a majority" (Thatcher 1967).

Much of Thatcher's speech reads like a more tactful reprise of Angus Maude's notorious 1966 article (although Thatcher added the characteristic touch that the pursuit of wealth was not wrong unless it became an end in itself, and that if the Good Samaritan had been impecunious "he too would have had to pass on the other side"). It was entirely apposite that the centrepiece of her 1975 leadership campaign – a *Daily Telegraph* article entitled "My Kind of Tory Party", which included an assertion that the postwar Conservatives had "failed the people" – was drafted by Maude, and that although Thatcher included him in her first cabinet, within two years he had been sacked as surplus to Thatcherite requirements (Moore 2013: 288). This was an ideological revolution

Margaret Thatcher: A besotted admirer cradles a
giant Edward Heath jigsaw puzzle at a Conservative
Party meeting, 1973

Source: Historical Picture Archive/Alamy Stock Photo.

which was perfectly prepared to feast on its grandparents; the cabinet
reshuffle which consumed Maude's eccentric political career also gob-
bled up Lord Thorneycroft, who had earned his place in the Thatcherite
pantheon by resigning as chancellor in 1958 (along with Enoch Powell)
in protest against Macmillan's obsession with economic "growth".

Mrs Thatcher's victory over two ballots in February 1975 – beating Heath by 130 to 119 in the first round, and Whitelaw along with three other challengers in the second – was emphatically not a sign of a wholesale ideological "conversion" among Conservative MPs. Julian Critchley, a moderate MP who himself voted for Thatcher, described the movement to unseat Heath as a "Peasant's Revolt" in which the rebel forces were united only by their desire for something different. Even as late as 1989, Philip Norton found that the parliamentary party remained resolutely "unThatcherised" (Norton 1990). In any case, like all good revolutionaries Thatcher had a well-developed aptitude for political timing, at least in her first two terms (1979–87). In her 1968 CPC speech she had conceded that all state-run industries could not be denationalized at once, and between 1979 and 1983 (apart from the highly successful sale of council houses to their tenants) the process of "privatization" was piecemeal. Even when it gathered momentum (with the sale of British Telecom, British Gas and other major utilities) Thatcher picked her targets carefully (the railways and coal, for example, were left to her hapless successor). The system of taxation was adjusted regressively, but again the most eye-catching shift did not take place until the triumphalist third term; in 1988 Chancellor Nigel Lawson slashed the top income tax rate to just 40 per cent compared to 98 per cent (on unearned income) when the government had taken office.

The Conservative Party's political dominance – some commentators even spoke of "hegemony" – in the 1980s owed a great deal to Thatcher's personal qualities, which were shown to greatest effect in her response to the invasion of the Falkland Islands (1982) and the IRA's assassination attempt at the 1984 party conference. Nevertheless, the roulette wheel kept on revolving in her favour. If, as Labour claimed, the Conservative Party had moved markedly to the right under Thatcher, its own rational course was to appeal to centrist voters. However, Conservatives like Coleraine and Joseph who had attacked the idea that British elections were best contested in the "middle ground" had plenty of counterparts in the Labour Party, whose own post-mortem on the 1979 general election concluded that the Wilson–Callaghan governments had themselves "failed the people" by being insufficiently socialist. The Social Democratic Party (SDP), formed in March 1981, offered centrist voters a new, media-friendly outlet, and quickly formed an alliance with the Liberals who had performed respectably on their own in the 1979 general election despite the coincidental trial for conspiracy and incitement to murder of their former leader, Jeremy Thorpe. When the SDP was founded, its policies were much more congenial to "consensual" Conservatives than the outlook of their own leader. However, as we have argued previously, many moderate postwar Conservatives would have been Liberals all along if that party had offered a realistic chance of furnishing them with a parliamentary seat, let alone a position in government. Despite Thatcher's ideological provocations, in 1981 her personal unpopularity, as unemployment soared towards interwar levels, meant there was still a chance that the so-called Conservative "wets" could reclaim their party; and despite the enthusiasm of activists within the Liberal–SDP alliance, it remained to be seen whether their socio-economic sources of support would be strong enough to secure an overall parliamentary majority under the disproportional first-past-the-post electoral system, rather than the familiar Liberal pattern of sporadic by-election shocks. For any One Nation Conservative who was tempted by the SDP, an important test was the attitude of Edward Heath who was a friend of SDP founder-member Roy Jenkins as well as a vociferous critic of the Thatcher government's early policies. But Heath remained studiously aloof from the venture. Ian Gilmour, a much closer friend of Jenkins, was tempted but decided not to jump ship; in March 1981 he was still a member of Thatcher's cabinet but knew very well that he would be tossed overboard before long. The approach to "Conservatism" which he had praised in *Inside Right* was in the process of being pushed to the party's extreme left.

Although in the abstract the SDP was (at least) equally attractive to dissident Conservatives as to moderate Labour MPs, only one of the former (Christopher Brocklebank-Fowler, who lost his seat in 1983) chose to defect. In 1968, Brocklebank-Fowler had served as chair of the Bow Group, an organization founded in 1951 by young Conservative intellectuals – a kind of extra-parliamentary youth wing of the One Nation group. It would not be unfair to say that aspirants to leading roles in the Bow Group during the 1960s saw this as a stepping-stone to a prominent career within the Conservative Party which at the time was dominated by consensus politicians (Barr 2001: 88–112). As such, it is worthy of note that three of Brocklebank-Fowler's Bow Group successors – Michael Howard (1970–71), Norman Lamont (1971–72) and Peter Lilley (1973–75) – turned out, in various ways, to be controversial

"Thatcherite" politicians after they found parliamentary seats. They had sniffed the ideological wind and charted their future courses accordingly.

Remaining moderates were prepared to accept ministerial positions; Chris Patten and William Waldegrave, indeed, played leading roles in the passage of Thatcher's most controversial policy, the Community Charge or "Poll Tax". Norton noted the continued predominance of "party loyalists" – usually older, less ambitious MPs – within the parliamentary ranks; but as Thatcher's leadership entered its second decade such individuals tended to equate loyalty to the party with unthinking comformity to the government's instructions. If the instinct for party unity did not suffice, Thatcher now enjoyed institutional resources to quash incipient rebellion. In April 1988 an amendment which would have transformed the Community Charge into something akin to a local income tax was defeated, with only 38 Conservatives supporting the change and 13 abstaining. Opposition within the party ran far deeper than these numbers suggested. The mover of the amendment, Michael Mates, was subsequently purged from the chairmanship of the Conservative Home Affairs Committee (Butler *et al.* 1994: 120).

While ideology played a role of sorts in Thatcher's own removal, her undiminished zest for economic liberalism was now less important than her style of leadership and her unbridled hostility towards "Europe". Contrary to a persistent media myth, there was no conspiracy to oust Thatcher – most of her cabinet were probably telling the truth when they promised to support her if she contested the second round of the 1990 leadership contest, although they might have been excessively keen to persuade her not to let her name go forward. Rather, there was a concerted effort to prevent the succession of Michael Heseltine, a genuine enthusiast for European integration whose views on economic intervention marked a partial reversion to the party's pre-Thatcherite position. Like Enoch Powell in his 1964 *Times* articles, Heseltine preached a more realistic assessment of Britain's global status, arguing that "There is no empire to sustain us; we are no longer an industrial super-power; we can no longer pretend that Britain is in any sense an equal partner of the United States. There is nowhere for us to go except as part of a European consortium". Heseltine thought that "few British citizens" would deny these propositions (Heseltine 1989: 14). He reckoned without his Conservative colleagues, the majority of the party's rank and file, and the English nationalism of the right-wing press.

With the communist bloc dissolving fast at the end of the 1980s and the Labour Party retreating from the left-wing posture it had adopted after 1979, many Conservatives began to suppose that they had won the battle of ideas. Thatcher's replacement John Major lacked her ideological fervour and spoke of creating "a nation at ease with itself" – implying that Thatcher had disturbed Britain's tranquillity – but in essence his policy ideas represented "Thatcherism with a human face". The furious European debate which dogged his premiership did not erupt simply because, by the time of the 1992 general election, Conservatives had exhausted other sources of contention. Although Major's skilful diplomacy had exempted Britain from aspects of the Maastricht Treaty, the resulting compromise still raised serious questions about national "sovereignty". While Thatcher and her allies tended to portray party divisions over Maastricht as a re-run of the "wet" versus "dry" debate, in reality some convinced economic liberals (notably the ex-chancellor Sir Geoffrey Howe) took a positive view of European integration. Indeed, the tendency of economic liberals to take a purist line on sovereignty in respect of the emerging European Union (EU) contrasted oddly with their stances on other issues, particularly the sovereignty-sapping "special relationship" with the US and the practical results of privatization, which often meant that industrial concerns of strategic importance fell under the control of non-British individuals and financial institutions.

After her departure from office Thatcher derided pro-European members of her party as "no-nation Conservatives". This was an unpleasant slur on many senior postwar party figures whose support for European integration had been fostered while they were fighting fascism, but the ex-leader's logic had been implicit in her 1988 Bruges speech, which argued that the European project could destroy Britain's sense of nationhood. Judging from the previous utterances of politicians she admired – Powell and Joseph – it was astonishing that "Britishness" had survived for so long. For Powell (1968), immigrants were the enemies of national identity; for Joseph (1974), the national stock was being undermined by unmarried mothers. It seemed that the Conservative Party was under an obligation to warn patriotic Britons about existential threats of one kind or another. Whatever their proximate sources, Conservative voters were easily convinced that ultimate responsibility for these developments lay with "socialists"; during the 1984–85 miners' strike Thatcher had pronounced such ideologues to be un-British, "the enemy within".

At no point, apparently, did any of these Conservative prophets of doom consider that the main solvent of national identity might be the consumerism which had taken root in the 1950s, when Michael Oakeshott was extolling the "conservative disposition" and Macmillan was misinterpreted as boasting that "You've never had it so good". Had they done so, it might also have occurred to them that further instalments of free-market individualism were likely to make matters worse.

The national humiliation of Britain's enforced exit from the European exchange rate mechanism (ERM) on "Black Wednesday" (16 September 1992) provided additional ammunition for those within the party who thought that Britain would be better off – materially as well as politically – if it left the EU. After the landslide Labour victory of 1997, which put an end to 18 years of Conservative rule, the obvious candidate to succeed John Major was Kenneth Clarke who had shown himself to be a dutiful Thatcherite in a succession of ministerial postings before proving his fitness for the top job as a combative but pragmatic chancellor of the exchequer. Unlike the majority of his colleagues, Clarke seemed comfortable in his own skin and capable of communicating with ordinary people. His undeniable qualifications merely increased the resolve of his opponents. He was duly beaten for the leadership in 1997 (by William Hague, who won the position too early) and in 2001 by Iain Duncan Smith (an improbable leader for a major party at any age or in any circumstances).

Although "Europe" was an obsessive preoccupation for most Conservatives under Hague and Duncan Smith, there was another hangover from Thatcherism which won considerable attention from more serious operators. "Modernisers" within the party argued that it had alienated voters by endorsing "traditional" views on moral matters. The best-remembered speech on this subject came at the 2002 Conservative party conference, when the then party chair, Theresa May, told her audience that "Our base is too narrow and so, occasionally, are our sympathies. You know what some people call us – the Nasty Party" (Guardian 2002). May was the daughter of an Anglican clergyman; even if she had been inclined to take full advantage of the hedonism of the 1960s she was born a bit too early (1956) to do so. Her personal biography made her insistence that the Conservative Party was somewhat behind the times in moral matters all the more arresting. For many attendees of the 2002 conference, a return to the moral framework of the 1950s was not only desirable but practicable. However, despite their occasional ill-advised forays into the moralistic field the Thatcher governments had signally failed to turn the clock back; indeed, on a range of issues British attitudes had shifted markedly since the 1960s, partially in a direction which reflected the "permissive" legislation of both major parties in that much-debated decade, but also in an unquantifiable loss of civility in daily dealings.

When running for the party leadership in 1975 Thatcher had portrayed herself as a champion of the middle class, and saw no need to apologise for espousing what she called "Victorian values". Some commentators have alighted on this as evidence that, in ideological terms, Thatcherism cannot be explained simply in terms of economic liberalism; there was also an element of "social conservatism". "Authoritarian" is a much less misleading term for this enduring outlook within the postwar Conservative Party. There is no reason to doubt that under Thatcher the Conservative Party attracted support from voters who craved social stability, and convinced themselves that the party's hard line on law and order was the most promising means of achieving this. However, Thatcher herself interpreted moral developments – and British history in general – through an economic lens which verified her views. The Victorian values she espoused were rationalized by Shirley Letwin as "vigorous virtues"; the ideal Thatcherite would be "upright, self-sufficient, energetic, adventurous, independent, loyal to friends, and robust against enemies" (Letwin 1991: 33). These, rather than the "softer virtues" – "kindness, humility, gentleness, cheerfulness, sympathy" – were what made Britain great during the nineteenth century. They epitomized the outlook of a tough-minded mill-owner rather than a philanthropic nineteenth-century Conservative politician like Lord Shaftesbury, who had frittered away his time trying to make human life a little less miserable.

Economic liberalism and social authoritarianism

Thatcher – unlike Powell – was an enthusiastic supporter of capital punishment, granting her a special connection with the grass-roots Conservatives who were regarded with distaste by most of her senior colleagues. However, she was neither particularly prudish nor prejudiced

– as she showed in her relationship with Mikhail Gorbachev, she could even acknowledge the human qualities of (selected) socialists. Like Letwin, she might have imagined that the correct application of the "vigorous virtues" in the 1980s excluded certain trades from free market activity. For example, as Letwin put it, "what could be more deleterious to the more vigorous values than free markets in drugs?" (Letwin 1991: 44). The cocaine-fuelled denizens of the Thatcher-worshipping City of London took a different position on this matter. Whatever Thatcher might herself have thought about specific activities, in the context of the 1980s the indiscriminate rhetoric of "freedom" was unlikely to deter thorough-going libertarians from regarding her Conservative Party as a congenial vehicle for their views. As a general rule, the government ensured that whenever economic arguments conflicted with traditional moral norms, the latter would have to give way. There was one apparent exception, when the government suffered a rare Commons' defeat on its proposal to abolish restrictions on Sunday trading. However, in that vote (April 1986) the 72 Conservative rebels rebuffed a three-line whip imposed by a government which denied that there was anything special about Sunday. It was left to the Major government to push through a relaxation of the laws, in 1994.

Social liberals and outright libertarians might not have formed a majority in many Conservative constituency associations, but they had logic as well as youth on their side. If governments should stand back and give free play to market forces, what was their warrant for inter-fering in morality? In her 1968 CPC lecture Thatcher had quoted only one philosopher – the nineteenth-century Conservative bogeyman, J. S. Mill ("Mankind are greater gainers by suffering each other to live as seems good to themselves than by compelling each to live as seems good to the rest"). When Thatcher's government infringed these improving sentiments, in Section 28 of the 1988 Local Government Act, it incurred widespread ridicule as well as richly-deserved odium. The clause, which had been inserted as a sop to the party's "Back to the 1950s" wing, was self-evidently unenforceable. If he had heard Theresa May's reference to "the nasty party", Mill would have muttered "and clearly still the stupid-est party, after all these years".

Despite May's warnings, the debate between consistent liberals and authoritarians ("Mods" and "Rockers", as they were dubbed) was decided in favour of the latter when the parliamentary party chose

Michael Howard to succeed Duncan Smith (another "Rocker") in 2003. The 2005 Conservative manifesto, adorned with the slogan "Are You Thinking What We're Thinking?", might as well have been a questionnaire to discover the extent of the party's irreducible core vote. It was as if Julian Critchley's prophecy of 1973 had finally been verified, and the Conservatives had turned themselves into "the party of the aggrieved motorist" (Critchley 1973: 410).

But Howard was only ever going to be a stop-gap leader, to ensure that the party held together after what was certain to be a third consecutive electoral defeat. Despite having piloted Section 28 through the Commons and served as a populist home secretary, Howard favoured the young social liberals, George Osborne and David Cameron, as candidates to succeed him. Cameron pulled off a feat worthy of a self-proclaimed "heir to Blair" by persuading a party still more than half in thrall to "nastiness" to give him a chance; and with Osborne as shadow chancellor it looked as if the Conservatives had finally entrusted their fortunes to liberals who were consistent rather than confused. When the 2010 general election produced a hung parliament, ministers in the ensuing Conservative–Liberal Democrat coalition were, in ideological terms, more united than any government since 1974 (Dorey & Garnett 2016).

The unity, however, did not extend far below elite level. The Conservative Party had an appetite for power, not for partnership; and once the euphoria of a return to office after 13 years of impotence had worn off, grass-roots members woke up to the threat of their party being absorbed in the tasteless soup of a post-Thatcherite consensus. Antipathy to the EU was the single remaining issue which could make them feel distinctive – and they were in danger of being out-flanked even here by the United Kingdom Independence Party (UKIP). Having failed in his mission to stop Conservatives "banging on about Europe", Cameron gambled on an in-out referendum whose outcome, hopefully, would bang some sense into his party. He made the pledge in January 2013, just two weeks before the second reading of a Marriage (Same Sex Couples) Bill, which was opposed by 136 Conservative MPs (with just 127 in favour) and flooded the correspondence columns of the *Daily Telegraph* with furious complaints from life-long party supporters.

Through their atavistic antipathy to the EU, the Conservatives had contrived to keep an issue which was toxic to themselves in the headlines even when voters showed little interest. The coverage by the right-wing press – whose proprietors had commercial reasons for disliking "Europe" – included fabricated stories which gave uniformed voters the impression that the EU provided no tangible benefits to Britain to set against innumerable disadvantages. In their pomp, the Conservatives had been able to detect dangerous developments on their right flank – usually flagged up by the creation of a "League" of some kind – and effortlessly to slide in that direction in order to neutralize the threat before it became serious. In the case of UKIP, the Conservatives had actually created the threat themselves, through anti-EU rhetoric which became compulsory for any senior figure (even the moderately-sceptical Cameron), and the promise of a referendum only encouraged them to keep feeding the beast. UKIP topped the poll in the European Parliamentary elections of May 2014, consigning the Conservatives to third place. In no national election since 1906 had a party other than the Conservatives or Labour won the popular vote.

It remained to be seen if UKIP could repeat this exploit in a general election. As it turned out, in 2015 the party won nearly 4 million votes (12.6 per cent) but only one seat, thanks to the electoral system. Despite its manifest unsuitability for what was now clearly a multi-party country, first-past-the-post had emerged unscathed from a 2011 referendum whose outcome had been swayed by Cameron's calculated distortions of the financial cost. Before a similar single-issue poll, held in 2014, the prospect that Scotland would opt for independence from the UK had been real enough to wrest last-minute concessions from the main Westminster parties, and any Conservative contribution to the victory for the status quo was dwarfed by an impassioned intervention from Labour's Gordon Brown. In an unguarded moment, Cameron revealed that the queen "purred" with satisfaction when he told her that the Union had been saved. Presumably she did not go on to point out that the danger to the Union had chiefly been caused by the Conservatives, who had piled up grievances north of the border during the Thatcher years and were now senior partners in a government which had responded to the global financial crisis of 2007–08 by applying economic "austerity" against the wishes of most Scottish voters.

Objectively, in the 2015 general election the interests of Cameron and his moderate Conservative colleagues were best served by a result which necessitated continued cooperation with the Liberal Democrats.

However, some old Conservative habits died harder than others, and no therapist could have persuaded the party to kick the primordial tribal itch to use a spell in coalition as a pretext to exterminate Liberals. Chiefly through the successful targeting of Liberal Democrat seats in 2015, Cameron's party was able to achieve a majority of ten, on a share of the vote (36.9 per cent) which was less than that achieved in the election of February 1974 – the defeat which had triggered more than four decades of "creative destruction" for the party and for Britain.

The slender 2015 victory effectively made the prime minister a hostage of Conservative "Eurosceptics", now organized far more effectively than the party's residual moderates. Whatever Cameron himself might have thought, in these circumstances he had no chance of forcing the cabinet to line up in support of a campaign for Britain to remain within the EU. In fact, his predicament created an irresistible opportunity for any minister who was tempted to agitate for withdrawal to win cheap applause from the party faithful. In another maladroit move, before the 2015 election Cameron had revealed that, regardless of the result, he would not be seeking a third term as prime minister. Whatever the overall verdict of the EU referendum, it was likely that most members of the Conservative Party – who, under rules adopted in 1997, enjoyed the decisive role in leadership elections – would vote in the referendum for what came to be known as "Brexit". If the overall national vote favoured "Remain", grass-roots Conservatives would be looking to replace Cameron with a leader who had fought valiantly but in vain for the righteous cause. If, against expectations, the country voted to leave the EU, the vacancy in Downing Street would appear ahead of schedule but the scenario for aspirants who had been courageous enough to campaign for "Leave" would be even more propitious.

Whether or not the decision to leave the EU was rational, it is puzzling that the majority of Conservative members (and so many MPs) should have invested so much passion in the cause. Since the downfall of Margaret Thatcher, party members had lost no opportunity to show their scorn for the unworthy upstarts at Westminster who were palpably unworthy to shine her shoes. After the Conservative rout in the 1997 general election, the party's MPs had been exposed to the unbridled wrath of grass-roots activists. In 2009, the parliamentary expenses scandal revealed by the pro-Conservative *Telegraph* newspaper group extended the indictment to the whole political class. In effect, then,

Conservative supporters of the "Vote Leave" campaign were seeking to wrest "control" of the nation's affairs from the EU and entrust it to people who were, allegedly, more corrupt and incompetent than any elected representatives in the nation's history.

If Conservatives troubled themselves about this question, their response would probably have been that the political class had failed and should now either take direct instructions from voters or find alternative employment. In short, a party whose initial purpose had been to preserve an hierarchical socio-political order had become anti-elitist, using "elite" as a short-hand term for anyone who (for whatever reason) disagreed with "Brexit". Theresa May, who succeeded Cameron after the referendum, was an unlikely agent of subversion, and, indeed, had unobtrusively supported "Remain" along with the dwindling cohort of Conservatives who preferred continuity to chaos. But once she became leader, she responded to the party's mood by attacking any institution which attempted to obstruct her own hardline version of Brexit. It was claimed that her opponents were "anti-democratic" even though, notoriously, no terms for "leaving" had been specified on the ballot paper. The *Daily Mail* branded High Court judges "Enemies of the People", and when May called a snap general election in April 2017 the paper which the philosopher R. G. Collingwood had once described as "a keen worker in the cause of corrupting the public mind" implored her to "Crush the saboteurs" (Collingwood 1939: 163).

The prolonged transformation of the Conservative Party from constitutional gamekeepers to populistic poachers was nearing completion. A less-noticed implication of the *Daily Mail*'s 2017 election headline was its contradiction of Edmund Burke's view that elected representatives should be held accountable for decisions based on their independent judgement, rather than acting as passive channels for the demands of their most raucous constituents. Burke, as we have seen, also argued that love of country depended on whether or not the country in question was truly lovable. The party was now addicted, not to Burke's patriotism but to a hollowed-out version of (English) nationalism. On this basis the party initiated the kind of heresy-hunt which it had always decried when Labour conducted its own inquisitions. The over-hyped "de-selections" championed by Labour's militants in the 1980s seemed innocuous by comparison to the decision to deprive 21 moderate MPs of the Conservative whip, in September 2019.

By that time the party had finally decanted Theresa May, who was replaced in July 2019 by Boris Johnson. It was Johnson's second attempt; first time round, in the contest to succeed Cameron, he had fallen victim to a genuine "saboteur", his fellow-Brexiteer Michael Gove, who announced his own candidacy because he doubted Johnson's leadership and team-building qualities. Long before Gove's unexpected intervention there was ample evidence that close acquaintance with Johnson was no guarantee of a favourable opinion. His former employer, the distinguished journalist and historian Max Hastings, wrote that Johnson was unfit for office because "it seems he cares for no interest save his own fame and gratification", and accused him of "cowardice, reflected in a willingness to tell any audience, whatever he thinks most likely to please, heedless of the inevitability of its contradiction an hour later" (Guardian 2019). Conservative party members decided to disregard this testimony in the 2019 leadership contest, even when it was supplemented by reports that, after the final ballot among MPs, police had been called to Johnson's flat because of a high-volume altercation between the aspiring prime minister and his girlfriend. Less than two months after Johnson received the endorsement of Conservative members, his brother, Jo, left the government, citing a conflict between family loyalty and the national interest. In July 2019 Rory Stewart, though never likely to win the contest against Johnson, had polled very respectably among MPs and attracted considerable public interest through an innovative campaign. By October he was no longer even a member of the party. Somehow, the Conservatives had managed to produce a leadership contest which was more surreal than that of 1922, when the least popular candidate won (see Chapter 2).

If Johnson had any principles, they were probably similar to those of Cameron and Osborne – i.e., a combination of economic and social liberalism rather than anything distinctively conservative. However, in Johnson's case there were always legitimate grounds for suspecting that these ideas were instruments of personal ambition rather than sincere conviction. During the coronavirus (Covid-19) pandemic which prevented Johnson from enjoying any kind of "honeymoon" after the comfortable Conservative election victory in December 2019, the prime minister's evident discomfort at the need to impose unprecedented restrictions on personal liberty arose from the likelihood of a negative reaction from Conservative backbenchers rather than a qualm of libertarian conscience (see Preface). He made some noises about "One Nation", but this phrase could not readily be associated with a divisive character who, at most, was willing to talk about "levelling up" regions which had never recovered from the economic effects of Conservative policies between 1979 and 1997. It was painfully evident that, for Johnson, the "Nation" in question did not include Scotland, whose preference for "Remain" (in every region) was brushed aside by Westminster's new anti-elitist elite. Remain had also registered a clear victory in Northern Ireland, whose anomalous situation if the UK as a whole voted to withdraw (given its land border with the EU) had been ignored prior to the referendum by the Leave camp, including Johnson whose interest in the Union was only activated when it seemed on the point of collapse. For the party faithful (in England, at least), Johnson's shortcomings were smothered by his bombastic sub-Churchillian rhetoric which, Conservatives imagined, would appeal to parts of the electorate inaccessible to other politicians. If Johnson was a passable facsimile of a Churchill, it was the caddish clap-trapper Lord Randolph, not the flawed genius Sir Winston.

The Conservatives had finally chosen a leader who would do anything at all to win votes; and that decision, taken in the face of notorious facts about Johnson, demonstrated that the same was now true of the party itself. The interlude of coherent liberalism, it seemed, had been only a momentary pause on the Conservative Party's postwar path from pragmatism to all-out populism. The leadership contest which followed Johnson's enforced resignation in July 2022 only confirmed that the party had made itself the prisoner of Brexit, which was associated with so many unrealistic promises. The brief ascendancy of Liz Truss – a populist whose unbridled enthusiasm for laissez faire easily overcame her meagre reserves of political judgement – was not an unforced error by the party, but rather an accident which had been waiting to happen for more than a century.

Conclusions: "Is Conservatism dead?"

By 1926, the descendants of Sir Robert Peel no longer occupied the property, Drayton Manor, whose purchase had guaranteed the family a seat in the House of Commons. Peel's stately pile was pulled down; only the clock tower remained to record the passing of time since the composition of the Tamworth Manifesto. After a sale in 1947 Drayton Manor was redeveloped as an amusement park. In 2020, while Boris Johnson's Conservative government was facing up to the task of "taking back control" from the EU, Peel's old property was acquired by a company with headquarters in Paris.

Just two years before the destruction of Drayton Manor Stanley Baldwin had evoked the sights and sounds of England. To the immemorial cry of the corncrake and the plough team rumbling over the hill, he could have added the destruction of historic houses as a phenomenon which was becoming increasingly familiar. The new burden of taxation, thanks particularly to death duties, had taken its toll on the aristocracy. The old ruling class was losing what was left of its political power and its fate was a matter of public indifference; the idea of preserving the past as a resource for future generations only took root after the Second World War. In England, more than a thousand historic houses were demolished during the twentieth century, and the losses in Scotland were proportionally higher.

These developments obviously held much more than symbolic importance, yet rumours of the death of "Conservative England" only began to circulate among journalists after the party's mauling in the 1997 general election (Wheatcroft 2005). Evidently the assumption that the Conservative Party always embodied "conservatism" had become so prevalent that such commentators would not be able to certify the death of an ideological tradition until the organization finally disbanded or (as it could easily have done on several occasions since the 1830s) adopted a less misleading name. It was not suggested that, in the process of killing the Liberal Party in the first half of the twentieth century, the Conservatives had found it necessary to adopt the ideological outlook of their less fortunate rivals.

However, as we have seen thanks to Thatcher the nature of conservative thought had finally become a topic of academic interest, and long before the 1997 election a handful of scholars (and more thoughtful MPs) had begun to question its relevance to an understanding of the contemporary party. In 1994 the Social Market Foundation (SMF) think tank published pamphlets by two prominent participants in the debate. Before joining the Commons in 1992, David (later Lord) Willetts had worked for Margaret Thatcher's Downing Street Policy Unit and headed the Centre for Policy Studies (CPS) which Thatcher had co-founded with Keith Joseph in 1974. The author of *Modern Conservatism* (1992), Willetts could be regarded as the party's most authoritative intellectual in the 1990s. In his 1994 pamphlet, *Civic Conservatism*, Willets argued that free markets were compatible with robust civic institutions; indeed, the main threat to such institutions was the over-mighty state. The Conservative Party's opponents had wrongly associated its policies with "neoliberalism" – a viewpoint which portrayed human beings as atomistic, "rational" economic actors with no sense of community. The conservative tradition, by contrast, emphasized that meaningful activity depends on a context of shared cultural understandings and ethical values, and the party had been faithful to that approach since 1979.

In *Modern Conservatism* Willetts had acknowledged his intellectual debt to John Gray, who had taught him at Oxford (Willetts 1992: vii). However, much had changed since the 1970s and the ex-student and his tutor were now sharply opposed. In *The Undoing of Conservatism*, John Gray argued that, in fact, neoliberalism had taken control of the party. For all their ideological triumphalism during the 1980s, Conservatives had introduced policies which ravaged long-established institutions, allowing traditional cultural and ethical understandings to be crowded out by market imperatives. The effect was to undermine any distinctively "conservative" project. Conservatism had been "undone" by a party which continued to bear the name but which could no longer be trusted to conserve anything of value to itself or to the British public as a whole.

The pamphlets were republished in a single volume after the 1997 election. Gray and Willetts provided postscripts in which they reflected on recent events. Willetts saw no reason for repentance. Like loyal Conservative spokespeople after a similar defeat in 1945, he repeated that the party's approach had been caricatured unfairly by its critics. However, even after the salutary lesson of 1997 Willetts continued to betray an antipathy towards the state which lent credence to John Gray's arguments. For example, he claimed that people in Britain are liable to forget the dangers of state encroachment "because of our optimistic belief in benign, rational, all-knowing government" (Willetts 1997: 179). In 1997 – after more than three decades of scoffing attacks on the state and "the establishment" from both the ideological right and the left – only a libertarian of the Herbert Spencer school could suppose that the British people were still deferential towards their rulers.

In his 1997 contribution, Gray could feel even more confidence in his assertion that conservatism had been "undone". It was conceivable that the Conservative *Party* might recover from its electoral catastrophe, but only if New Labour threw away the opportunity which Thatcherism had provided. Even then, the Conservative Party "cannot hope to put Tory Britain back together. That has been broken into pieces". Gray noted that "Traditional conservatism, in Burke, Disraeli and Coleridge" had contested optimistic Enlightenment assumptions about human nature. However, "Latter-day conservatism is a caricature of that Enlightenment view" (Gray 1997: 163, 155). "Conservatism", in short, had wrought havoc within British institutions because the party which still bore that name now accepted uncritically a worldview which its greatest exponents had explicitly rejected. In their heedless ideological fervour, Thatcherite neoliberals had forgotten that stable institutions were preconditions for their own cherished "free" market economy, thus exhibiting the self-defeating nature of their creed.

Even those who were willing to accept Gray's argument could feel that more supporting evidence would help. In particular, Gray claimed that "Tory England was once a living, flesh-and-blood reality. It was destroyed by global economic changes and by the social effects of Conservative economic policies" (Gray 1997: 157). However, this implies that in 1979 a recognisably "Tory England" still existed, albeit on the eve of destruction. Since Gray rightly attributes considerable political importance to ideas, this scenario implies that conservatism, properly understood, must have been a potent political force in the preceding years. Yet, of the "traditional conservatives" whom Gray thought worthy of mention, the most recent (Disraeli) died in 1881. This left a considerable chronological lacuna, which the present book has attempted to address.

The Conservative Party and conservatism

Recent scholarship has confirmed that the Conservative Party's name was not adopted in explicit homage to Edmund Burke. However, James Fitzjames Stephen noted that while "Whig" and "Tory" had been nicknames, "Liberal" and "Conservative" "aim not merely at identifying political parties, but at describing their principles" (Stephen 1862: 70). One might argue that the early "Conservatives" were Burkeans without realizing it. Those who thought about such matters believed that their party stood for a hierarchical, interdependent society in which duties were more important than rights and preponderant power was rightly entrusted to a hereditary aristocracy; and Burke, though a Whig, had provided a principled argument to justify an order of that kind.

From an "ultra-Tory" perspective the ideological rot set in at the start. Peel's Tamworth Manifesto essentially set out the conditions under which the Conservative Party could cooperate with moderate Whigs. His acceptance in 1846 of the Whig argument for repeal of the Corn Laws was regarded by many Conservatives as a compromise too far – that, in the terms used by Keith Joseph in 1974, he was "not a Conservative". However, the protectionist rump which disavowed Peel's leadership had limited prospects of winning office under the reformed electoral system. Derby and Disraeli offered a variation of Peel's formula: the party could win even if the franchise was extended further, if it embraced a degree of populist nationalism in its presentation of religious and foreign policy issues. The survival of the party as an institution was prioritized over any semblance of ideological coherence, in accordance with Disraeli's witty allusion to "Tory men and Whig measures".

However, Lord Salisbury, rather than Disraeli, is the pivotal figure in the ideological evolution of the Conservative Party. Distinctively conservative in his principles, his practice was far more ecumenical. Deeply antipathetic to changes which he regarded as inevitable, he convinced himself that national ruin could at least be postponed so long as representatives of the Conservative Party were in charge of change. The Liberal Party's divisions over Irish Home rule and "collectivism" offered opportunities too good to miss. By the end of his career Salisbury's allies included laissez-faire liberals, quasi-socialists like Joseph Chamberlain, and a mass movement (the Primrose League) which could only be nourished on a diet of populism. None of these tendencies could be pleasing to Salisbury's jaundiced eye, but they were the price for keeping his show on the road. The struggle for survival could not last long; Salisbury was in earnest when he speculated about being "the last of the Conservatives".

By the end of the First World War, continued Liberal divisions ensured that, in a two-party system, the forthcoming battle would lie between Labour and a Conservative Party which was now regarded as the most effective champion of property in general rather than the political wing of the landed classes. Since Britain was now (almost) a fully-fledged democracy as well as a manufacturing power dominated by urban settlements, there could no question of a return to the full Burkean agenda. Laissez-faire liberalism would please the property-owners and provide the sharpest ideological challenge to Labour's alleged "socialism"; but it was difficult to reconcile with the vote-winning idea that the Conservatives were the party of national unity. In Stanley Baldwin, the party had an interwar leader who, even after the confrontation of classes in the 1926 General Strike, personified the idea of unity. His marked preference was for pragmatic, piecemeal state intervention – in essence, the approach adopted by all governments since Disraeli, but now enjoying intellectual support from "new" liberal followers of the Oxford philosopher, T. H. Green. After the Second World War the majority of Conservatives accepted that a continuation of that approach was the only way to avoid the electoral oblivion which seemed possible given the disastrous 1945 result.

This approach, which is now commonly designated by the Disraelian "One Nation" tag, did include some vestiges of distinctive conservative thought. As well as its explicit echo of Disraeli's national unity theme, it could be presented as a recipe for social stability, and the resulting policy ideas could be implemented in conformity with Burkean pragmatism. However, the *substance* of the Burkean tradition – its inegalitarianism, its emphasis on duties over rights, and (especially) its adamant opposition to democracy – had to be left on the cutting-room floor in an era of mass parties and universal suffrage. Now that the party's leading lights were distinctively liberal by nature, it might have been more logical to become Liberal by name. However, the effects of the electoral system had consigned the Liberal Party to the fringes of political debate, and the Conservative Party offered ideological liberals of various kinds a chance to pursue their favoured causes under a much more successful brand name. With the help of party propagandists, senior members of the party elite could follow Baldwin in convincing themselves that their own liberal variant *was* "conservatism"; or, rather, that conservatism was whatever the party wanted it to be, so long as the people in charge could be certified as free from the taint of dogma. In any case, for obvious reasons even leaders who were interested in ideas tended to be more impressed by electoral results and opinion polls. Even Macmillan, who as a backbencher had produced a very plausible theoretical defence of the Middle Way presented by liberal interventionism, ended up inviting grassroots Conservatives to acclaim the creation of a purely pragmatic party.

This was always pretty thin gruel, and it proved distinctly unappetising once "events" had turned against the pragmatic men with their practical measures. When the postwar liberal-social democratic consensus collapsed in the mid-1970s the opponents of "One Nation" found it easy to argue that the supposed virtues of its approach had proved in practice to be vices. Under its influence, successive Conservative leaders had simply played catch-up with the Labour Party. The obvious alternative was laissez-faire – a doctrine which, its votaries claimed, had never been given a fair trial by the Conservative Party even though it was possible to claim (thanks to Lord Hugh Cecil *et al.*) that it had always been one of conservatism's "converging streams". These enthusiasts never seemed to consider that laissez-faire had been resisted because moderate leaders had deemed it too electorally and economically divisive. After Margaret Thatcher became leader, a new cohort of apologists was encouraged to imply that their party had always leant towards laissez-faire, but "true conservatism" had been "betrayed" by leaders who either lacked the courage of their real convictions or, more likely, had themselves been infected by the socialist virus. Even well-read Thatcherites easily accepted this revisionist line. Thus, for example, in 1994 David Willetts insisted that the denial of free-market economics as an element of conservatism was "bad history", because "Edmund Burke went into politics as a follower of Adam Smith" (Willetts 1997: 73). This claim could easily feature in an examination for courses on ideology, where it would be accompanied by the word "Discuss". Credit would only be given to candidates who noted that Burke "went into politics" with firm convictions on a range of issues, and that the dogmatic economic views which he expressed shortly before his death were a caricature of Smith's message as well as being incompatible with the writings which earned his reputation as the founder of conservatism.

Whatever might have inspired Edmund Burke to pursue a political career, it was evident that David Willetts himself had gone into politics as a follower of Adam Smith, and in this respect he was fairly representative of a new breed of earnestly Thatcherite Conservative MPs. The policies of the 1979–90 governments were as divisive as One Nation Conservatives had predicted, but Thatcher continued to talk tough and seemed to be vindicated by two further election wins. Symptoms of social breakdown could even be turned to the party's advantage, thanks to its scarcely-deserved reputation for dealing effectively with problems of law and order. Nevertheless, party strategists attributed the 1997 electoral defeat, at least in part, to an "uncaring" image. The obvious solution, now that the party had become a hostile environment for opponents of laissez-faire, was to embrace a complementary libertarian outlook on social matters. Thus when the Conservatives chose David Cameron as their leader in 2005 they seemed to have brought their tortuous ideological course to an end. Having been liberal in its orientation since 1918, the party had finally endorsed a form of liberalism which was reasonably coherent (although for presentational reasons Cameron preferred to characterize his position as "liberal conservative").

In retirement, Lady Thatcher was less squeamish about her true ideological identity. In a 1996 lecture in memory of Keith Joseph, she recalled how they had "reshaped Conservatism". She went on to explain that their kind of Conservatism "would be best described as 'liberal' – in the old-fashioned sense. And I mean the liberalism of Mr Gladstone not of the latter-day collectivists" (Thatcher 1996). To emphasize the point, the title of the lecture was "Liberty and Limited Government". It could have been "Herbert Spencer, take a bow" (although of course Spencer thought that Mr Gladstone had betrayed the cause of "Liberty and Limited Government"). Shortly before his death in 1990, Michael Oakeshott conceded in private correspondence with the present author that Thatcher was not a "conservative ruler". Gradually the ideological penny began to drop amongst objective scholars. Despite continuing to think of conservatism in terms of "varieties", in 2002 Ewen Green concluded that "As the Conservative Century came to an end, it seemed that even if the Conservative Party had survived, conservatism had not" (Green 2002: 290).

However, the Conservative Party rank and file were not interested in such nuances. Since 1990 they had become a kind of tribal tribute act to the martyred Thatcher, and now demanded that their elected representatives should attest to their "tax-cutting instincts" while denigrating "bureaucracy" whenever its activities were disobliging (i.e., in almost every respect apart from the administration of pensioner benefits). Abetted by an alarmist right-wing press increasingly infected (as Churchill had predicted a hundred years before) by the ideas of ideological fellow-travellers across the Atlantic, the party's social authoritarians felt licenced to fulminate against aspects of the Britain which their party had done so much to create. Occupying an echo-chamber of double-standards, they found no difficulty in excoriating benefit fraud while envying the exponents of tax evasion. A semblance of consistency was supplied by a determination to thwart any policy initiatives which could be attributed to "left-wing thinking". Thus there was an incandescent reaction, at all levels of the party beneath the coalition cabinet, to Cameron's open support for same-sex marriage. Although the prime minister delivered the longed-for election victory in 2015, resentment had not died away by the time of the 2016 referendum and his involuntary departure was, for some members, even sweeter than the thought of freedom from the EU.

After a brief and unsatisfactory flirtation with One Nation-style pragmatism in the shape of Theresa May, Conservative MPs and constituency members alike were ready to embrace a warped version of Disraeli's populist legacy, plumping for a new variant which could forge an unlikely alliance between the party's tax-dodging donors and Powellite elements within the working class. Whatever his private opinions, Boris Johnson was never going to let principle impede his prospects. All that mattered, to the membership, was that he could tickle Tory tummies with the appropriate bombastic rhetoric. It was no accident that his resignation was lamented loudly by the populist right-wing newspapers; only the heavyweight *Telegraph* remained resolutely unimpressed by his record in office. At least Johnson's career sets at rest any notion that his party remains addicted to "social conservatism". Not even the *Telegraph*, previously renowned for a sanctimonious adherence to traditional moral standards, condemned Johnson for his lurid lifestyle and his disregard even for rules which his own government had made. If anything, the newspaper's columnists thought he was insufficiently libertarian, while the party's Brexit-besotted members seemed attracted rather than repulsed by his cheerful disregard for personal and political responsibility.

Initially, at least, the substitution of Liz Truss for Johnson in September 2022 produced an outburst of libertarian over-excitement in the Conservative-supporting press. "At last!" crowed the *Daily Mail* in response to the government's first economic package, "A *True* Tory Budget" (Daily Mail 2022). In reality, the Truss interlude looked likely to be the final instalment of a long-running saga; after all, the new prime minister was yet another recruit from the "Liberal" ranks who had changed her partisan allegiance without modifying a level of libertarian passion from which even a reincarnated Herbert Spencer would have recoiled. If an individual who took pride in her capacity to be "disruptive" really *was* a "true Tory", Truss had at least performed the public service of proving that her party's "disposition" was incompatible with "conservatism" in any acceptable sense of that contestable word.

The conservative ideological tradition

The story of modern British conservatism, by comparison, is briefly told. It would be too simplistic to say that, as a distinctive political ideology, it "begins with Burke" and ends with the death of Robert Southey in 1843, but that chronology is not wholly misleading. We have argued that ideologies do not change; rather, people can change their minds under the weight of "events", and even those who remain consistent to their underlying principles can be confronted with social and political developments which cause them to reorder their priorities. In short, there is a continuous relationship of mutual moulding between "principles" and "practice".

Just two years after Southey's death, John Stuart Mill wrote of the 1832 Reform Act that:

> its indirect consequences have surpassed every calculation. The series of events, commencing with Catholic Emancipation, and consummated by the Reform Act, brought home for the first time to the existing generation a practical consciousness of living in a world of change. It gave the first shock to old habits. It was to politics what the Reformation was to religion – it made reason the recognized standard, instead of authority. By making it evident to the public that they were on a new sea, it destroyed the force of the instinctive objection to new courses. Reforms have still to encounter opposition from those whose interests they affect, or seem to affect; but innovation is no longer under a ban, merely as innovation. (Mill 1845: 502)

Mill's account was exaggerated, but not excessively so. He had identified what might be called a shift in the "climate of opinion". In themselves, expressions of distinctively conservative views remained no less persuasive than they had been before the reforms of 1828–32. But the context had changed in a way which made such views seem far less *relevant* to public questions. Conservative beliefs had lost much of their potency as the basis for *political action*; and this, as we have seen, is a key element in the definition of an ideology. Instead of reading an article and resolving to resist reform at all costs, the average subscriber to the *Quarterly Review* would now agree with its sentiments and regret the necessity of acquiescence in the latest step towards the deplorable democratic endgame, in which their imposing country estates might even be reconfigured as amusement parks.

As so often, the experience of the Third Marquess of Salisbury elucidates the point. As a politician, within a few years he had apparently forgotten his fulminations against the 1867 Reform Act and was prepared to join a government led by the dubious Disraeli. When in turn he became prime minister, as we have seen, he proved willing to countenance a series of uncongenial measures if this was necessary cost to keep his party (and himself) in office or as an effective opposition. Judged purely on the decisions of the governments he led, Salisbury would best be characterized as a pragmatic, moderate liberal. Yet as soon as he picked up a pen – even when engaged in private correspondence – Salisbury's distinctive conservatism returned with something which was not far removed from "a vengeance". It was as if Hatfield House had become the venue for a real-life enactment of Robert Louis Stevenson's 1886 novella *Dr Jekyll and Mr Hyde*.

Salisbury's son Lord Hugh Cecil persuaded himself that Jekyll and Hyde could be reconciled, by drawing a distinction between "natural" and "political" conservatism. In itself, this was a significant departure from Burke, whose *Reflections* can be regarded as an attempt to explain how "natural conservatism" – an instinctive antipathy to radical change – can be applied to political questions. By 1912, when Cecil published *Conservatism*, the process of change instigated by the industrial revolution had ramified through every aspect of life in Britain, even affecting privileged individuals like the author himself. The question for "political conservatives" was, the extent to which the state should try to ameliorate its social and economic effects. Superficially, Cecil's answer was that such matters should be approached in a pragmatic spirit; but his discussion is heavily coloured by his distinctively liberal leanings on the proper scope of government activity and the rights of property. Mr Hyde had won: "natural conservatives" might still regard the Conservative Party as an appropriate refuge in a world of disorientating change, but only for want of a viable alternative.

It was unfortunate as well as ironic that a laissez-faire liberal should write a book which was quickly recognized as a classic of conservatism, but as we have seen Cecil was merely providing additional authority to a long-established trend. When ideological conservatives addressed the work of John Stuart Mill, there was limited scope for a productive exchange. Accordingly, Mill's best-known critics were not conservative in a distinctive sense; like Fitzjames Stephen and Arnold, they tended to be liberals who were unwilling to follow Mill and take their own principles to logical conclusions. The next generation of writers who have been associated with "conservatism" were less equivocal in their liberalism, but have been misidentified because they were bitterly disillusioned with the direction of Liberal *Party* policy under Gladstone. Their sympathy with Herbert Spencer – perhaps the least disputable exemplar of late-Victorian ideological liberalism – should have been sufficient to set the record straight. However, their incorporation into the "converging streams" of conservatism by liberals like Cecil and F. C. Hearnshaw was allowed to pass without serious challenge, not least because of a relative lack of academic interest. If laissez-faire radicalism could be accepted as a "variety of conservatism", the party's interwar intelligentsia would have little difficulty in squeezing the pragmatic liberalism offered by Baldwin and Neville Chamberlain into the same elastic tradition.

The swing towards laissez-faire under Thatcher produced the level of academic interest in conservative thought which would have been so helpful in clarifying the situation during the postwar consensus. However, much of the literature still reflected traditional academic hostility towards "the stupidest party" and its apologists. Thus, for example, Ted Honderich happily accepted Thatcherite claims and equated conservatism with laissez-faire; as such, it was much easier to insist that conservatism, and the Conservative Party, had *always* been chiefly concerned to furnish a cynical defence of economic inequality. Before Thatcher, his critique would have applied with far more justice to the position of self-styled Republican "conservatives" in the United States (Honderich 1991). The intellectual vanguard of Thatcherism seemed perfectly content to be tarred with the same brush. Sir Keith Joseph even allowed himself to be named as co-author of a polemical attack on the idea of equality, which was inspired by the American libertarian Robert Nozick (Joseph & Sumption 1979).

Thatcherism did not kill conservatism – indeed, John Gray's own writings testify that rumours of its extinction, as a distinctive ideological position, have been exaggerated. Some eloquent authors with connections to the Conservative Party have tried in recent years to deflect its members from the neoliberal course to which they are irredeemably committed, thanks to the party's idolatry of Thatcher and the influence of its non-domiciled donors (Blond 2010; Timothy 2020). More relevant to what was now usually described as "traditional conservatism" – i.e., conservatism as a distinctive ideology rather than a mongrel branch of the liberal family – was the turn towards environmental concerns exhibited in the work of John Gray, along with Roger Scruton (a member of Thatcher's fan club in the Conservative Philosophy Group who nevertheless remained highly critical of neoliberalism: Gray 1994; Scruton 2012). The descendants of Cecil's "natural conservatives" have an obvious interest in the conservation of nature, and this outlook can of course inform a wide-ranging agenda for political action. Predictably, the advocates of laissez-faire regard environmental activism – or even acceptance of any link between climate change and human activity – as hallmarks of a "lefty", such is the debasement of political discourse in the Anglophone world. The final irony is that this aspect of conservative ideology would not have assumed such prominence without the ecological vandalism inflicted on the planet and its inhabitants since the industrial revolution, and justified from the outset in the name of "freedom" by deluded people who sincerely consider themselves to be good conservatives.

A chronology of conservatism and the Conservative Party

1790	Publication of Edmund Burke's *Reflections on the Revolution in France*.
1793	Whig opponents of the French Revolution break with the party and support "Tory" Pitt government.
1828–29	Tories, led by the Duke of Wellington and Robert Peel, acquiesce in "liberal" religious reforms, alienating supporters of established order in "Church and State".
1830	Samuel Taylor Coleridge publishes *On the Constitution of the Church and State*
1832	Passage of "Great" Reform Act; establishment of Carlton Club; appearance of "Conservative" as a party label.
1834	Formation of short-lived (minority) Conservative government under Peel, who issues Tamworth Manifesto before general election of January 1835.
1841	Election of first majority Conservative government despite 1832 reforms which Peel and his party had opposed.
1846	Party schism over Peel's removal of agricultural protection ("the Corn Laws"). Peel's opponents become known as "Protectionists", led after 1848 by the 14th Earl of Derby and the former radical Benjamin Disraeli.
1867	Derby government – the third minority administration he led – pass a second and much more radical Act to extend the electoral franchise.
1868	On Derby's retirement, Disraeli becomes Conservative leader and (briefly) prime minister.
1874	Disraeli's party wins decisive election victory under new franchise.
1880	Liberals under rejuvenated Gladstone win general election.
1881	Death of Disraeli (now Lord Beaconsfield); disputed succession eventually falls to 3rd Marquess of Salisbury.
1884	Further electoral reform, manipulated by Salisbury for party advantage.
1885	Short-lived minority Conservative government under Salisbury.
1886	Liberal Party splits over Gladstone's proposals for Irish Home Rule; Salisbury forms second government with support of "Liberal Unionists"

1892	General election sees Conservatives win most seats but not enough to remain in government.
1895	General election – comfortable Conservative majority.
1900	"Khaki" election – Salisbury's Conservatives win easily again in early (successful) stages of the imperialist Boer War.
1902	Salisbury retires from premiership due to ill-health; succeeded by ineffectual nephew Arthur Balfour.
1903	Staunch imperialist and Liberal Unionist Joseph Chamberlain resigns from Balfour's government to campaign for "tariff reform", splitting the party.
1906	Conservatives routed in general election; Liberals return to office.
1909	Lloyd George's "People's Budget" voted down by the House of Lords.
1910	Two inconclusive general elections caused by constitutional crisis over the veto powers of the House of Lords.
1911	Parliament Act curtails powers of Conservative-dominated House of Lords; Balfour resigns from Conservative leadership, succeeded by obscure former junior minister, Andrew Bonar Law.
1912	In a public speech Bonar Law endorses armed resistance to Home Rule; Lord Hugh Cecil, who combines extreme economic liberalism with a visceral hatred of Catholic Britons, publishes the first book on "conservatism" with any claim to be authoritative.
1916	Fatal divisions within wartime Liberal cabinet lead to coalition under Lloyd George, including Bonar Law's Conservatives as well as Arthur Greenwood representing the recently-founded Labour Party.
1918	Votes for all (males) aged 18 and over; "Coupon" election returns large Conservative majority which remains within Lloyd George coalition.
1921	Bonar Law resigns due to ill health; replaced by Austen Chamberlain.
1922	Conservative opponents of Lloyd George, assisted by Bonar Law and Stanley Baldwin, rebel against continuation of coalition. Lloyd George replaced as prime minister by Bonar Law.
1923	Retirement and death of Bonar Law, replaced as prime minister by Baldwin who calls general election on issue of tariff reform. Conservatives win most seats but Labour forms first (minority) government.
1924	General election; Conservatives secure overwhelming majority.
1926	General strike; Conservative Party reveals marked bias against working class and Baldwin struggles to maintain his conciliatory approach.
1929	Foundation of the Bonar Law Memorial College at Ashridge, Hertfordshire to expound "conservatism" (as determined by the party's leadership), and

establishment of a Conservative Research Department (CRD) to assist front-bench speakers; general election makes Labour the largest parliamentary party for the first time, although without an overall majority.

1931   Collapse of minority Labour government amidst economic crisis; formation of a Conservative-dominated National Government which receives over-whelming endorsement in general election.

1935   Baldwin becomes prime minister on retirement of Ramsay MacDonald.

1937   Baldwin retires and is succeeded by Neville Chamberlain (a Liberal Unionist rather than a Conservative).

1939   Outbreak of Second World War marks failure of Chamberlain's policy of "appeasement".

1940   Chamberlain resigns; succeeded by former Liberal Winston Churchill at the head of a coalition government.

1944   Publication of Friedrich von Hayek's *The Road to Serfdom*, the bible of neolib-erals within the Conservative Party.

1945   Labour wins landslide in general election despite Churchill's inspired wartime leadership.

1947   Publication of Quintin Hogg's *The Case for Conservatism*, the classic defence of the pragmatism of the Conservative Party's elite; party accepts similar posi-tion as expressed in *The Industrial Charter*.

1951   Conservatives return to office under Churchill; broad acceptance of Labour's postwar mixed economy and welfare state.

1955   Churchill succeeded by Anthony Eden, whose position is confirmed by 1955 snap general election.

1956   Suez crisis exposes extent of Britain's global decline and realities of "special relationship" with the US.

1957   Eden resigns and is succeeded by Harold Macmillan.

1959   Conservatives re-elected amid growing middle-class "affluence" in era of consumerism.

1962   Britain's belated bid to join European Economic Community (EEC) is rebuffed by France's President de Gaulle.

1963   Macmillan resigns through ill-health; succeeded by Sir Alec Douglas-Home after controversial "consultations".

1964   Conservatives lose office after narrow defeat in general election.

1965   Home resigns and is replaced by Edward Heath, the first leader to be elected by MPs.

1966   General election; Labour secures decisive victory.

1968   Leadership fights off challenge from Enoch Powell's neoliberal populism.

1970   Unexpected Conservative victory in general election.

1973   Britain joins EEC; within months, world economy hit by dramatic rise in commodity prices.

1974   Heath government fails to secure renewed mandate in "Who Governs?" election (February) amid widespread industrial conflict, power cuts and crisis of price inflation; similar result in second election (October) sees Labour returned with a slender majority.

1975   Heath defeated by Thatcher in first formal leadership challenge; Conservatives overwhelmingly support continued EEC membership in referendum.

1979   Conservatives win general election as Labour seems incapable of meeting economic and industrial challenges.

1981   Thatcher maintains hardline neoliberal rhetoric despite deepening economic problems and inner-city disturbances.

1982   Thatcher demonstrates leadership qualities in Falklands conflict.

1983   Conservatives easily re-elected thanks to "Falklands factor", signs of economic recovery and divided opposition forces.

1987   Thatcher's party wins third successive election as economic gloom replaced by short-lived "boom".

1990   Thatcher fails to fight off leadership challenge due to increasing public unpopularity and backbench fears of impending electoral defeat; replaced by John Major.

1992   Signature of Maastricht Treaty which creates a European Union; Britain excepted from provisions concerning single European currency and social legislation; Conservatives win general election (April) but majority now vulnerable to "Eurosceptic" rebels; "Black Wednesday" (September) increases salience of European issue and destroys party's reputation for economic competence.

1997   Labour wins landslide majority in general election, with Conservatives tainted by financial and sexual scandals as well as being divided over "Europe"; Major resigns as party leader and is replaced by William Hague; new rules give final choice of future leaders to party membership.

2001   Conservatives soundly beaten in general election; Hague resigns and is replaced by Iain Duncan Smith, an advanced Eurosceptic with no ministerial experience.

2003   Duncan Smith deposed; parliamentary party engineers unopposed succession of Michael Howard.

2005   Conservatives avoid a third landslide defeat in general election but make lit-
        tle progress against Labour which is divided and discredited by Iraq War;
        Howard resigns and is succeeded by David Cameron, who offers combination
        of social and economic liberalism.

2008   In response to global economic crisis, Conservatives adopt policies of
        "austerity".

2010   General election leads to hung parliament and formation of coalition between
        Conservatives and Liberal Democrats.

2013   Passage of legislation legalizing same-sex marriage; Cameron agrees to hold
        referendum on EU membership if re-elected.

2015   Conservatives secure narrow victory in general election; Cameron effectively
        the prisoner of Eurosceptics.

2016   Referendum results in vote for EU withdrawal; Cameron resigns and is
        replaced by Theresa May.

2017   May calls snap election in ill-fated bid to secure parliamentary support for her
        proposed "Hard Brexit"; needs support from Northern Ireland's Democratic
        Unionists to retain parliamentary majority on key votes.

2019   Unable to win parliamentary support for her negotiated terms of EU with-
        drawal, May resigns and is replaced by Boris Johnson; having finished only
        fifth in the EU parliamentary election of May 2019, Conservatives win com-
        fortable majority in December's general election

2020   Coronavirus pandemic presents unprecedented challenge to government;
        Johnson himself almost succumbs to the virus (April).

2022   Rocked by a succession of scandals and faced by adverse opinion polls,
        Johnson survives vote of no confidence (June) but is forced to resign the fol-
        lowing month. In the final ballot of the ensuing leadership contest, Liz Truss
        defeats Rishi Sunak but is herself forced to resign after less than two months
        in office. Despite strong grass-roots support for a Johnson comeback, Sunak
        becomes leader without a final vote of party members.

Further reading on conservatism and/or the Conservative Party

Bale, T. 2016. *The Conservative Party: From Thatcher to Cameron.* Second edition. Cambridge: Polity.

Ball, S. 2013. *Portrait of a Party: The Conservative Party in Britain, 1918–1945.* Oxford: Oxford University Press.

Dorey, P. 2010. *British Conservatism: The Politics and Philosophy of Inequality.* London: I. B. Tauris.

Garnett, M. & K. Hickson 2009. *Conservative Thinkers: The Key Contributors to the Political Thought of the Modern Conservative Party.* Manchester: Manchester University Press.

Hayton, R. 2012. *Reconstructing Conservatism? The Conservative Party in Opposition, 1997–2010.* Manchester: Manchester University Press.

Heppell, T. 2014. *The Tories: From Winston Churchill to David Cameron.* London: Bloomsbury.

Neill, E. 2021. *Conservatism.* Cambridge: Polity.

O'Hara, K. 2012. *Conservatism.* London: Reaktion.

O'Sullivan, N. 1976. *Conservatism.* London: Dent.

Quinton, A. 1978. *The Politics of Imperfection: The Religious and Secular Traditions of Thought in England from Hooker to Oakeshott.* London: Faber.

Bibliography

Adonis, A. 1993. *Making Aristocracy Work: The Peerage and the Political System in Britain 1884–1914.* Oxford: Clarendon Press.

Barker, E. 1928. *Political Thought in England from 1848 to 1914.* London: Thornton Butterworth.

Baldwin, S. 1926. *On England and Other Addresses.* London: Philip Allan.

Baldwin, S. 1935. *This Torch of Freedom: Speeches and Addresses.* London: Hodder & Stoughton.

Baldwin, S. 1937. *Service of Our Lives: Last Speeches as Prime Minister.* London: Hodder & Stoughton.

Ball, S. (ed.) 1999. *Parliament and Politics in the Age of Churchill and Attlee: The Headlam Diaries, 1935–51.* Cambridge: Cambridge University Press.

Ball, S. 2005. *The Guardsmen: Harold Macmillan, Three Friends and the World They Made.* London: HarperPerennial.

Barr, J. 2001. *The Bow Group: A History.* London: Politicos.

Bates, S. 2020. Obituary of Sir Peregrine Worsthorne. *The Guardian,* 6 October.

Bell, D. 1960. *The End of Ideology: On the Exhaustion of Political Ideas in the Fifties.* New York: Free Press.

Bentinck, H. 1918. *Tory Democracy.* London: Methuen.

Berkeley, H. 1977. *The Odyssey of Enoch: A Political Memoir.* London: Hamish Hamilton.

Berthezène, C. 2015. *Training Minds for the War of Ideas: Ashridge College, the Conservative Party and the Cultural Politics of Britain, 1929–54.* Manchester: Manchester University Press.

Blake, R. 1955. *The Unknown Prime Minister: The Life of Times of Andrew Bonar Law, 1958–1923.* London: Eyre & Spotiswoode.

Blond, P. 2010. *Red Tory: How Left and Right Have Broken Britain and How We Can Fix It.* London: Faber.

Boyd-Carpenter, J. 1980. *Way of Life.* London: Sidgwick & Jackson.

Brinton, C. 1962. *English Political Thought in the 19th Century.* New York: Harper.

Brinton, C. 1926. *The Political Ideas of the English Romanticists.* New York: Oxford University Press.

Bryant, A. 1929. *The Spirit of Conservatism.* London: Methuen.

Buckle, G. 1920. *The Life of Benjamin Disraeli, Earl of Beaconsfield: Volume V.* London: John Murray.

Butler, D., A. Adonis & T. Travers 1994. *Failure in British Government: The Politics of the Poll Tax.* Oxford: Oxford University Press.

Burke, E. 1816. *Speeches,* Vol. III. London: Longman.

Campbell, J. 1993. *Edward Heath: A Biography*. London: Jonathan Cape.

Catterall, P. (ed). 2011. *The Macmillan Diaries: Volume II, Prime Minister and After, 1957–1966*. London: Macmillan.

Cecil, H. 1912. *Conservatism*. London: Thornton Butterworth.

Churchill, R. 1883. "Elijah's Mantle". *Fortnightly Review*, 1 May.

Churchill, R. 1884. "Lord Randolph Churchill at Birmingham". *The Times*, 16 April.

Churchill, W. 1970. *The People's Rights*. London: Jonathan Cape.

Clark, J. C. D. 2000. *English Society 1660–1832: Religion, Ideology and Politics under the Ancient Regime*. Cambridge: Cambridge University Press.

Coleraine, Lord 1970. *For Conservatives Only: A Study of Conservative Leadership from Churchill to Heath*. London: Tom Stacey.

Collingwood, R. G. 1939. *An Autobiography*. Oxford: Oxford University Press.

Collini, S. (ed.) 1993. *Arnold: Culture and Anarchy and Other Writings*. Cambridge: Cambridge University Press.

Cooke, A. & S. Parkinson (eds) 2009. *Tory Policy-Making: The Conservative Research Department 1929–2009*. London: Conservative Research Department.

Cowling, M. (ed.) 1978. *Conservative Essays*. London: Cassell.

Cranborne, Lord 1867. "The Conservative surrender". *Quarterly Review*, October.

Crick, B. 1972. *Political Theory and Practice*. London: Allen Lane.

Critchley, J. 1973. "Stresses and strains in the party". *Political Quarterly* 44: 401–410.

Daily Mail 2022. Front page, 24 September. Available at https://www.tomorrowspapers. co.uk/daily–mail–front–page–2022–09–24/.

Dangerfield, G. 1961. *The Strange Death of Liberal England 1910–1914*. New York: Capricorn.

Denham, A. & M. Garnett 2001. *Keith Joseph: A Life*. Chesham: Acumen.

Dicey, A. V. 1905. *Lectures on the Relation between Law and Public Opinion in Britain during the Nineteenth Century*. London: Macmillan.

Dorey, P. 2009. *British Conservatism and Trade Unionism, 1945–1964*. Farnham: Ashgate.

Dorey, P. & M. Garnett 2016. *The British Coalition Government, 2010–15: A Marriage of Inconvenience*. London: Palgrave Macmillan.

Driver, C. 1946. *Tory Radical: The Life of Richard Oastler*. New York: Oxford University Press.

Eccleshall, R. 1990. *English Conservatism Since the Restoration*. London: Unwin Hyman.

Eden, A. 1947. *Freedom and Order: Selected Speeches, 1939–1946*. London: Faber.

Elliot, W. 1927. *Toryism and the Twentieth Century*. London: Philip Allan.

Feiling, K. 1924. *A History of the Tory Party 1640–1714*. Oxford: Clarendon Press.

Feiling, K. 1930. *What is Conservatism?* London: Faber & Faber.

Feiling, K. 1936. *The Second Tory Party 1714–1832*. Oxford: Clarendon Press.

Fisher, N. 1977. *The Tory Leaders: Their Struggle for Power*. London: Weidenfeld & Nicolson.

Freeden, M. 1985. "Review of Greenleaf's *The British Political Tradition*, Vols 1 and 2". *English Historical Review* 100(397).

Gamble, A. 1974. *The Conservative Nation*. London: Routledge & Kegan Paul.

Gash, N. 1965. *Reaction and Reconstruction in English Politics 1832–1852*. Oxford: Clarendon Press.

Gash, N. 1986. *The Political Significance of the Tamworth Manifesto*. Tamworth: Peel Society.

Gaunt, R. (ed.) 2006. *Unrepentant Tory: Political Selections from the Dairies of the Fourth Duke of Newcastle-under-Lyne, 1827–38*. Woodbridge: Boydell & Brewer.

Gilbert, M. 1991. *Churchill: A Life*. London: Heinemann.

Gilmour, I. 1978. *Inside Right: Conservatism, Policies and the People*. London: Quartet.

Gilmour, I. 1992. *Riot, Risings and Revolution: Governance and Violence in Eighteenth-Century England*. London: Hutchinson.

Gilmour, I. & M. Garnett 1997. *Whatever Happened to the Tories? The Conservatives since 1945*. London: Simon & Schuster.

Gray, J. 1994. *Beyond the New Right: Markets, Government and the Common Environment*. London: Routledge.

Gray, J. & D. Willetts 1997. *Is Conservatism Dead?* London: Social Market Foundation.

Green, E. H. H. 1993. *The Crisis of Conservatism: The Politics, Economics and Ideology of the British Conservative Party, 1880–1914*. London: Routledge.

Green, E. H. H. 2002. *Ideologies of Conservatism: Conservative Political Ideas in the Twentieth Century*. Oxford: Oxford University Press.

Greenleaf, W. H. 1966. *Oakeshott's Philosophical Politics*. London: Longman.

Greenleaf, W. H. 1983. *The British Political Tradition, Volume Two: The Ideological Heritage*. London: Methuen.

Grenville, J. 1964. *Lord Salisbury and Foreign Policy: The Close of the Nineteenth Century*. London: Athlone.

Guardian 2002. "Full text: Theresa May's conference speech". *The Guardian*, 7 October 2002. https://www.theguardian.com/politics/2002/oct/07/conservatives2002.conservatives1.

Hailsham, Lord 1976. *Elective Dictatorship*. London: BBC.

Hansard HC Deb. Vol. 11, cols 450–63, 19 March 1832. https://api.parliament.uk/historic-hansard/commons/1832/mar/19/parliamentary-reform-bill-for-england#S3V0011P0_18320319_HOC_35.

Hansard HL Deb. Vol. 12, col. 1029, 17 May 1832. https://hansard.parliament.uk/Lords/1832-05-17/debates/4d6d4d4e-8074-4e14-ac83-bc2c1c7ace5c/LordsChamber.

Hansard HC Deb. Vol. 183, col. 1591, 31 May 1866. https://api.parliament.uk/historic-hansard/commons/1866/may/31/committee-adjourned-debate#S3V0183P0_18660531_HOC_32.

Hansard HL Deb. Vol. 300, cols 333–56, 31 July 1885. https://hansard.parliament.uk/lords/1885-07-31/debates/5a8f9d0e-0513-45df-92fd-8379bcda9681/LordsChamber.

Hansard HC Deb. Vol. 123, col. 194, 28 May 1903. https://api.parliament.uk/historic-hansard/commons/1903/may/28/fiscal-policy-of-the-country#S4V0123P0_19030528_HOC_223.

Hansard HC Deb. Vol. 148, col. 857, 3 July 1905. https://api.parliament.uk/historic-hansard/commons/1905/jul/03/aliens-bill-1#S4V0148P0_19050703_HOC_492.

Hansard HC Deb. Vol. 28, cols 1517–20, 25 July 1911. https://api.parliament.uk/historic-hansard/commons/1911/jul/25/parliament-bill-home-rule#S5CV0028P0_19110725_HOC_149.

Harris, R. 1969. *Romanticism and the Social Order*. London: Blandford.

Hastings, M. 2019. "Opinion: I was Boris Johnson's boss: he is utterly unfit to be prime minister". *The Guardian*, 24 June 2019. https://www.theguardian.com/commentisfree/2019/jun/24/boris-johnson-prime-minister-tory-party-britain.

Hearnshaw, F. 1933. *Conservatism in England: An Analytical, Historical and Political Survey*. London: Macmillan.

Heath, A. 2021a. "Decadent Britain is sleepwalking into a vortex of decline". *Daily Telegraph*, 23 June.

Heath, A. 2021b. "Boris's shameful Tory betrayal guarantees the total victory of socialism in Britain". *Daily Telegraph*, 9 September.

Heath, E. 1970. Leader's speech, Blackpool. http://www.britishpoliticalspeech.org/speech-archive.htm?speech=117.

Heffer, S. 1998. *Like the Roman: The Life of Enoch Powell*. London: Weidenfeld & Nicolson.

Heseltine, M. 1989. *The Challenge of Europe: Can Britain Win?* London: Weidenfeld & Nicolson.

Himmelfarb, G. 1984. *The Idea of Poverty: England in the Early Industrial Age*. London: Faber.

Hoffman, J. 1964. *The Conservative Party in Opposition 1945–51*. London: McGibbon & Kee.

Honderich, T. 1991. *Conservatism*. London: Penguin.

Hogg, Q. 1947. *The Case for Conservatism*. London: Penguin.

Howe, P. (ed.) 1932. *The Complete Works of William Hazlitt, Volume VII*. London: Dent.

Hutcheon, W. (ed.) 1913. *Whigs and Whiggism: Political Writings by Benjamin Disraeli*. London: John Murray.

Inge, W. 1920. *The Idea of Progress*. Oxford: Clarendon Press.

Jenkins, R. 1998. *The Chancellors*. London: Macmillan.

Jones, E. 2015. "Conservatism, Edmund Burke, and the invention of a political tradition, c.1885–1914". *Historical Journal* 58(4): 1115–39.

Joseph, K. 1976. *Stranded on the Middle Ground*. London: Centre for Policy Studies.

Joseph, K. & J. Sumption 1979. *Equality*. London: John Murray.

Kirk, R. 1954. *The Conservative Mind*. London: Faber.

Law, R. 1950. *Return from Utopia*. London: Faber.

Letwin, S. 1992. *The Anatomy of Thatcherism*. London: Fontana.

Lexden, Lord 2020. "The first Conservative college". 1 April. https://www.alistairlexden.org.uk/news/first-conservative-college.

Lindsay, T. & M. Harrington 1974. *The Conservative Party, 1918–1970*. Basingstoke: Macmillan.

Lucy, H. 1886. *A Diary of Two Parliaments*. London: Cassell.

Macaulay, Lord 1898. *The Works of Lord Macaulay: Essays and Biographies Volume 1*. London: Longmans Green.

McDowell, R. (ed.) 1991. *The Writings and Speeches of Edmund Burke, Volume IX*. Oxford: Clarendon Press.

McDowell, R. & J. Woods (eds) 1970. *The Correspondence of Edmund Burke, Volume IX*. Cambridge: Cambridge University Press.

McKenzie, R. & A. Silver 1968. *Angels in Marble: Working-Class Conservatives in Urban England*. London: Heinemann.

Macmillan, H. 1966. *The Middle Way*. London: Macmillan.

Macpherson, C. 1980. *Burke*. Oxford: Oxford University Press.

Maine, H. 1970. *Popular Government*. Indianapolis, IN: Liberty Press.

Mallock, W. 1909. *A Critical Examination of Socialism*. London: John Murray.

Mallock, W. 1920. *Memoirs of Life and Literature*. London: Chapman & Hall.

Marsh, P. 1978. *The Discipline of Party Government: Lord Salisbury's Domestic Statecraft, 1881–1902*. Sussex: Harvester.

Maude, A. 1966. "Winter of Tory discontent". *Spectator*, 14 January.

Maude, A. 1969. *The Common Problem: A Policy for the Future*. London: Constable.

Mill, J. S. 1840. "Coleridge". *Westminster Review*, March.

Mill, J. S. 1845. "The claims of labour". *Westminster Review*, April.

Mitchell, L. G. (ed.) 1989. *The Writings and Speeches of Edmund Burke, Volume VIII, The French Revolution 1790–1794*. Oxford: Clarendon Press.

Morrow, J. 1990. *Coleridge's Political Thought: Property, Morality and the Limits of Traditional Discourse*. Basingstoke: Macmillan.

Norman, J. 2014. *Edmund Burke*. London: William Collins.

Norton, P. 1990. "'The lady's not for turning'. But what about the rest? Margaret Thatcher and the Conservative Party 1979–89". *Parliamentary Affairs* 43(1): 41–58.

Oakeshott, M. 1962. *Rationalism in Politics and Other Essays*. London: Methuen.

Orwell, G. 1968. *The Collected Essays, Journalism and Letters, Volume 1: An Age Like This*. London: Secker & Warburg.

Percy, E. *et al.* 1935. *Conservatism and the Future*. London: Heinemann.

Petrie, C. 1938. *The Chamberlain Tradition*. London: Lovat Dickson.

Pitchford, M. 2011. *The Conservative Party and the Extreme Right, 1945–75*. Manchester: Manchester University Press.

Prothero, R. (ed.) 1896. *Private Letters of Edward Gibbon, Volume 2*. London: John Murray.

Pugh, M. 1985. *The Tories and the People, 1880–1935*. Oxford: Blackwell.

Ramsden, J. 1978. *The Age of Balfour and Baldwin*. London: Longman.

Ramsden, J. 1998. *An Appetite for Power: A History of the Conservative Party since 1830*. London: HarperCollins.

Rhodes James, R. 1991. *Bob Boothby: A Portrait*. London: Hodder & Stoughton.

Rockrow, L. 1925. *Contemporary Political Thought in England*. London: Allen & Unwin.

Roberts, A. 1999. *Salisbury: Victorian Titan*. London: Weidenfeld & Nicolson.

Roberts, D. 1979. *Paternalism in Early Victorian England*. London: Croom Helm.

Rossiter, C. 1962. *Conservatism in America: The Thankless Persuasion*. New York: Vintage.

Sack, J. 1993. *From Jacobite to Conservative: Reaction and Orthodoxy in Britain c.1760–1832*. Cambridge: Cambridge University Press.

Salisbury, Lord 1883. "Disintegration". *Quarterly Review*, October.

Sandbrook, D. 2010. *State of Emergency*. London: Allen Lane.

Scruton, R. 2012. *Green Philosophy: How to Think Seriously about the Planet*. London: Atlantic.

Shannon, R. 1992. *The Age of Disraeli, 1868–1881: The Rise of Tory Democracy*. London: Longman.

Shepherd, R. 1994. *Iain Macleod: A Biography*. London: Hutchinson.

Skidelsky, R. 1983. *John Maynard Keynes: Hopes Betrayed, 1883–1920*. London: Macmillan.

Southey, R. 1831. "Moral and political state of the British Empire". *Quarterly Review*, January.

Spectator 1923. "The Philip Stott College". *The Spectator*, 16 June 1923. http://archive.spectator.co.uk/article/16th-june-1923/5/the-philip-stott-college.

Spencer, H. 1969. *The Man Versus the State*. Harmondsworth: Penguin.

Stanhope, Earl 1879. *The Life of the Right Honourable William Pitt*, Volume I. London: John Murray.

Stanley, T. 2017. "The virtues of conservatism have to be explained". *Daily Telegraph*, 11 July.

Stephen, J. F. 1862. "Liberalism". *Cornhill Magazine*, January.

Stephen, J. F. 1993. *Liberty, Equality, Fraternity*. Indianapolis: Liberty Press.

Stephen, L. 1895. *The Life of Sir James Fitzjames Stephen*. London: Smith, Elder.

Stewart, R. 1971. *The Politics of Protection: Lord Derby and the Protectionist Party 1841–1852*. Cambridge: Cambridge University Press.

Stewart, R. 1978. *The Foundation of the Conservative Party 1830–1867*. London: Longman.

Taylor, H. 1931. *Smith of Birkenhead: Being the Career of the First Earlo of Birkenhead*. London: Stanley & Paul.

Timothy, N. 2020. *Remaking One Nation: The Future of Conservatism*. London: Polity.

Thatcher, M. 1967. Speech to Conservative Party Conference, Brighton, 20 October. https://www.margaretthatcher.org/document/101586.

Thatcher, M. 1996. Keith Joseph Memorial Lecture ("Liberty and Limited Government"). 11 January. https://www.margaretthatcher.org/document/108353.

Torrance, D. 2001. *Noel Skelton and the Property-Owning Democracy*. London: Biteback.

Tominey, C. 2021a. "The Tories have lost touch with Conservatism". *Daily Telegraph*, 4 September.

Tominey, C. 2021b. "We have just witnessed the PM sound the death knell for Conservatism". *Daily Telegraph*, 8 September.

Trollope, A. 1982. *The Eustace Diamonds*. London: Penguin.

Trollope, A. 1980. *An Autobiography*. Oxford: Oxford University Press.

Viereck, P. 1956. *Conservatism: From John Adams to Churchill*. Princeton, NJ: Van Nostrand.

Wheatcroft, G. 2005. *The Strange Death of Tory England*. London: Allen Lane.

White, R. 1950. *The Conservative Tradition*. London: Nicholas Kaye.

Young, H. *et al.* 1967. *The Zinoviev Letter*. London: Heinemann.

Young, H. 1989. *One of Us: A Biography of Margaret Thatcher*. London: Macmillan.

Index

Gilmour, Sir Ian 119–20, 134, 137, 150
Gladstone, Sir John 31
Gladstone, William 40, 41, 43, 48, 49,
    52–3, 55, 57, 58, 59, 62, 67, 70, 74,
    107, 169, 173
Gordon Riots (1780) 11
Goschen, George 60
Gove, Michael 159
Graham, Sir James 38, 41
Gray, John 164–6, 174
Green, T. H. 109, 129, 167
Green, E. H. H. 77, 170
Greenleaf, W. H. 4–7, 50–51, 74, 96, 114,
    129–30
Grey, 2nd Earl 32–3, 37

Hague, William 153
Hailsham, Lord (see Hogg, Quintin)
Halifax, 1st Earl of 80
Halifax, Viscount 112
Halsbury, 1st Earl of 64
Hardy, Thomas, 80
Harrington, James 18
Harris, Ralf 112
Hastings, Max 159–60
Hayek, Friedrich von ix, 112, 116–17,
    119, 120, 146
    not a conservative 116
Hazlitt, William 17, 31
Headlam, Cuthbert 109, 125-6
Hearnshaw, F. C. 48, 50, 59, 106–107,
    108, 173
Heath, Allister viii
Heath, Edward 117, 119, 129, 135–7, 138,
    140, 141–5, 148, 150
Henderson, Arthur 90
Heseltine, Michael 151
Himmelfarb, Gertrude 12–14
Hinchingbrooke, Lord 131, 132
Hitler, Adolf 108
Hobbes, Thomas 70
Hogg, Quintin 110–12, 113, 118–19, 121,
    122, 125, 128, 134, 139, 140
Home, Alec 119, 134–5, 136, 137
Honderich, Ted 174
House of Lords 57, 59, 62, 64–5, 72, 87,
    88, 90, 91, 94, 132

Howard, Michael 150, 155–6
Howe, Sir Geoffrey 152
Hume, David 1, 24

ideology 3–7, 27–8, 85, 106–107, 111,
    115, 121–2, 129, 130, 151, 152–3,
    163–4, 166, 167, 169, 171, 172, 173
Industrial Charter 126–7
Inge, William 80
Inglis, Sir Robert 34, 41
Institute of Economic Affairs (IEA)
    112–13
Irish Home Rule 4, 58, 62, 75, 79, 85, 90,
    91, 107, 139, 167

Jenkins, Roy 87, 89, 150
Johnson, Boris viii, 159–60, 170–1
Johnson, Jo 160
Joseph, Sir Keith xii, 117–18, 119–20,
    122, 123, 145, 146, 149, 152, 164,
    166, 169, 174

Kant, Immanuel 18
Keynes, John Maynard 15, 24, 90, 96, 97,
    103, 108, 114, 128, 130
Kirk, Russell 8, 25, 26, 77, 115

Lamont, Norman 150
Laski, Harold 78, 115
Law, Andrew Bonar 89–90, 91–2, 102,
    103, 107, 115, 139
Lawson, Nigel 149
League of Empire Loyalists (LEL) 131
Lecky, William 74, 116
Letwin, Shirley 120, 154
liberalism (and laissez-faire) 4, 6, 21,
    24–6, 61, 65, 68–72, 74, 80, 81,
    85, 91, 97, 104, 105–107, 109, 110,
    112–13, 114, 121, 122, 123, 130,
    133, 146–7, 151, 152, 153, 154, 156,
    160, 161, 164, 165, 167, 169, 171,
    173, 174
Liberal Unionists 60–61, 74, 85, 86, 89, 96
Liberty and Property Defence League
    (LPDL) 61, 74, 76, 80
Lilley, Peter 150
Liverpool, 2nd Earl of 19–20